Differentiated Instructional Strategies

for the

Block Schedule

Differentiated Instructional Strategies

— for the —

Block Schedule

Gayle H. Gregory · Lynne E. Herndon

CORWIN
A SAGE Company

For information:

Corwin
A SAGE Company
2455 Teller Road
Thousand Oaks, California 91320
(800) 233-9936
Fax: (800) 417-2466
www.corwin.com

SAGE Ltd.
1 Oliver's Yard
55 City Road
London EC1Y 1SP
United Kingdom

SAGE India Pvt. Ltd.
B 1/I 1 Mohan Cooperative
    Industrial Area
Mathura Road, New Delhi 110 044
India

SAGE Asia-Pacific Pte. Ltd.
33 Pekin Street #02-01
Far East Square
Singapore 048763

Printed in the United States of America

Library of Congress Cataloging-in-Publication Data

Gregory, Gayle.
Differentiated instructional strategies for the block schedule/Gayle H. Gregory, Lynne E. Herndon.
    p. cm.
Includes bibliographical references and index.
ISBN 978-1-4129-5096-1 (pbk.)
    1. Block scheduling (Education) 2. Individualized instruction. I. Herndon, Lynne E. II. Title.
LB3032.2.G74 2010
371.2'42—dc22   2010016128

This book is printed on acid-free paper.

10   11   12   13   14   10   9   8   7   6   5   4   3   2   1

Acquisitions Editor:	Hudson Perigo
Associate Editor:	Joanna Coelho
Editorial Assistant:	Allison Scott
Production Editor:	Melanie Birdsall
Copy Editor:	Paula L. Fleming
Typesetter:	C&M Digitals (P) Ltd.
Proofreader:	Cheryl Rivard
Indexer:	Sheila Bodell
Cover Designer:	Rose Storey

Contents

Additional materials and resources related to
Differentiated Instructional Strategies for the Block Schedule
can be found at http://www.corwin.com/distrategies

Acknowledgments

We are indebted to all professional educators for making a difference in the lives of children and rising to the challenge of meeting the needs of all learners.

Special thanks go to Paul Herndon for his technical assistance and support throughout this project.

We are blessed to have worked with such talented staff at Corwin and appreciate their patience and professionalism throughout this project.

Special thanks to the Northeast Foundation for Children, Greenfield, Massachusetts 01301.

PUBLISHER'S ACKNOWLEDGMENTS

Corwin gratefully acknowledges the contributions of the following reviewers:

Jodi Mulholland
Principal
Stoneybrook Elementary School
Kinnelon, NJ

Gabriela Mafi, EdD
Assistant Superintendent
Secondary Education Garden Grove Unified School District
Garden Grove, CA

Delphia Young
Coordinator of Special Projects for Secondary Instruction
Jonesboro, GA

About the Authors

 **Gayle H. Gregory** is an internationally known consultant who has specialized in brain compatible learning and differentiated instruction and assessment.

She presents practical teacher-/student-friendly strategies grounded in sound research that educators find easy to use. Her interactive style and modeling of strategies help teachers and administrators transfer new ideas with ease.

She has had extensive experience in elementary, middle, and secondary schools, and in community colleges and universities. Gayle has also had district leadership roles, including that of curriculum coordinator and staff development director. She has worked with Instructional Leadership Teams in many schools and districts throughout the country focusing on data analysis; using assessment, both formative and summative; and differentiating instruction based on readiness, learning profiles, and interests.

Her areas of expertise include brain-compatible learning, block scheduling, emotional intelligence, instructional and assessment practices, differentiated instructional strategies, using data to differentiate, literacy, presentation skills, renewal of secondary schools, enhancing teacher quality, coaching and mentoring, managing change, and building professional learning communities.

Gayle is affiliated with many organizations, including the Association for Supervision and Curriculum Development and the National Staff Development Council, and is the author and co-author of numerous publications for teachers and administrators.

Gayle believes in lifelong learning for herself and others.

Gayle may be contacted at 905-336-6565 or 716-898-8716, or by e-mail at gregorygayle@netscape.net. Her website is www.gaylehgregory.com.

Lynne E. Herndon has over twenty years experience teaching science at the middle school, high school, and college level, five of which have been in a block schedule. Lynne currently teaches in the Clark County School District in Las Vegas, Nevada. She has conducted workshops at the local, state, and national levels in the areas of classroom management, curriculum mapping, differentiated instruction, integrating technology, and teaching in a block schedule, and she also has experience working in staff development and school improvement planning. Lynne's educational background includes a bachelor's degree in general science from Buena Vista University and a master's degree in science education from the University of Northern Iowa. Lynne is dedicated to providing research-based growth opportunities that have practical applications for classroom teachers.

Lynne's written works include *Thinking Inside the Block Schedule* (1998), written with co-authors Pam Robbins and Gayle Gregory, and *Thinking Inside the Block: The Teacher's Day Planner* (1998), written with co-author Pam Robbins, both published by Corwin. Lynne may be contacted at 702-269-4872 or by e-mail at lynne.herndon@herndons-net.com.

1 Introduction

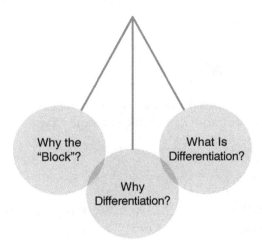

Why the "Block"?

What Is Differentiation?

Why Differentiation?

*B*lock scheduling, simply defined, creates large segments of instructional time for staff and students. These longer-than-usual periods provide several opportunities. Many teachers have used this extended time as a resource to integrate the curriculum, providing enriched student learning experiences. Others have used the additional minutes of instructional time to afford students the chance to delve deeper into subject areas, enhancing student understandings. Schools have used block scheduling to increase the number of credits that students may take in a given year. Many schools report several benefits derived from longer periods of instructional time: fewer discipline referrals, better student attendance, enhanced staff-student relationships, and more students on the honor roll. Students report that block scheduling has prepared them for college and is "less stressful" than a traditional schedule. Block scheduling success relies heavily on how instructional time is used. It is also well known that every learner is unique. This book is devoted to these two factors.

WHY THE "BLOCK"?

In short periods of time, there is little hope of providing a full range of instructional strategies to meet the various preferences and learning styles of diverse learners. Often time is sufficient only to present content or skill through teacher direction and insufficient for anything other than delivery. In a block of time, students get a chance to rehearse new learnings through a variety of instructional tasks and assessment. Teachers get a chance to know the students at a deeper level and begin to identify their learning styles and multiple intelligences as well as their strengths. In addition, flexible groups can be established for interaction and clarification, enrichment, and reteaching.

WHY DIFFERENTIATION?

Teachers have always been driven by student success. Today, teachers face a challenging landscape that is in constant flux. Many factors influence the constantly changing classroom:

- *Standards-Based Classrooms.* Targeted outcomes are set by districts, states, and counties.
- *High Expectations for All Students.* No longer can we leave students behind and just "spray and pray" for success.
- *Multicultural Diversity.* Continuous immigration means some students have little or no communication skills or competencies in English.
- *Diversity of Student Population.* Students have individual learning styles, different levels of multiple intelligences, and unique learning profiles.
- *Continuous Growth of Cognitive Research on Human Learning.* Our knowledge of the brain, including how it develops memory, makes meaning, and engages in the learning process, is constantly improving.
- *Constant Societal and Technological Change.* Political and economic revolutions influence what and how learning takes place.

WHAT IS DIFFERENTIATION?

Differentiation in a nutshell is providing the opportunity for every student to succeed and reach his or her potential. Back when the earth was cooling, we used a "bell curve" to spread out the learners; only some could achieve at high levels, and some wouldn't make it. We went through a cycle of "teach, test, and hope for the best." If they did not "get it," it was just too bad. In education today, we have a quest to "leave no child behind," but to achieve that end, we must plan strategically, using all the knowledge and skill at our disposal. We must create an inviting, supportive classroom environment and have a tool kit of instructional and assessment instruments to provide variety and be responsive to the learner.

This is not a simple task for one teacher and many different types of learners. Teachers are doing an amazing job, but there is always room to grow. Differentiation is like the story of the elephant and the six blind men: there are many facets to differentiated instruction, and if you touch just one part, you may be missing others.

Differentiation may be accomplished through varying the following (see Figure 1.1):

- Content
- Process
- Product

Figure 1.1 Content, Process, and Product

Content	Process	Product
The *what* we are teaching: Students can develop competencies and big ideas through varied content that sparks their interest and meets their needs.	The *how* we teach: Students can get to the same goal in a variety of ways. Thus elaborate rehearsal of content may vary from student to student or group to group.	The *result* of learning: Students process information and demonstrate understanding or competence in a variety of ways.

Differentiation can also be accomplished through attention to the following (see Figure 1.2):

- Readiness
- Interest
- Learning profile (learning styles, preferences, multiple intelligences)

Differentiation is a process or journey for the teacher and students. You cannot differentiate "everything, every day, in every way." However, you can become more responsive over time. Celebrate successes on the way. Just get started, and you will find you are doing more each week, month, and year (see Figure 1.3).

Start small and think big!

Figure 1.2 Readiness, Interest, and Learning Profile

Readiness	Interest	Learning Profile
What is the prior knowledge or experience of the learner? Pre-assessments are key to determining readiness. Respond to differentiated readiness with • varied texts, • supplementary materials, • tiered tasks and products, • compacting, • coaching, and • scaffolding.	How can the learner be "hooked" or engaged? • Exploring of materials to find an interest • Various entry points • Student choice • Group investigation • Negotiated tasks • Contracts	Consider the learner's • learning styles (visual, auditory, tactile, kinesthetic); • opportunity for self-expression through multiple intelligences; • ability to benefit from a flexible learning environment; • preferred organizational choice; and • agenda.

Figure 1.3 Easy Beginnings and Advanced Differentiation

Easy Beginnings	More Advanced Differentiation
• Start building up a variety of reading materials that will grow each year. • Give choices for homework. • Assign partner work. • Use simple cooperative structures. • Provide more opportunity for student interaction and dialogue. • Vary questioning. • Give quick pre-assessments to get a starting point for planning. • Use more graphic organizers. • Give students learning choices related to the standard. • Vary the pace of instruction. • Adjust the complexity of material. • Reteach content in small groups. • Scaffold to support learners. • Begin to assemble more concrete materials and manipulatives.	• Use multiple texts and layered books. • Tier assignments. • Use tiered centers. • Increase the variety of assessments. • Use contracts. • Use individual agendas. • Compact content. • Allow opportunities for group investigation. • Use choice and tic-tac-toe boards. • Use simulations. • Employ problem-based learning. • Use rubrics for assessment. • Allow students to form interest groups and study self-selected topics. • Introduce students to a variety of methods of note taking and summarizing. • Make thorough use of evidence-based instructional strategies. • Provide a full range of visual, auditory, and bodily/kinesthetic learning opportunities.

What Can Be Varied?

When teachers plan any lesson, certain variables can be adjusted to meet the needs of the diversity of learners in the classroom. Some of the factors listed below are done on a daily basis, often randomly and unconsciously, yet need to be considered in the overall planning process.

Differentiating Content and Materials (DCM)

Sometimes students will exhibit a particular interest in some aspects of the unit of study and will want to go deeper into this area. For example, in a unit on the American Revolution, the students may be interested in different individuals who had an impact or major role in the Revolution. Whether learning more about Thomas Jefferson or Paul Revere, students may investigate an outstanding individual of choice and still arrive at the understandings or beliefs of a "freedom fighter." Likewise, they can take this approach to concepts such as fascism or democracy.

Reading materials may be differentiated based on the needs of the readers. Content may be accessed from a variety of materials and resources, from books to the Internet.

Differentiating Communication/Technology (DCT)

Students may select from a variety of communication methods, from role-play to essay to presentation, depending on their needs or their interests. Technology may be integrated based on students' needs or expertise.

Differentiating for Multiple Intelligences (DMI)

Projects, problem-solving tasks, and learning centers may be created to engage different multiple intelligences. This differentiation allows students to find a comfort area or area of strength or perhaps an area that needs attention and bolstering.

Differentiating by Readiness (DR)

Students may be grouped by readiness or sometimes by their ability to deal with a learning situation that is just beyond their level of expertise.

Differentiating by Interest/Choice (DI)

Students are allowed to choose an assignment based on their interests or choice. Contracts, projects, and tic-tac-toe boards are useful in facilitating this.

Differentiating by Process (DP)

Students may use different methods to process information. Activities that are varied and engaging allow all students to rehearse information and skills and apply them in a variety of ways to increase retention and understanding.

In the chapters that follow, specific attention is given to enhancing the use of instructional time with respect to a variety of dimensions: what is known about how the brain learns, teaching strategies, ways to promote attention, working with inclusion students, active participation, review strategies, grouping techniques, approaches to curriculum, assessment practices, classroom management, dealing with student absences, promoting student responsibility, time management, and using technology. In addition, this book will discuss how to select a schedule conducive to the needs and goals of the particular school and its community.

Teachers and administrators today are experiencing continuous pressure to help students meet or exceed national- and state-level academic standards. At the same time, they are facing an educational population that is increasingly diverse—culturally, academically, socially, and emotionally. This complex environment puts schools in the difficult position of being compelled to focus on academics with a population of youths who often lack prerequisite skills or who are emotionally or socially needy. That is, the students may come from households where stress is high because of failed relationships and/or where financial, ethical, and moral support is lacking. Students in such situations are often more concerned with immediate basic needs than with academic concerns. Remarkably, the one place where these same students may find a source of solace is in school.

Teachers who are asked to fill multiple roles, from social worker, counselor, and educator, may well feel overwhelmed by the challenge. However, in these times school truly must be a place for the heart and the mind. A caring, supportive environment goes a long way to welcome each learner and provide nurturing of the heart as well as stimulation for the mind.

2 Who Are the Learners?

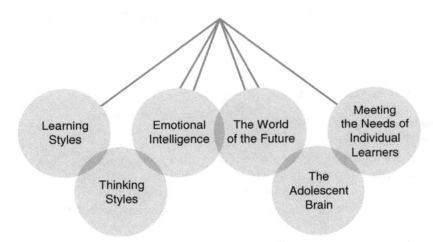

*What is the reality of the young adolescent in
the digital millennium?
What is the contextual environment of these learners?
What do we know about their brains and expectations for success?*

All human beings, regardless of age, race, or space, need certain conditions to thrive. They must feel as though they

- belong and are included.
- have some worth and value.
- are safe in all aspects: physically, emotionally, and cognitively.
- have some choice and freedom related to their environment and activities.
- can be successful.
- are appreciated for who they are.

In classrooms, schools, and playgrounds, these expectations need to be met so that students may thrive and succeed.

Cognitive research tells us that every brain is unique. Even children born into the same family with the same nature (genes) and nurture (environment) do not look or act alike. Each has formed dendrite connections based on experiences and circumstances. Each has a preferred learning style and will thrive better in a visual, auditory, tactile, or kinesthetic environment. Some like natural light, some a musical background, some a quiet space. Some students need hands-on, "being-there" experience, while others appreciate analogy. Some need movement and activity and collaboration, while some need quiet time for contemplation and reflection. Most brains are naturally curious and seek understanding and meaning.

The anonymous poem "Children Are Like Trees" captures these differences.

Children Are Like Trees

Children are very much like trees,
They differ in kind and form.
Some have grown in the open with lots of space to expand,
The crowded forest around them has affected others.
Some have been tied to sticks to keep them straight,
While others have been allowed to develop naturally with a minimum of pruning.
Some children are made of hard wood; others, of soft.
Like trees which may be best for shade, or fruit, or decoration,
Children have their best uses.
Some are better to look at; some are better in groups;
Others are better standing alone.
Some grow strong and sturdy; others need protection from the elements, but every wood, every tree, and every child has a unique and different value.
We may try to graft the characteristics of a child onto another, but we know we cannot make a palm tree into an oak or vice versa.
The best we can do is to accept the tree as it is, to feed it, to give it light, and to prune it gently to its natural shape.
And we need to remember that in working with children, as well as in working with wood . . .
For best results, always sand with the grain.

—Author Unknown

Many researchers, behaviorists, and physiologists have theories to support these differences.

LEARNING STYLES

Ken and Rita Dunn (1987) suggested one learning-styles model that classifies personal styles as auditory, visual, tactile, and kinesthetic.

Auditory Learners

Auditory learners appreciate spoken and heard material and like to be involved in aural questioning rather than reading materials. They engage and absorb more through discussion and interaction. They prefer listening to lectures, stories, and songs, and they enjoy variation such as voice inflection and intonational pitch. They like to discuss their learning with other students. They not only like to hear ideas but enjoy the sound of their own voice as well.

> **Applications**
>
> Suggestions for auditory learners include the following:
>
> - Have students read out loud to each other as partners and in small groups that are safe and supportive.
> - Ask students to paraphrase what they have heard before answering a question.
> - Use audiotapes, CDs, and DVDs to explain concepts. Have students create their own.
> - Use stories that give examples or illustrations.
> - Use "Say and Switch," "Think-Pair-Share," and "Turn and Talk."
> - Have students verbalize directions while performing a task.
> - Create raps, rhymes, or mnemonics to support memory of key points.
> - Have students form cooperative groups where they can explain ideas, test hypotheses, make creative suggestions, and debate ideas.

Visual Learners

Visual learners appreciate and learn from information that they see or read. They create and seek illustrations, pictures, and diagrams. Graphic organizers are useful tools for visual learners, as they help them to construct meaning visually. Color has an impact on their learning. Visual stimuli help them make memories "in the mind's eye," and they can often easily recall ideas, concepts, and ideas that have been presented in a visual way or for which they have created symbolic or pictorial representation.

Applications

Suggestions for visual learners include the following:

- Use descriptive language as well as metaphors and analogies.
- Use presentation materials that are bright and engaging.
- Use SMART boards, DVDs, and television.
- Have students work with objects and other materials that can be examined.
- Use directed observation.
- Decorate classrooms in colorful and appealing ways.
- Evoke guided imagery (e.g., "Picture this . . .").

Tactile Learners

Tactile learners appreciate best the handling of materials, writing, drawing, and being involved with concrete experiences. When they ask to see something, their hands are out ready to examine the resource fully. These are often the students who are tapping pencils, doodling, and so forth, as their hands need to be busy to engage their minds. They are "mild" kinesthetic learners.

Applications

Suggestions for tactile learners include the following:

- Use manipulatives.
- Evoke the sense of touch.
- Provide opportunities to learn through touching and feeling.
- Provide opportunities to fiddle with materials and handle and examine them.
- Use models and dioramas.
- Engage students in learning through active practice.
- Allow students to create collections related to the topic.

Kinesthetic Learners

Kinesthetic learners appreciate best the opportunities to learn by doing and moving; that is, by becoming physically involved in learning activities that are meaningful and relevant in their lives. Creating models and constructing samples and examples allow their muscles to "make memories."

Applications

Suggestions for kinesthetic learners include the following:

- These students remember what is done rather than what is said.
- Engage them in role-playing and simulations.
- Take field trips.
- Have students work with others to create meaning.
- Allow for the spontaneous application of new ideas and concepts.
- Have students create representations of understanding through concrete materials.

Tactile/kinesthetic learners want to be physically involved in the learning process. They appreciate role-playing and simulations and like the freedom and opportunity to move about the classroom. "Sitting and getting" frustrates these learners, and they will become disengaged or distracted when their needs aren't met. Such stress can cause the release of adrenaline and cortisol in the bloodstream, which if present continuously is harmful to the cardiovascular system. Movement helps reduce the adrenaline, cortisol, and sodium in the bloodstream.

Applications

Suggestions for tactile/kinesthetic learners include the following:

- Have students engage in imitation and repetition.
- Ensure that learning involves more than "sit and get."
- Allow students opportunity for movement and change of "scenery."
- Provide a variety of learning environments.

In a differentiated block of time, all types of learners may have time to engage in their preferred mode of learning. More important than labeling students is that when we are planning, we build into our instruction multiple interactions that will at some point satisfy the different styles of learners.

So we ask ourselves as planners for diverse learners, Are there opportunities for

- discussion and listening?
- creating or using pictures, video, SMART boards, charts, diagrams, and split-sheet note taking?

- hands-on examination of materials and manipulatives?
- role-playing, stations and centers, and physical movement?

Figure 2.1 lists some products that might appeal to the various types of learners. For more ideas, check out www.learningabledkids.com.

Figure 2.1 Approaches to Engaging Different Learners

Auditory	Visual	Bodily/Kinesthetic
• Dialogue • Presentations • Auditory recording • Song lyrics • Oral report • Press conference • Interviews • Cooperative learning • Literature circle • Debate or panel • Speech • Travelogue	• Poster • Advertisement • Brochure • Collage • Comic strip • Bulletin board • Graphic organizer • Computer program • Magazines • Photo essay • Pamphlet with illustrations • Cartoons • Photographs • Slide show • Video web	• Role-play • Simulations • Collections • Dance • Mime • Tableau • Exhibits • Model • Learning center • Play or skit • Puppet show • Rap or rhyme • Photography • Experiments

THINKING STYLES

Anthony Gregorc (1985) of the University of Connecticut developed a theory of thinking styles based on two variables: our view of the world (whether we see the world in an abstract or concrete way) and how we order the world (in a sequential or random order). Gregorc combined these variables to create four styles of thinking:

The Beach Balls: Concrete Random Thinkers

These thinkers, who enjoy experimentation, are also known as divergent thinkers. They are eager to take intuitive leaps in order to create. They have a need to find alternate ways of doing things. Thus in the classroom, these types of thinkers need opportunities to make choices about their learning and about how they demonstrate understandings. They enjoy creating new models and practical things that result from their new learning and concepts they develop.

The Clipboards: Concrete Sequential Thinkers

These thinkers are based in the physical world as identified through their senses. They are detail oriented, appreciate order, and don't particularly like "out of the ordinary" in the classroom. They appreciate structure, frameworks, timelines, and organization to their learning. They like lecture and teacher-directed activities. Randomness unnerves them.

The Microscopes: Abstract Sequential Thinkers

These thinkers appreciate being in the world of theory and abstract thought. Their thinking processes are rational, logical, and intellectual. They are happiest when involved with their own work and investigation. These learners need to have the time to examine fully the new ideas, concepts, and theories that have been presented. They seek out support for the new information by investigating and analyzing so that the learning makes sense and has real meaning for them.

The Puppies: Abstract Random Thinkers

These thinkers make sense of information through sharing and discussing. They live in a world of feelings and emotion and learn best when they can personalize information. These learners like to discuss and interact with others as they learn. Cooperative group learning, centers or stations, and partner work facilitate their understanding.

Figure 2.2 shows the four styles of thinking, their characteristics, and implications for the classroom.

Applying the Four Thinking Styles in the Classroom

To identify the thinking styles present in the classroom, a teacher might have students rank the four styles or symbols from 1 to 4, based on their understanding of themselves. Teachers can point out that we all have some

Figure 2.2 Different Thinking Styles: Characteristics and Applications

Thinking Style	Characteristics of Learners	Implications for the Classroom
Concrete Random 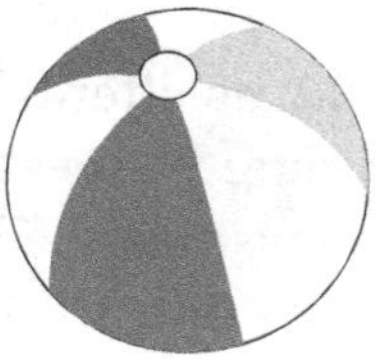	Have an experimental attitude and behavior; are intuitive; are divergent thinkers; enjoy finding alternate ways of solving problems.	These learners need opportunities to make choices about their learning and how they will demonstrate understanding. They like independent work without teacher intervention. They respond to a rich environment.
Concrete Sequential 	Derive information through hands-on experience; are based in the physical world as identified through their senses; prefer concrete materials.	These learners require structure, frameworks, timelines, and organization to their learning. They like lecture and teacher-directed activities with step-by-step procedures.
Abstract Sequential 	Prefer to decode written, verbal, and image symbols; delight in theory and abstract thought; thinking processes are rational, logical, and intellectual.	These learners prefer presentations and lectures that have substance and are rational and sequential in nature. They defer to authority. They have low tolerance for distractions
Abstract Random 	Live in a world of feelings and emotion; associate the medium with the message; evaluate learning experience as a whole; organize information through sharing and discussing.	These learners prefer to receive information in group discussion. They gather information and delay their reaction to it. They organize material through reflection. Cooperative groups, partners, learning centers, and stations facilitate learning.

characteristics of each type but that students' top two choices show the way they would prefer to learn and the types of activities that would be most comfortable for them.

Dr. Robert Sternberg, in his book *Successful Intelligence* (1996), suggested that intelligent people who will be successful in life are able to use information or knowledge in practical, analytical, and creative ways. Learners with different styles bring their natural ability to be practical, analytical, and creative to the group. Thus, it is valuable to organize learning so that a variety of students' strengths are working together. Different ways of thinking are not a detriment to group interaction but rather a gift when different perspectives are represented and shared.

Teachers may want to take time to examine what each of the four style preferences would appreciate in the classroom. For example, Beach Balls want to keep moving, be creative, and be free to go where they wish. Therefore, in a classroom, they want choice and options in their learning and the opportunity to be creative and move freely, using centers and so forth. One group of teachers generated the following list of what they thought the four types would value in the classroom:

Beach Ball

- Variety of resources
- Adaptive environment
- Various manipulatives
- Choice of activities
- Spontaneity
- Extensions to activities
- Personal freedom

Clipboard

- Organization
- Structure
- Visual directions
- Clear closure
- Sequential learning
- Clear procedures
- Consistent routines
- Clear expectations

Microscope

- Investigative learning
- Critical thinking
- Verifying information
- Analyzing concepts
- Deep exploration
- Discussions
- Focus on details
- Ownership

Puppy

- Comfortable environment
- Encouraging atmosphere
- Supportive grouping
- Safe climate
- Respectful colleagues
- Empathic listeners
- Sensitive peers

Which style delineator a teacher uses is not as important as the teacher's recognizing that different students have different preferences and designing learning so that the diverse clientele in the classroom have their needs satisfied at some point (see Figure 2.3).

Figure 2.4 is an example of how all four objects can relate to a unit on the Great Depression. Not only do the activities appeal to the different learning styles, but they also facilitate thinking at a variety of levels, from recall to application.

EMOTIONAL INTELLIGENCES

Another distinguishing characteristic that makes brains unique is emotional intelligence (Goleman, 1995), or the ability to use one's emotions intelligently. Emotion intelligence includes five domains (see Figure 2.5). Students differ dramatically with respect to demonstrating competencies in each of these domains.

Self-Awareness

Self-awareness is the ability to recognize a feeling as it happens. Our feelings influence our personal decision making. "People with greater certainty about their feelings are better pilots of their lives" (Goleman, 1995, p. 43). In

Figure 2.3	Lesson-Planning Checklist: Have You Done Your Best to Know Every Learner in Your Classroom?

Considering Beach Balls	☐ Have a chance to make choices. ☐ Are able to be self-directed for some time. ☐ Are in a competitive situation on occasion. ☐ Are allowed to experiment through trial and error. ☐ Get a chance to brainstorm and deal with open-ended options. ☐ Engage in hands-on activities. ☐ Are encouraged to create and use their imagination.
Considering Clipboards	☐ Receive clear directions and expectations. ☐ Environment is orderly, consistent, and efficient. ☐ Timeline of assignments and grading guidelines are shared clearly and accurately. ☐ Materials are available; models or samples are shown. ☐ Real experiences invoked; genuine need for learning established. ☐ Concrete examples, not theories, used. ☐ Thrive with procedures, routines, and predictable situations. ☐ Access practical, hands-on applications. ☐ Engage in guided practice for successful results.
Considering Microscopes	☐ Have expert and ample references and sources. ☐ Feel confident and comfortable. ☐ Can work alone part of the time. ☐ Have time for thorough investigation. ☐ Can write analytically. ☐ Can learn from lecture and reading. ☐ Can think in abstract terms and language. ☐ Get a chance to delve into interest areas important to them.
Considering Puppies	☐ Have opportunities to work with others. ☐ Time provided for self-reflection. ☐ Receive feedback; connect with teacher and other learners. ☐ Have a rationale for the learning. ☐ Feel included and get some personal attention and support. ☐ Environment is safe for taking risks and is mostly noncompetitive. ☐ Open communication exists; their ideas are accepted.

Figure 2.4 Sample Differentiated Lesson on the Great Depression

For the Beach Balls . . . Do something interesting with the content.	☐ Create a role-play to depict the political situation during the Depression. ☐ Create a role-play to depict the social ramifications of the Depression. ☐ Create a role-play to depict some of the Depression's major events. ☐ Create a visual to show how people lived during the Depression.
For the Clipboards . . . Work with concrete information.	☐ Describe the political and social situation during the Depression. What were the contributing factors? ☐ List the causes of the Depression in rank order from your perspective. Have a rationale for your ranking.
For the Microscopes . . . Connect with the deeper meanings of the topic.	☐ What was life like for people during the Depression? ☐ Why did the Depression occur? How might it have been avoided? ☐ If the Depression happened today, how would people react? How would they spend their time?
For the Puppies . . . Connect with the personal aspects of the topic.	☐ How do you think people felt during the Depression? ☐ What was done to raise the spirits of those who were struggling? ☐ Interview three or four people who lived through the Depression. Prepare at least 10 questions, from narrow to broad, for the interview.

Figure 2.5	Five Domains of Emotional Intelligence
Self-Awareness	One's ability to recognize one's own emotions
Managing Emotions	One's ability to express and control emotions as the situation dictates
Self-Motivation	One's ability to persist in the face of setbacks or obstacles
Empathy	One's ability to recognize emotions in others and to feel with others
Social Skills	One's ability to deal with and manage the emotions of others

Source: Adapted from Salovey, in Goleman (1995).

addition to recognizing their feelings, those with a well-developed sense of self-awareness can describe those feelings in their own words. They also possess strategies to manage moods. For example, if they are in a bad mood, they have several ways to deal with that mood—perhaps exercising, talking with a friend, or listening to music. Teachers who can articulate their feelings and encourage students to do the same help build students' emotional vocabulary. Helping students identify a range of emotions, such as anxious, depressed, angry, excited, and joyful, helps them expand their emotional language beyond sad, mad, glad, and bad.

Managing Emotions

The skill of managing emotions follows self-awareness. Managing emotions is a capacity to deal with feelings so that they are appropriate in a particular circumstance. This domain of emotional intelligence includes the ability to soothe or calm oneself, control anger, deal with irritability or failure, and dispel feelings of anxiety. Teachers report that many students have not had experience managing emotions or seen this skill modeled. One teacher organized several lessons around this domain. She showed popular videos with scenes in where individuals did either a good or poor job of managing their emotions. After viewing each clip, the class analyzed the decision making embedded in the scenario. When an actor "lost control," the class discussed what alternatives might have been used and the possible consequences of each. The class then explored conflict resolution options. After identifying these methods and practicing them, class members were able to handle situations more skillfully.

Self-Motivation

Motivation is the ability to "keep on, keeping on," even in tough situations. Motivating oneself and delaying gratification are key skills that enable a student to focus, resist the urge to give up when the "going gets tough," and pursue goals. These abilities often create a sense of optimism and future accomplishment. Goleman (1995) wrote about entering a "flow state":

> Being able to enter flow is emotional intelligence at its best; flow represents perhaps the ultimate in harnessing emotions in the service of performance and learning. . . . Flow is a state of self-forgetfulness. . . . People in flow are so absorbed in the task at hand that they lose all self-consciousness, dropping the small preoccupations. . . . In flow, people exhibit a masterly control of what they are doing, their responses perfectly attuned to the changing demands of the task. And although people perform at their peak while in flow, they are unconcerned with how they are doing, with thoughts of success or failure—the sheer pleasure of the act itself is what motivates them. (pp. 90–91)

One teacher asked students to bring in examples of people who were in a state of flow. Students identified artists, athletes, writers, musicians, and mechanics. Then she asked students to consider, "Have you ever experienced a flow state?" After some dialogue, students were asked to do a "quick write" about flow states they had encountered or imagined.

Empathy

Empathy—the ability to "walk a mile in another's shoes"—is predicated on self-awareness. Violent criminals, such as murderers, rapists, child molesters, and psychopaths, seem to lack this domain. The Net Generation views many violent acts on television, on the Internet, and in video games, and some students have become desensitized to others' feelings. Parents who are sensitive to others often foster empathy in children by asking how a person in a particular circumstance might feel. For example, if a child read a story in which a pet was hurt, the parent might ask how the pet feels, or if the child had a fight with his or her best friend, the parent might ask how the friend feels. These questions help children consider others and to change their perceptions. Teachers, with many standards focused on point of view or perspective taking, can approach teaching empathy while simultaneously building critical competencies in language arts and reading.

Social Skills

Having social skills, or managing relationships, is the ability to handle emotions in other people. This is the ability to read body language and anticipate another individual's needs. Individuals who do this well are often described as "socially adept." They are popular and well liked. They are often charismatic. They are adept in leadership roles and frequently demonstrate the same in interpersonal relationships. In one class, students were asked to identify someone who they thought demonstrated exemplar social skills, and each student wrote a paragraph about why this particular individual was a model of this domain of emotional intelligence.

Applying the Five Emotional Domains in the Classroom

These domains can be both modeled and addressed in the classroom in a variety of ways. Figure 2.6 suggests ways to foster each of the emotional intelligence domains and strategies to apply in classroom activities to promote standards.

THE WORLD OF THE FUTURE

It has been said that parents and teachers prepare students for a world they will never know. It is a world unfamiliar. For example, Alvin Toefler, a well-known futurist, offered that the "literacy of the future" will not be the ability to read and write but rather the ability to learn, unlearn, and relearn. This prediction is based on the forecast that new information will emerge and transform rapidly. Other futurists tell us that a person under age 25 will be expected to change careers every 10 years and jobs every 4 years. The Secretary's Commission on Achieving Necessary Skills (1991) outlined five competencies that will be essential to thrive in the future. (The Conference Board of Canada [2000] identified similar employability skills.) The five competencies are an ability to

1. identify, organize, plan, and allocate resources.

2. work with others.

Figure 2.6 Fostering Emotional Intelligence in the Classroom

Intelligence	How to Foster Emotional Intelligence	Strategies for Application
Self-Awareness One's ability to sense and name a feeling when it happens	• Help students discuss their feelings in different situations.	• Reflection • Logs and journals
Managing Emotions Recognizing and labeling feelings, then dealing with them appropriately	• Use "teachable moments" to help students learn to manage emotions.	• Deep breathing • Counting to 10 • Time out • Physical movement
Self-Motivation Competencies such as persistence, goal setting, and delaying gratification	• Help students find their niche. Help them to persist in difficult or challenging situations.	• Goal setting • Persistence strategies • Problem solving
Empathy Ability to feel for another person	• Encourage students to "stand in another's shoes." • Help students to think about another's pain.	• Modeling empathy • Discussing empathic responses to persons studied
Social Skills Competencies that one uses to "read" and manage emotional interactions	• Teach social skills explicitly. • Have students practice social skills while doing group tasks.	• Modeling social skills • Using explicit language to describe behaviors so students can practice the skill

3. acquire and use information.

4. understand complex interrelationships (systems).

5. work with a variety of technologies.

Extended periods of instructional time provide opportunities for these life skills to be developed.

A national survey of what employers are looking for in entry-level workers found that specific technical skills are now less important than the underlying ability to learn on the job. After that, employers listed the following:

• Listening and oral communication
• Adaptability and creative responses to setbacks and obstacles

- Personal management, confidence, motivation to work toward goals, a sense of wanting to develop one's career and take pride in accomplishments
- Group and interpersonal effectiveness, cooperativeness and teamwork, skills at negotiating disagreements
- Effectiveness in the organization, wanting to make a contribution, leadership potential (Carnevale et al., as cited in Goleman, 1998, pp. 12–13)

As one reflects on workplace realities, it becomes apparent that rigorous academic standards have been designed to assist students in meeting future challenges. Some schools are recognizing that it will take unconventional means—like restructuring time and varying teaching methodology—to prepare students to meet these necessary ends.

Characteristics of the Digital Natives

Just as the world is changing, requiring different skill sets to survive and thrive, so are students changing. The students who are entering classrooms today have never known a world without e-communication. Technology is as natural to them as breathing. They also share a set of Net Generation norms (Tapscott, 2009).

Net Generation Norms

- Digital natives need their freedom, including of choice and expression. For example, they value having a choice of where and when they work, of job and career path, and of the way in which they express themselves.
- They require personalization and customization. They like to manipulate information and customize it to their needs and interests.
- They avail themselves of information, particulary from the Internet, to meet their needs.
- They examine potential employers for integrity and values similar to their own.
- They just "wanna have fun," whether at work or play. About 87 percent of American children from the ages of 2 to 17 are regularly involved in video games. They are accustomed to interactive experiences and learning.
- They appreciate expediency, as they are used to rapid communication, such as during real-time chats.
- They are innovators who want the latest technology and consistently seek innovative ways to collaborate, entertain themselves, work, and learn.

Source: Tapscott, D. (2009). *Grown up digital: How the Net Generation is changing your world.* New York: McGraw Hill, pp. 34–36.

THE ADOLESCENT BRAIN

During the teen years, significant evolution occurs in the activity, neurochemistry, and anatomy of the brain. Neural pruning occurs in earnest in early childhood, as the brain makes connections and eliminates unused or designated neurons to increase brain efficiency. The brain picks up this process again through the adolescent years into the early 20s.

Change happens mainly in several areas of the brain.

Frontal Lobes

This area is found behind the forehead. Jay Giedd and colleagues at the National Institutes of Mental Health (NIMH) used functional magnetic resonance imaging (fMRI) to scan 1,000 healthy children and adolescents ages 3 to 18 and discovered that a huge spurt of brain development takes place from ages 9 to 10. Millions of new synapses that process information form. Then at 11 years of age, substantial pruning takes place, which then continues throughout the teen years (Spinks, 2002).

Axon Myelination

Myelination is the coating of the axons of the brain cells with a fatty material called myelin. The myelin sheath winds around the axons of the neurons (brain cells) and allows for faster and more efficient transport of electrical impulses. Any action or thinking process repeated habitually is strengthened by myelination to a higher level of maturity. Brain scans of the frontal lobes of teens ages 12–16 show considerably less myelination than those of young adults ages 23–30 (Spinks, 2002).

Executive Control

The prefrontal cortex (immediately behind the forehead) is often referred to as the "CEO of the brain." It is responsible for

- making sound judgments;
- goal setting and prioritization;
- organization and planning of tasks;
- controlling impulses; and
- controlling emotions.

Young adolescents seem to be lacking these executive control functions. This is probably due to a huge number of unpruned synapses and incomplete myelination of axons. Their brains are simply not finished preparing for these complex decisions.

Emotional Thinking

In the limbic system, the small almond-shaped structure called the amygdala supports emergency responses. The amygdala was responsible for the survival of the species on the savannah. Giving a threatening signal, the amygdala immediately short-circuited the thinking response to "flight or fight" to save the individual. Adolescents for the most part are using this method of response rather than making decisions with logic and reason and the considered weighing of consequences, all of which would take place in the prefrontal lobes. At Harvard's McLean Hospital, Dr. Deborah Yurgelun-Todd and her team used fMRI to compare how teens and adult brains reacted to emotion. Teens repeatedly had more activity in the amygdala, while adult brains showed more in the frontal lobes (Spinks, 2002).

The results of this study also showed that adolescents

- are not as adept at reading facial expressions and body language; and
- make poor choices, reacting from an emotional rather than rational stance.

Circadian Rhythms and Sleep Patterns

Dr. Mary Carskadon (2002) at Brown University's Bradley Hospital has found that adolescents need at least nine and a quarter hours of sleep a night, while prepuberty children need 10 hours. This becomes a challenge when their circadian clock changes and they no longer become sleepy in time to get enough rest without sleeping in in the morning. Given all the societal demands of homework, part-time jobs, sports, and family commitments, plus the media draw of television, computer, e-communication, and so forth, they can't seem to get to bed at an hour that would allow them to get nine and a quarter hours of sleep each night. Teachers of early classes note that students are there in body but not in mind.

Continuous lack of sleep has an effect on the amount of deep, rapid eye movement (REM) sleep that is necessary for the consolidation of new learning in the neocortex and students' ability to be attentive to and absorb new information and skills.

Many districts are rethinking their daily schedules in middle and high schools to accommodate the circadian rhythms of young adolescents. They are starting later in the morning and rotating periods so that students don't always have the same subject during their sleepiest time of day.

Applications

Although we can't change the biology of the brain, the National Sleep Foundation (n.d.) suggests adolescents do the following:

- Avoid caffeine and nicotine in the afternoon.
- Stop using the TV and computer and stop heavy studying right before bed so the brain has a chance to slow synaptic firing and activity.
- Make sure the bedroom is dark and quiet at bedtime but open the blinds/draperies and turn on the lights in the morning to start the body's wakening cycle.
- Keep weekend sleeping like that on weeknights as much as possible to avoid confusing the brain's circadian rhythms.

MEETING THE NEEDS OF INDIVIDUAL LEARNERS

Planning to meet individual needs requires that lesson plans be flexible and incorporate strategies that differentiate instruction. Not only must teachers decide upon specific strategies they could use for teaching the content, but they must build into the lesson plans key elements that will focus on meeting the needs of students. Listed are examples of these key elements.

- Environment
- Pre-assessments
- Curriculum compacting
- Grouping strategies
- Choice boards
- Differentiated assessments
- Multiple intelligences
- Bloom's taxonomy

With all we now know about styles, the way people think, and physiological realities of the youthful brain, we are challenged to faci........ their opportunities to learn in optimal ways. Let's proceed to examine differentiated ways to provide learning for diverse learners within a block schedule. We'll begin in the next chapter by looking at how to plan for differentiated instruction in the block schedule.

3 Planning for Instruction

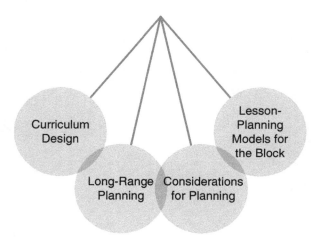

CURRICULUM DESIGN

Teaching is an art form that requires the use of multiple resources. For teachers to make decisions about instructional planning, it is essential that they identify the "what" that needs to be taught. In other words, curriculum must be designed with a vision of student learning outcomes. *Curriculum* is derived from the Latin *currere*, meaning "to run." The oval track known as the *curriculum* on which Romans raced chariots has evolved from a racecourse to an abstract concept (Oliva, 2001). Oliva interpreted curriculum both in terms of subjects taught and as the learning experiences of students.

According to Oliva, curriculum can be interpreted as the following:

- That which is taught in schools
- A set of subjects
- Content

- A program of studies
- A set of materials
- A sequence of courses
- A set of performance objectives
- A course of study
- Everything that goes on within the school, including extra-class activities, guidance, and interpersonal relationships
- Everything that is planned by school personnel
- A series of experiences undergone by learners in a school
- That which an individual learner experiences as a result of schooling

Moving to a block schedule provides the opportunity to revisit the curriculum and determine the essential content objectives. The amount of information that could be taught increases daily, and it is impossible to pour all possible information into all curricula. Rather, appropriate content needs to be selected to achieve the targeted learner outcomes. Teachers using a block schedule have often referred to this process of revisiting content as "cleaning out the closet." Teachers often have favorite topics they like to teach, but with the standards movement and the focus on backward design, teachers must ask, Is this content what students need to know and be able to do to achieve the desired results of learning?

The standards movement has increased educator awareness of how curriculum design should be related to expectations and competencies desired for all learners. Standards provide a road map for instruction, creating the need to begin with the end in mind. Essential learnings can be considered achievement targets that set a limit on teacher responsibility while at the same time building in accountability. The achievement targets need to be clear and appropriate, thus validating expectations for the student. When planning for instruction, teachers must take into account the type of achievement target. The following is a list of such targets.

- *Knowledge Mastery (Declarative)*. What students need to know and what they can retrieve
- *Reasoning Proficiency (Procedural)*. Analysis and problem solving
- *Skill (Procedural)*. What students should be able to do well
- *Products (Procedural)*. Tangible products that provide evidence of mastery
- *Dispositional*. Attitudes, values, and interests we want to instill in our students (Stiggins, 1997)

Standards are a description of what students should understand and be able to do following instruction. Benchmarks articulate what students should understand and be able to do at developmentally appropriate levels. This standards-based focus or approach has caused many to revisit and reexamine the practice of designing curriculum. A new way of designing curriculum has often been called "designing down" or backward mapping (Wiggins & McTighe, 1998). It enables the teacher to streamline the planning process and maximize the quality of instructional time. Figure 3.1 presents two ways of approaching the learning process—the traditional versus designing-down model.

Figure 3.1 Designing Down

Traditional Approach	Designing Down
Lesson Design Based On . . .	*Lesson Design Based On . . .*
Content goals ↓	Desired results of student learning (essential learnings) ↓
Course goals ↓	Content standards ↓
Classroom objectives ↓	Benchmarks (by grade level) ↓
Classroom activities/strategies ↓	Assessments that directly measure each content standard and/or benchmark ↓
Assessments	Units, lessons, and activities that align with student needs, standards, benchmarks, and assessments

Figure 3.2 Seamlessly Informing and Facilitating Learning

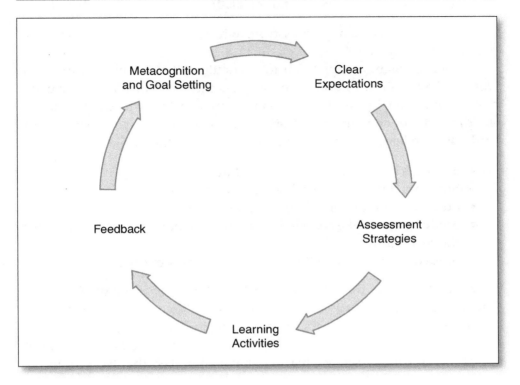

One approach to planning is to use the learning cycle model, which is a seamless process of targeting, planning, and assessing student growth (see Figure 3.2). Content needs to be selected carefully so as to include what is essential in the curriculum as a foundation for that particular discipline. Following are the steps involved in this process:

1. Carefully select expectations and identify content.

2. Design appropriate strategies for collection and feedback (assessment tools).

3. Immerse students in learning activities that will explore the content and develop targeted skills.

4. During the learning process, data are collected on how students are progressing toward standards; this information is valuable to teachers and students in assessing student achievement.

5. Design strategies for student reflection time and goal setting (Robbins, Gregory, & Herndon, 2000).

Figure 3.3 offers many tools from which teachers can choose while planning lessons.

Constructivism, an approach to curriculum that developed from the work of Piaget, allows students to construct their own meaning from experiences provided by the teacher. This approach leads to deeper understanding of the content by the student. Some of the many benefits for students who learn in a constructivist manner are these:

- Students become actively engaged in learning.
- Students develop higher-level thinking skills.
- Students gain ownership of their learning.
- Students can make connections between what they are learning and the real world.
- Students can improve their social and communication skills.

An instructional model of constructivism developed by the Biological Science Curriculum Study (BSCS) employs the "five E's," summarized in Figure 3.4. Each phase has a specific function. With the popularity of using coordinated sequencing of lessons, learning cycles, and instructional models, many science teachers have embraced the BSCS 5E model of instruction.

LONG-RANGE PLANNING

One of a teacher's responsibilities is to pace the curriculum so as to align content with standards and benchmarks and to ensure that students master the content. Students today are often exposed to informational overload, and the teacher has to make sure that time is not spent on repetition and content not addressed in the standards. The expression "less is more" is often heard in teachers' conversations. Many educators find themselves asking, Where do I begin?

At the beginning of each school year, teachers use many strategies to identify the needs of students. Pre-assessments and learning style profiles are two examples. As mentioned above, long-range planning that uses a backward design allows teachers to see the big picture; they can align content, activities, and assessments with the required standards as they plan. Doyle and Strauss (1976) used the analogy that gum is the content teachers bring to the learners and that chewing the gum is the process of understanding and learning. Bob Garmstom, a well-known educator and organizational

Figure 3.3 Tools for Success When Teaching in Extended Instructional Blocks

Instructional Models	Collaborative Structures	Grouping Strategies
Concept attainment Concept formation Inquiry Advance organizer Mnemonics Role-play Synectics Direct instruction Lecture Simulations Group investigation	Think-pair-share Think-pair-share-write-draw Wheel in a wheel Take a stand Checkmate Interview team Round the block Collaborative corners Jigsaw Brainstorming	Cards Counting off Statistics Chairs Smell your way to a group Assignments Name tags Candy Team formation
Roles	**Collaborative Skills**	**Active Learning**
Encourager Questioner Clarifier Summarizer Prompter Gatekeeper Recorder Reporter Materials manager Timekeeper Researcher Liaison Observer	Listening Taking turns Encouraging others Using positive statements Using quiet voices Participating equally Staying on-task Asking for help Checking for understanding Asking for clarification Following directions Accepting difference Disagreeing (agreeably)	Carousel brainstorming Shaping up a review Ticket Out the Door Rhyme Divide and conquer Talk walk Experiments Dramatization Crosswords Graphic organizers Investigations
Multiple Intelligences	**Assessment Tools**	**Authentic Tasks**
Verbal/linguistic Musical/rhythmic Bodily/kinesthetic Logical/mathematical Naturalist Visual/spatial Intrapersonal Interpersonal	Rubrics Contracts PNI Six hats Logs and journals 3-2-1 Reflection stems Portfolio Conferences	Exhibitions Presentations Demonstrations Debates Speeches Models Products Posters Projects

Source: Reprinted from Robbins, P., Gregory, G., & Herndon, L. E. *Thinking Inside the Block Schedule: Strategies for Teaching in Extended Periods of Time.* Copyright © 2000 Corwin.

Figure 3.4 BSCS 5E Instructional Model

Phase	Summary
Engagement	The teacher or a curriculum task accesses the learners' prior knowledge and helps them become engaged in a new concept with short activities that promote curiosity and elicit prior knowledge. The activity should make connections between past and present learning experiences, expose prior conceptions, and organize students' thinking toward the learning outcomes of current activities.
Exploration	Exploration experiences provide students with a common base of activities within which current concepts (i.e., misconceptions), processes, and skills are identified and conceptual change is facilitated. Learners may complete lab activities that help them use prior knowledge to generate new ideas, explore questions and possibilities, and design and conduct a preliminary investigation.
Explanation	The explanation phase focuses students' attention on a particular aspect of their engagement and exploration experiences and provides opportunities to demonstrate their conceptual understanding, process skills, or behaviors. This phase also provides opportunities for teachers to directly introduce a concept, process, or skill. Learners explain their understanding of the concept. An explanation from the teacher or the curriculum may guide them toward a deeper understanding, which is a critical part of this phase.
Elaboration	Teachers challenge and extend students' conceptual understanding and skills. Through new experiences, the students develop deeper and broader understanding, more information, and adequate skills. Students apply their understanding of the concept by conducting additional activities.
Evaluation	The evaluation phase encourages students to assess their understanding and abilities and provides opportunities for teachers to evaluate student progress toward achieving the educational objectives.

Source: Bybee, R. W., Taylor, J. A., Gardner, A., Van Scotter, P., Carlson Powell, J., Westbrook, A., & Landes, N. (2006).

BSCS developed the BSCS 5E Instructional Model in the 1980s. Since that time, BSCS has used this model in its curriculum development programs as well as its professional development programs. The BSCS 5E Instructional Model has been widely disseminated and used as an effective instructional model that allows students to construct their understanding across time. Used with permission from BSCS, www.bscs.org.

change consultant, suggests that for students to internalize and understand learning, they should be provided with perhaps less gum (content) and more time to chew (process the information; Garmston & Wellman, 1995). An analysis of the Third International Mathematics and Science Study (TIMSS) testing showed that curricula in U.S. schools are a "mile wide and an inch deep" (National Center for Education Statistics, 1996). It is crucial instead to focus on facilitating mastery of key concepts rather than on trying to cover all that is in the curriculum (Robbins et al., 2000).

With extended time blocks, learners can have time "to chew and construct meaning," thus enhancing understanding. Many teachers and students who have experienced block scheduling say that the frantic classroom pace is slowed, that teachers can be more intentional about targeting standards, and that students can delve more deeply into the curriculum through a variety of meaningful learning activities (Robbins et al., 2000).

One process used for long-range planning is to design a curriculum map. Curriculum mapping is a calendar-based technique for recording the curriculum that is to be taught. A curriculum map can include standards, objectives, essential questions, content, skills, activities, and assessments. These maps need to be tailored to the needs of the students and the school culture. The rationale for mapping is

- to acquaint teachers with the entire curriculum.
- to focus instruction.
- to define achievement targets.
- to provide opportunities for professional discussion about curriculum articulation.
- to determine if instructional components support district standards and initiatives.
- that the map can serve as a planning tool.
- that the map can be used to plan the ordering of materials and supplies.
- that the map is a pedagogical tool.
- that maps are flexible and can be revised.

Curriculum mapping can create a basis to differentiate instruction. Once standards for mastery are established, teachers can accommodate the variance among learners in their classrooms as well as differentiate by content, process, product, and learning environment.

There are many ways to map curriculum—some teachers map each quarter, while others choose to map units, semesters, or the entire year. Figure 3.5 shows a template that can be used to map curriculum for one semester. Figure 3.6 is a sample map showing curriculum for one month of each of three high school courses.

Long-range planning provides opportunities to assess the scope and sequence of the curriculum and to analyze the parts and interpret the whole. Long-range planning invites teachers to regulate the pace of curriculum delivery. During the course of the school year, teachers may revise the curriculum maps and make adjustments to meet the needs of students. Throughout the year, as teachers modify and adjust the curriculum, they should also modify and change the data to reflect the actual, or taught, curriculum. Individual teachers or groups of teachers can peruse the following list of questions as they analyze and redesign the curriculum as a work in progress:

- Are the essential learnings included?
- Do the topics connect with one another? Are transitions provided between topics?
- What transitional bridges are or could be used?
- Would this order make sense to the learner?
- Have standards been sufficiently explored?
- Are higher-level thinking skills built in?
- Do the assessments demonstrate learning?
- Are the assessments tangible products or observable performances?
- Do the instructional processes/learning strategies have enough variety to reach the diverse group of learners?
- Are metacognition, self-reflection, and goal setting built in?
- Do the learning activities interest, intrigue, and capture the attention of the learners?
- Are the opportunities for making connections, relating and developing understanding, and demonstrating competencies adequate?
- Has adequate time for practice and feedback been built in?

Completed curriculum maps can be shared with other teachers at the same grade level and be reviewed for consistency. Repetitions and gaps in the curriculum can be identified. Maps are often shared across grade levels and disciplines so teachers can develop an understanding of what students experience as a whole. As a result, areas of possible theme integration can be identified. If curriculum is to include what students need for life and learning will endure beyond the test, it is essential that teachers within and across departments go through this culling process. In doing so, many teachers come to recognize that they have missed opportunities to integrate subjects across disciplines and to facilitate movement toward

Figure 3.5 Template for One-Semester Curriculum Map

	August	September	October	November	December	January
Essential Questions						
Standards/ Benchmarks/ Objectives						
Content						
Skills/ Activities						
Assessment						

Figure 3.6 Sample Curriculum Map

	September/Chemistry	October/Math	November/English
Essential Questions	• How will I use math/algebra in chemistry? • How can I use my calculator as a problem-solving tool? • What value does the SI system/metrics have in chemistry and my life? • What can I do to stay safe in a chemistry lab? • How can I write a quality lab report?	• Why is it important to rewrite common formulas for any variable? • How can we use operations of real numbers? • How can we solve real-world problems using a problem-solving plan? • How are graphs used in society today?	• How can knowledge of Greek and Latin root words improve vocabulary skills? • How can writing be evaluated fairly? • Why is composing quality writing important in the workforce?
Standards/ Benchmarks	• Insert district standards.	• Insert district standards.	• Insert district standards.
Content	• SI units, metric prefixes • Metric conversions • Significant digits • Scientific notation • Graphing calculator use • Graphing skills • Safe lab procedures • Scientific inquiry design	• Whole numbers, integers • Rational and irrational numbers • Exponent, base, power • Like terms • Linear inequalities, compound inequalities • Absolute value • Tolerance • Algebraic properties	• Greek and Latin root words • Oral language conventions • Six traits of writing • Creating compound complex sentences • Ideas and organization • Word choice • Sentence fluency • Voice • Transitions
Skills/Activities	• Identify SI units. • Demonstrate correct use of metric prefixes. • Use calculator. • Solve algebraic equations. • Produce graphs by hand. • Produce graphs in Excel. • Use lab equipment. • Write lab reports.	• Graph and order real numbers. • Use operations of real numbers. • Evaluate algebraic expressions. • Simplify like terms. • Solve linear equations. • Rewrite equations with more than one variable. • Rewrite common formulas. • Use a problem-solving plan to solve real-world problems. • Solve simple and compound inequalities. • Solve absolute value equations.	• Apply standard English conventions when writing. • Apply a variety of strategies to expand vocabulary. • Write in narrative, expository, descriptive, and persuasive voice.
Assessment	• Class assignments • Homework worksheets/projects • Lab rubrics • Quizzes • Informal assessment/questioning • Peer grading/assessment • Lab notebooks	• Oral questioning • Rubrics • Written quizzes • Board work • Group work • Daily work • Unit test	• Notebooks • Oral discussions • Vocabulary quizzes • Prewriting assessments • Final drafts of essays • Six-traits writing rubric

standards (Robbins et al., 2000). Some schools have used an integrated curriculum as a way to make education relevant and thus keep students interested in school. Most real-world problems are multidisciplinary; thus, discipline-based curriculum should be changed to an integrated curriculum (Kain, 1993). The checklist in Figure 3.7 can be used for curriculum map review work.

CONSIDERATIONS FOR PLANNING

Many educators find that teaching in shorter periods of time restricts creativity, promotes daily routines that can be stifling, and limits the depth of content covered. Longer class periods, on the other hand, allow educators to design lessons that use a variety of teaching strategies, differentiate instruction, and accommodate the ways students learn. Designing effective lessons requires many decisions and considerations on the part of the teacher. Planning lessons to meet the needs of students is a complex, multifaceted process.

Many school districts provide teachers with curriculum guides to ensure that content aligns with standards and benchmarks. Designing lessons from such a document requires teachers to ask more questions as they plan for instruction.

- What are the state-/district-mandated standards and objectives for the subject/grade level?
- What are the specified achievement targets?
- What content would align with these standards and objectives?

Teachers using curriculum maps often begin lesson planning by using the backward-design model to come up with a weekly plan. The weekly template shown aligns with the format used for curriculum mapping. This weekly plan format can be used to write detailed lesson plans that accommodate differentiation. For example, when taking into consideration how students learn, cognitive research has taught us that the following are key considerations.

- *Primacy-Recency Effect.* The brain remembers best what it encounters first, remembers second best what comes last, and remembers least what is in the middle. In longer class periods, teachers need to chunk information into mini lessons in order to create several "firsts" and "lasts" (Fitzgerald, 1996).
- *Processes of Memory* (short-term to long-term)
  o Attention
  o Memory

Figure 3.7 Checklist for Reviewing and Analyzing Curriculum Maps

Items for Review	Notes
☐ Identify gaps.	
☐ Identify repetitions.	
☐ Identify potential areas for integration.	
☐ Do assessments align with standards?	
☐ Identify content and learning activities to be differentiated.	
☐ Review for timeliness.	

      o Rehearsal (working memory)

      o Context

      o Recall

- *Multiple Intelligences.* Select activities that represent student intelligences.

Using the information about the process of memory is useful for teachers as they plan for lessons. Teachers may want to ask these questions:

- What do I want students to do or be able to do because of this learning experience?
- What do they already know, and what are they already able to do?
- How will we judge success?
- How can attention be captured and sustained?
- What will be the "emotional" hook for the learner?
- How will the new information and skills be acquired?
- How will students practice or rehearse to make meaning and understanding?
- How will they receive ongoing feedback during and after the learning? (Gregory & Chapman, 2007)

The teacher should also keep in mind these considerations while planning for a lesson in a block class:

- Learning must engage the entire person (cognitive, affective, and psychomotor domains).
- The human brain seeks patterns in its search for meaning.
- Emotions are an integral part of learning, retention, and recall.
- Past experience always affects new learning.
- The brain's working memory has a limited capacity.
- Lecture usually results in the lowest degree of retention. Rehearsal is essential for retention.
- The brain is a parallel processor, performing many functions simultaneously.
- Practice does not make perfect.
- Each brain is unique (Jensen, 2003).

LESSON-PLANNING MODELS FOR THE BLOCK

Various lesson-planning models have been proposed. Whichever model one chooses, the following considerations for lessons in the block should be kept in mind:

- Divide the time into three or four chunks to provide several beginnings, ends, and middles (BEMs). Consider changing topics or activities related to a particular standard. This promotes alertness, attention, and engagement.
- Chunk the content so that students can develop "mental files" of related ideas and information.
- Vary teaching strategies to address and honor the diversity of learners in the class.
- Provide a variety of learning experiences so that each learner is in a state of "flow" (Csikszentmihalyi, 1990) at some time during the period. Consider selecting activities representative of the multiple intelligences in the group.
- Build in opportunities for interactive dialogue, movement, and hands-on tasks, as well as for intrapersonal moments of reflection.
- Consider the cognitive research on how humans make meaning and develop memories of key learnings.
- Build assessment strategies into the learning cycle to give the learners ongoing feedback based on their progress toward targeted standards. Vary the type of assessment strategies so that all learners may thrive (Robbins et al., 2000).

One of the most familiar lesson-planning models is Madeline Hunter's (Russell & Hunter, 1976) seven-step lesson plan. As we look at this model, we can see that each step effectively links to the research about how the brain learns and makes meaning.

1. *Anticipatory or Mental Set.* Capture student attention through *sensory* stimulation (visual, auditory, tactile, or olfactory). This sets the stage for the learning that is to come.

2. *Sharing the Purpose.* Provide an overview of the lesson or unit to give students a sense of security about the lesson's direction and how they will get there.

3. *Providing Input.* Taking into account the broad standards targeted and the subject discipline expectations, choose content or subject material to create a high-quality, meaningful learning experience.

4. *Demonstrating and Modeling. Modeling* is a visual representation of what is being learned. In most cases, modeling is presented at the same time as or after teaching information.

5. *Checking for Understanding.* The teacher monitors students to determine whether they understand the material. The teacher assesses students' competency in using the skills that have been introduced.

6. *Guided and Perfect Practice.* Students apply or rehearse what they have learned. *Guided practice* includes coaching with or by peer groups or working with teacher observation and monitoring.

7. *Closure.* Revisit the purpose of the lesson and the expectations or targets. Often, closure addresses the transfer process and helps students reflect on where this new information or skill will be useful in the real world. Typically, *independent practice* follows closure. This engages students in developing fluency and speed in applying new learnings on their own.

Brain research recognizes that closure of a lesson helps students consolidate their learning and allows them to reflect actively on it. Students can also demonstrate to themselves their understanding of what they have learned. Teachers and students get so engaged in activities during the lesson, however, they often find that time runs out before the lesson is closed. Having a tool box of strategies for closure and careful planning and time management will ensure that students get the time for reflection they need.

A "Ticket Out the Door" is one strategy that will engage students in metacognition and allow teachers to assess student understanding of the overall lesson. The template in Figure 3.8 can be copied onto brightly colored paper, then cut into three strips so as to conserve paper. These strips can be placed in a box as the students leave the classroom.

As outlined above, the seven-step lesson plan may seem linear and straightforward. However, it can be as creative as the repertoire the teacher has at his or her disposal. The steps do not have to be in a specific order, and the time spent on each step is not necessarily the same in each lesson. As long as several beginnings, ends, and middles are chunked during the class period to take advantage of the primacy-recency effect, the teacher can be flexible in designing learning by using a variety of strategies and tools to reach the desired standards. The teacher must consider not only the variety of instructional strategies but also the importance of varying learning experiences to include active, passive, kinesthetic, and reflective tasks.

Figure 3.9 shows an example of a lesson plan structure that accommodates these elements. This lesson plan model incorporates three mini lessons, thus taking into consideration the primacy-recency effect.

Figure 3.8 Black Line Master for Ticket Out the Door

Name _____	**Ticket Out the Door**
Period _____	Describe 3 things you learned from today's lesson (be specific).
Date _____	1.
	2.
	3.

Name _____	**Ticket Out the Door**
Period _____	Describe 3 things you learned from today's lesson (be specific).
Date _____	1.
	2.
	3.

Name _____	**Ticket Out the Door**
Period _____	Describe 3 things you learned from today's lesson (be specific).
Date _____	1.
	2.
	3.

Figure 3.9 Real-Time Lesson Plan Template for a Block Schedule

Time	Task	Description
2–3 minutes	Essential Learning (This is often posted on the board for students to see as they enter the room.)	Describe the observable performance or behavior. Can be in the form of an objective or essential question.
4–6 minutes	Warm-Up/Bell Ringer/Anticipatory Set	Capture attention; help students visualize what they will be learning and how they will achieve mastery.
10–15 minutes	First Mini Lesson	Engage the full range of Gardner's multiple intelligences.
15–20 minutes	Second Mini Lesson	Mini lecture: Use teaching aids to promote long-term memory, such as mind maps and visualizations—engage students!
15–20 minutes	Third Mini Lesson	This time can be used for students to apply what they are learning. Can be accomplished via group activities, simulations, role-playing, etc.
20–30 minutes	Evaluation	Know what behaviors are to be observed that support the learner outcomes.
5–10 minutes	Closure	Can be time for reflection using journals or class discussion.
	Independent Practice	Homework.

Alternatively, the lesson design shown in Figure 3.10, which includes time for a transitional activity, may be preferble. Figure 3.11 shows a sample social studies lesson that uses this design.

Good teaching is an art form that requires knowledge not only of how students learn but of best practices and effective lesson design. Expert teachers are constantly refining their skills and stay focused on the essentials. They ask, What do we want students to know and be able to do? How can we meet the needs of all students? Good lesson design addresses these questions. Therefore, using a backward-design model for planning and differentiating instruction is essential for effective lesson planning.

Figure 3.10 Real-Time Lesson Plan Template

Lesson Title: _____ Date: _____

Time in Minutes	Activity
1.	*Opening.* Review, overview, use of prior knowledge, discussion of homework.
2.	*Introduction of Concept/New Knowledge.* Lecture, demonstration, directed reading, multimedia.
3.	*Transitional Activity.* Class discussion, time for reflection, regrouping, movement.
4.	*Application and Use of New Knowledge.* Hands-on activity, small-group projects, problem-solving activity, laboratory experiments.
5.	*Student Assignment.* In-class independent work, homework. (Post directions with due dates.)
6.	*Closure.* Summaries, reflections, journal writing, report outs, Ticket Out the Door.

Figure 3.11 Social Studies Real-Time Lesson Plan (85 minutes)

Lesson Title: <u>Local Government</u>   Date: _____

Time	Activity
1. 15 minutes	*Opening.* Students will work in cooperative groups and discuss why they think local government is necessary. They will brainstorm their ideas and record them on a large sheet of paper. Each group will share its results with the entire class.
2. 20 minutes	*Introduction of Concept/New Knowledge.* PowerPoint presentation on the structure and function of local government and its connections to state and national government. Students will record the information in their interactive notebooks using Cornell note-taking style.
3. 10 minutes	*Transitional Activity.* Students will pick up dictionaries from the shelf and define the following words in their notebooks: *services, department, represent, mayor, council,* and *participant.*
4. 15 minutes	*Application and Use of New Knowledge.* In the left side of their interactive notebooks, using their notes, newspapers, and textbooks, students will construct a flowchart showing the organization of the local government. The chart will include names of current elected officials.
5. 10 minutes	*Student Assignment.* Directions for homework: Students will construct a scrapbook that includes 10 articles from local newspapers that are relative to the actions of local government. Students will explain how the contents of each article may impact themselves, family, and community. Explain the assessment rubric and expectations for this assignment. Time permitting, let students cut out some articles from newspapers for them to take home.
6. 15 minutes	*Closure.* Students will use their notes and information gained from previous activities to answer the following questions in their notebooks: • Why is local government important to the community? • Which people have the greatest influence on local government? • How is local government structured? Students will share their answers with the class.

The following is a list of what teachers do when they are guided by the principles of backward design and differentiated instruction (Tomlinson & McTighe, 2006):

1. Identify the desired results for student learning.

2. Determine acceptable evidence of student learning.

3. Plan learning experiences and instruction based on the first two principles.

4. Regard learning differences as inevitable, important, and valuable in teaching and learning.

5. Address learners' affective needs as a means of supporting student success.

6. Periodically review and articulate clear learning goals that specify what students should know, understand, and be able to do because of each segment of learning.

7. Use systemic pre-assessment and ongoing assessment aligned with designated goals to make instructional decisions and adaptations.

Lesson plans that utilize these essential elements and are guided by the backward-design principles contain the following categories:

- Learning goals
- Materials needed
- Differentiation strategies
- Warm-up
- Teacher focus
- Student focus
- Assessment
- Closure
- Homework

Various instructional strategies and assessment tasks may be selected, depending on targeted standards and content. The lesson plan template in Figure 3.12 helps the teacher focus on the needs of the students and ways to differentiate instruction. Figure 3.13 shows the lesson plan template applied to instruction on healthy nutritional choices; it provides students with choices as to how they will demonstrate their learning.

There are many daily lesson plan models to choose from, and teachers often create their own designs to meet their needs. School districts often have lesson plan templates they prefer their teachers to use, which simplifies the decision-making process for the teacher. Figure 3.14 shows four other models that can be used to plan instruction that are specific for classes that are 90 minutes in length.

Those teachers currently on a block schedule offer the following suggestions for planning, some of which have already been addressed in this chapter.

- Develop plans for the year or semester (curriculum mapping).
- Provide opportunities to engage higher-level thinking skills (Bloom's taxonomy).

Figure 3.12 Daily Lesson Plan

Learning Goals	Warm-Up	Assessment
• Standards • Objectives • Essential questions • Key questions	• Challenge of the day • Preview • Advance organizers • Prior knowledge • Freewriting • Vocabulary	• Monitor for progress • Performance tasks • Reflective questions • Criteria • Rubrics • Academic prompts • Journals • Quizzes • Tests
Materials	**Teacher Focused**	**Closure**
• Textbooks • Websites • WebQuests • Magazines • Classroom supplies	• Direct instruction • Mini lectures • Demonstrations • Modeling • Class discussion • Guided practice • Check for understanding • Guided discovery • PowerPoint • Questioning	• Clarifying misconceptions • Summarizing • Students sharing work • Wrap-up • Major points • Vocabulary review • Ticket Out the Door
Differentiation	**Student Focused**	**Homework**
• IEP accommodations • Content differentiation • Process/skills differentiation • Multiple intelligences • Bloom's taxonomy • Instructional scaffolding • Layered curriculum • Compacting curriculum • Student interests • Student choices • Adjusting questions • Peer teaching • Learning styles • Learning contracts	• Independent practice • Group work • Inquiry-based projects • Application • Problem-based learning • WebQuests • Simulations • Role-playing • Graphic organizers • Reading • Interactive notebooks	• Homework rubric • Homework policy • Clear/purposeful • Modified to student needs • Focused strategy • Less is more

Figure 3.13 Lesson Plan: Nutrition Healthy Choices

Learning Goals	Warm-Up	Assessment
• *Standard.* Students will make informed decisions for a healthy life. • *Objectives.* Students will identify options for healthy snacking based on knowledge of good nutrition. • *Essential Question.* How do we know if a snack is considered healthy?	• Have students in *small groups* examine a selection of snacks and prioritize their preferences. Or • Suggest *a think-pair-share* in which students share with their *partners* the snacks they had yesterday and record on self-sticking notes. Develop a web as a *large-group* activity. Or • *Small groups* can examine several advertisements and list the snacks recommended and the reasons given for eating these choices.	• Rubrics for poster, brochure, and song. • Students will present their rap or song to the class. • Students will explain their poster or brochure to the class.

Materials	Teacher Focused	Closure
• Textbooks • Websites • Magazines • Classroom supplies	• *Mini lecture* using a PowerPoint presentation outlining the nutritional requirements of and suggestions for healthy snacks. • Students will list key points. Or • Students view a *short video* outlining the nutritional requirements of and suggestions for healthy snacking. Students list key points to remember.	• Students will reflect on their analysis and write a response in their journal. • Students will set goals for themselves about their snack choices.

Differentiation	Student Focused	Homework
• IEP accommodations • Content differentiation • Process/skills differentiation • Multiple intelligences • Bloom's taxonomy • Student interests • Student choices • Learning styles • Learning contracts	Choices: • Students will create a *rap or song* to encourage others to choose healthy snacks. • Students will design a *poster* sharing information about selecting healthy snacks. • Students will create a *brochure* that could be seen in a doctor's office that highlights nutritional requirements for healthy living.	• Based on what they learned, students will develop a *survey* to be used for gathering data on people's eating habits. Or • Students will *record* their snacks for the next 3 days. They will bring in their recorded lists and analyze their snacks, using their knowledge of nutrition. They may use a *computer* program to analyze their snack intake.

Figure 3.14 Lesson Plan Models for 90-Minute Class Periods

Lesson Plan Model A

First 30 minutes
- Detailed review
- Instructional objective
- Teacher-directed (lecture/demonstration/discussion)

Second 30 minutes
- Student small groups
- Investigate, discover, or complete tasks.
- Students practice or experiment.

Last 30 minutes
- Debriefing with students and teacher
- Closure of the lesson

Lesson Plan Model B

Review previous lesson	10–15 minutes
Mini lecture	25–30 minutes
Guided practice	15–20 minutes
Reteach	10–15 minutes
Closure	5–10 minutes

Lesson Plan Model C

Warm-up	5 minutes
Mini lecture	20 minutes
Check for understanding	10 minutes
Guided practice	10 minutes
Group activity	20 minutes
Assessment	15 minutes
Closure	10 minutes

Lesson Plan Model D

Homework review	15 minutes
Mini lesson	20 minutes
Graphic organizer	20 minutes
Mini lesson	20 minutes
Closure	15 minutes

- Integrate technology.
- Reorganize the good pieces of previous lessons into new units of instruction.
- Vary instructional approaches.
- Collaborate with peers in planning.
- Consider using a thematic approach.
- Include a product-orientated activity—let students implement what they have learned by engaging in more hands-on activities.
- Include in-class writing.
- Use cooperative learning strategies.
- Build in daily checks for learning and lesson closure.
- Design homework that is used not only as a practice activity but also as a foundation for the next day's lesson.
- Use "open-ended" closure with your lessons.
- Incorporate direct silent reading; follow up with a question-and-answer session.

The demands upon the classroom teacher for accountability are forever increasing. This increases the importance on the planning process. A well-designed curriculum provides the framework to develop curriculum maps from which teachers can draw to construct lessons. The planning approach described here uses the backward-design model in which standards are aligned with assessment and content. The models provided can assist the classroom teacher with planning lessons for a block schedule.

In addition to planning curriculum and lessons, it is critical to plan for effective classroom management. As the next chapter discusses, planning for management of a diverse class, especially in the longer class periods in a block schedule, maximizes learning time and helps provide each student with an optimal learning environment.

4 Classroom Management

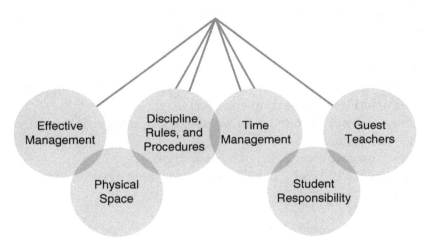

Research today tells us that the single most important factor affecting student achievement is the teacher (Marzano, 2007). Teachers wear many hats, one of which is that of a manager. Teachers who organize their classrooms and manage the behavior of their students will achieve positive educational outcomes. Managing extended blocks of time in a classroom requires teachers to reevaluate their classroom management and adopt new techniques.

EFFECTIVE MANAGEMENT

Canady and Rettig (1995) suggested that a lesson in a block should have a ratio of 75 percent direct instruction and 25 percent classroom management. Moreover, as mentioned in Chapter 3, the primacy-recency effect tells us that the beginning and end of a lesson are the most remembered. Therefore, clerical tasks should be saved for the middle of the lesson.

J. Allen Queen (2000) and colleagues identified important teaching skills necessary for success in a block class. Those related to classroom management are listed below:

- The skill to design and maintain an environment that allows for great flexibility and creativity
- The desire and skill to be an effective classroom manager
- The freedom to share the ownership of teaching and learning with the students

Evertson and Harris (1992) studied past research and field studies on effective classroom management and identified several strengths of teachers who are effective managers. These teachers

- use time efficiently.
- implement group strategies with a high level of student involvement and low levels of misbehavior.
- choose lesson formats and academic tasks conducive to high student achievement.
- communicate clear rules of participation.
- prevent problems by implementing a system at the beginning of the year.

More recently, Robert J. Marzano (2007) conducted a meta-analysis of classroom management that included 100 separate reports to be able to say with more certainty which strategies work and which do not. Based on this analysis, seven research-based elements of effective classroom management were identified:

1. Rules and procedures

2. Discipline and consequences

3. Teacher–student relationships

4. Mental set

5. Student responsibility

6. Getting off to a good start

7. Management at the school level

Three components of classroom management are outlined in Figure 4.1.

| Figure 4.1 | Components of Classroom Management |

Planning (Before School Starts)	Implementation (Beginning of School Year)	Monitoring (Ongoing)
• Arrange classroom furniture. • Place stations in room for student work, etc. • Establish rules and procedures. • Organize materials and supplies. • Plan activities for first week of school. • Create a learning environment. • Conduct lesson planning.	• Create class rules with students. • Post class rules. • Teach rules and procedures. • Model rules and procedures. • Role-play rules and procedures. • Communicate expectations. • Create class climate conducive to learning. • Conduct student surveys.	• Monitor behavior. • Praise positive behavior. • Consistently enforce rules and procedures. • Use progressive discipline. • Differentiate instruction. • Provide positive feedback. • Monitor student progress. • Communicate with parents.

PHYSICAL SPACE

Creating a learning environment for students is one aspect of classroom management that begins before school starts. Effective teachers spend a great deal of time organizing materials and preparing the physical environment. Resource-rich classrooms can motivate learners to explore their environment. Bulletin boards that display relevant materials help students focus on the content and processes of the curriculum.

Furthermore, the use of color is important when setting up a room for the school year. The effects of color on moods and the way we think have been studied for many years. Due to the different backgrounds and experiences students bring with them to the classroom, there will be some variability in the moods colors create. However, some universal reactions to color apply to almost everyone. When teachers prepare visual displays for their classrooms, they should choose posters and create notices that take into account these reactions.

Applications

Some universal reactions to color apply to almost everyone:

Red. The fire color; can bring feelings of warmth and excitement.

Blue. The color of skies and lakes; associated with cleanliness and tranquility.

(Continued)

(Continued)

Yellow. The color of sunlight and fruit; brings feelings of cheer, hope, and vitality.

Orange. The color of sunsets and fire; evokes feelings of energy and excitement.

Purple. Can evoke creativity.

Teachers will reap the rewards of their efforts when students enter a classroom the first day and it is inviting as well as conducive to learning. Teachers and students will spend many hours together in the classroom, so it is imperative that it be welcoming and aesthetically pleasing.

The arrangement of furniture in a classroom can affect the teacher's ability to manage the class effectively. The room should be arranged so that students feel free and comfortable. A classroom crammed with furniture not only is difficult to manage but can inhibit student interaction. There are many factors to consider when organizing classroom space, including the following:

- Arrange desks according to your teaching techniques.
- Allow for mobility for both yourself and the students.
- The teacher's desk and chair should be located so they are easily accessible to students and provide the teacher with a clear view of the students.
- Sit in the students' seats to visualize the room from their perspective.
- Try not to change the arrangement too often so students can develop ownership of their space.
- Try to maintain the same seating for assessment, since students often make physical/spatial associations while learning.
- Review all safety policies, such as fire drills, and leave space for students to exit the room in a timely manner.

One tool freely available for those teachers who like to create a floor plan of their classroom is Classroom Architect, which can be found at http://classroom.4teachers.org. This tool allows one to produce a layout of the classroom without the heavy lifting. One inputs the basic dimensions of the room, and once items are arranged on a grid, one can print out the layout.

Materials students will need during the school year should be readily accessible. All items should be clearly labeled and easy to read. Designate a corner or place in the room where all student supplies are located. Color coding items will assist students in returning them to the correct place. Use clear plastic containers to hold items such as scissors, tape, glue, and colored pencils. Some teachers assign corresponding numbers to desks and plastic containers that hold all items a student may need. This way the student is responsible to make sure all items are returned or replaced when used up. Another technique is to assign a color for each class and give the items for that class labels of the same color. Baskets for work to be turned in can also be labeled with class colors. Having a set color for each class can help the teacher organize class work and class notes by using colored binders, sticky notes, and folders.

Set aside a space where students will be able to display their work. Some classrooms have separate bulletin boards. In those that do not, save some wall space for future work. Students often need a place to store work that has been completed and assessed for future reference. Plastic crates that hold file folders are especially useful for this purpose. Student names are printed on labels, which are attached to manila folders. These folders provide easy access to student work for parent-teacher conferences, reviewing to prepare for assessment, or for any other purpose. It will be necessary to have a procedure in place for students to file their work.

DISCIPLINE, RULES, AND PROCEDURES

Increasing student achievement should be a goal of all educators. This is achieved by decreasing behavioral problems by using positive behavioral strategies that lengthen instructional time. Classroom teachers feel more in control and more competent when they have a formal plan for discipline and procedures in place (Charles, 1996). Likewise, students cannot function well in a chaotic environment. Students actually prefer structure or routines; they want to know exactly what they are supposed to do. Effective teachers create a classroom climate that is structured and caring and one in which students feel safe. Effective teachers also center their classroom management on a philosophy of differentiating instruction.

Rules and procedures are necessary for a climate in which students and teachers work together. Time invested at the beginning of the school year on rules and procedures will foster a climate conducive to learning with few disruptions. Students need to feel they belong, and allowing them to share in the development of the classroom rules and procedures will provide student ownership. In turn, student ownership of the rules and procedures will more likely lead to students consistently following them. Rules should be

- specific;
- student–teacher generated;
- understandable;
- practical/doable;
- manageable;
- consistent with school rules;
- written in positive terms;
- appropriate for the context in which teaching occurs; and
- limited to no more than five.

Some sample rules are these:

- Be in your assigned seat ready to work when the bell rings.
- Raise your hand and wait to be recognized before speaking.
- Respect the rights and property of others.
- Begin the bell activity within one minute after the bell rings.

Certain areas of study require more than one set of rules. For example, science teachers may have a separate set of rules for laboratory exercises, and physical education teachers may have rules for the locker room and rules for the gymnasium.

Figure 4.2 is an example of a set of rules for a science classroom that were established by students with the teacher's guidance.

Figure 4.2 Classroom Behavioral Expectations

Classroom Behavioral Expectations

- *Be On Time.* Students are expected to be in their seats ready to work when the bell rings.
- *Be Prepared.* Bring all necessary materials to class every day.
- *Be Respectful.* Respect your teacher, your classmates, school property, and yourself.
- *Be Safe.* Follow all laboratory safety procedures.
- *Be Involved.* This is part of the learning process; you are expected to participate.
- *Be Responsible.* Complete assignments on time, including makeup work when absent.
- *Be a Great Classroom Citizen.* Use appropriate language and follow all classroom procedures and protocols.

Sometimes students have difficulty following classroom rules and procedures. Students who show negative behaviors can disrupt the learning environment. Having a progressive discipline policy in place sends a message of consistency and fairness to all students. These types of policies provide opportunities for teachers to change students' negative behavior. Many school districts have progressive discipline policies in place to ensure that discipline is enforced consistently among teachers. Here is one example of such a policy:

First Offense. Verbal warning

Second Offense. Parent contact

Third Offense. Teacher detention

Fourth Offense. Counselor referral

Fifth Offense. Dean's referral

When students know what to expect, as they will in a structured environment, they will feel safe and work with greater confidence. Therefore, it is necessary to have procedures for all activities and events that happen in a classroom. A *procedure* is a method or process of how a teacher wants things done. Procedures are necessary for an effective classroom for several reasons.

- Procedures are statements of expectations necessary to function effectively in the classroom environment.
- Procedures allow for activities to take place effectively.
- Procedures increase time on-task and reduce classroom disruption.
- Procedures tell students how things operate in a classroom.

Many procedures, such as for turning in assignments, will need to be discussed and modeled at the beginning of the school year. Other procedures should be explained at the time of the event, as, for example, when the first test is given. One method for teaching procedures is to use a three-step approach:

1. *Explain.* State, explain, model, and demonstrate the procedure.

2. *Rehearse.* Have students ehearse and practice the procedure under the teacher's supervision.

3. *Reinforce.* Reteach, rehearse, practice, and reinforce the procedure until it becomes a classroom habit or routine (Wong & Wong, 1991).

TIME MANAGEMENT

Using time effectively is an essential component of effective teaching. The goal of any teacher is to increase the amount of time spent on instruction and learning, because doing so increases student learning and achievement (Wong & Wong, 1991). Wong and Wong described four types of time at school: allocated time, instructional time, engaged time, and academic learning time. The following is a breakdown of how these times are allocated. (The percentages add up to more than 100 because the teacher and students may be working simultaneously.)

Allocated time: 100%

Instructional time: 90%

Engaged time: 75%

Academic learning: 35%

In an extensive research study conducted in 2005 by 24/7, here is what was observed in 1,500 classrooms:

Behaviors	Percentage
Evidence of clear learning goals	4%
Worksheets	52%
Lecture	31%
Monitoring with no feedback	22%
Use of high-yield, research-based instructional strategies	2%
Communication-rich environment	2%
Fewer than half the students engaged	82%
Bell-to-bell learning	1%

Source: Adapted from Learning 24/7, cited in Schmoker (2006, p. 18).

Extended periods can increase instructional time but can also increase the amount of time wasted if good management strategies are not in place. Block schedules often have 90-minute periods, and keeping students on-task can be challenging for teachers. Effective teachers optimize engaged time and academic learning time. A new principal addressing his staff for the first time explained he had consulted the aliens as to what was happening in the classrooms. He informed the staff that these aliens observed young humans watching old humans working very hard. He challenged the staff to reverse this situation—he wanted to see older people watching the younger ones working very hard. This approach to teaching, in which the teacher takes on the role of facilitator, requires the use of many time management techniques. Effective classroom managers are very well organized, have all materials ready and easily accessible, plan well ahead, use research-based strategies, and foster a safe learning environment in which all students can learn.

Applications

To prevent wasting allocated time, teachers can do the following:

- Plan and organize lessons ahead of time.
- Have all materials and resources in place.
- Collaboratively establish classroom procedures at the beginning of the year.
- Always start on time. Modeling timeliness encourages students to begin on time.
- Have music playing during passing time and stop the music when class begins. This provides an auditory signal to students and establishes a routine.
- Use timers for student activities. Make sure students know how much time they are allowed for activities.
- Use student responsibility forms (described later in this chapter; see Figure 4.8).
- Build in time for students to reflect upon their work.
- Provide opportunities for student movement.
- Differentiate instructional activities.
- Use prep time effectively, taking care of miscellaneous tasks that arise.
- Keep a calendar of tasks that need to be accomplished and prioritize tasks.
- Allocate time each week to work undisturbed.
- Utilize volunteers to complete mundane tasks such as cutting, coloring, sign making, and so forth.
- Keep the room organized and clean. File papers as soon as possible to avoid having piles accumulate.
- With some exceptions, grade only assignments that determine future instruction by telling whether reteaching is necessary or if the class can move forward with the content.
- Assign students roles to assist in handing out papers and collecting student work.

(Continued)

(Continued)

- Use Ready/Working signs when students are working. These are especially useful when students are in cooperative groups. They provide a visual aid to inform the teacher which students are still working on the assignment and which have completed their work. Students are responsible for making sure the working side is facing forward while they are working and the ready side is facing forward when they are finished. (To make the Ready/Working signs from the blackline master in Figure 4.3, fold the paper in half and then in half again. Overlap the top portion and the bottom portion so that they meet in the middle crease. Staple each end of the paper to hold the paper together. These signs can be copied onto colored paper and laminated to increase durability.)
- Minimize open-ended discussions that are not related to the lesson objective.
- To avoid repeating directions, it may be necessary to have directions posted on the board or available to students by technological means.

Managing paperwork can be overwhelming. Many types of documents come across the teacher's desk during the school year. Use three-ring binders with dividers to store papers immediately for future reference. Using binders can prevent piles of papers from accumulating on the desk. Using binders also is a way of modeling organizational skills for students. Label presentation binders so they can easily be identified on a shelf. Suggestions for the contents of binders include the following:

- *Student Information.* Demographic data, skill surveys, learning style surveys, discipline records, and health records (See an example of a student information sheet in Figure 4.4.)
- *Lesson Plans.* Daily/weekly lesson plans, emergency lesson plans, curriculum guides, lists of resources, and lists of videos and other items needed for writing lesson plans
- *School Binder.* Handouts from staff meetings, master schedules, calendars, school policies, technology information, school improvement plans, emergency plans, fire drill information, and lists of phone numbers of school personnel
- *Parent Binder.* Lists of parent contacts, log for parent communication, copy of letters and documents sent to parents, and parent conference procedures (See an example of a parental communication log in Figure 4.5.)

Figure 4.3 Ready/Working Sign

Ready

Working

- *Grade Book.* Hard copy of grades, student information, Individualized Instruction Programs (IEPs) and modifications (this is confidential information to which students should not have access), and grading policies and rubrics used for assessment
- *Guest Teacher.* Teacher's schedule, list of responsible students, lesson plans, documents for recording the day's activities, list of substitutes with contact information, discipline policy and classroom rules and expectations, list of where important items may be found, school floor plan, seating charts, lunch schedule, and phone numbers of key school personnel
- *Professional Development.* Lists of classes offered locally, lists of books to read, copies of articles, handouts received on staff development days, copies of courses taken, evaluation procedures, copies of evaluations, copies of licenses, calendar of offerings, and mailings received

One task that shows the importance of procedures is handling student papers. Much time can be wasted handing out and collecting student papers. Assign two students to perform these tasks for a week. Students like to assist, and giving them a title such as Teacher Assistants (TAs) will create a feeling of ownership and build self-esteem. Numbering student desks can make for more efficient paper passing. Students write their desk number on the paper, and the TAs collect them in order. When corrected papers are returned to students, they will already be in the order students are seated. Some teachers seat students alphabetically so papers are collected in the same order students are posted in the grade book. This technique makes for faster entry of student grades. Students who can be discipline problems often make excellent TAs, become more respectful toward the teacher, and hence improve their own behavior.

Have baskets in place for each class to place work to be graded. Label the baskets with a different color for each class. Color coding classes not only helps the teacher organize student work but also prevents students from placing work in the wrong basket. Colored paper clips can also be used to keep work from different classes separated.

Having a separate basket for students who have been absent or are turning in work late for some other reason will keep these papers separate from the current assignments. Students can complete a form and attach it to their work to let the teacher know which student work is from students who were absent and which from students who are simply turning it in late. Students are responsible for completing the forms shown in Figures 4.6 and 4.7 as applicable. On the Absent Work Form, they must state which days they were absent. On the Late Work Form, they must explain why the work is late.

Figure 4.4 Student Information Sheet

Student Information

Please provide the following information and return the signed form to Mrs. Herndon.

Last Name: _____ First Name: _____

Period: _____ Birthday: _____

Home Address: _____

Home Phone: _____ Other Phone: _____

Preferred Phone Number for Mrs. Herndon to Contact Parent/Guardian: _____
_____

Do you have access to a computer outside of the classroom? (Mark with an X)
_____ Yes _____ No

Parent E-mail: _____

Student E-mail: _____

Book Number: _____ (To be completed at the time of book distribution)

Student Signature: _____

Parent/Guardian Signature: _____

Figure 4.5 Parent Communication Log

Teacher/Parent Communication Record

Student Name	Parent Name	Date	Notes/Parental Requests/ Teacher Recommendations

Figure 4.6 Absent Work Form

Absent Work	Absent Work
Directions: Fill in this form COMPLETELY! Staple this form to your late assignment(s). Put your late assignment(s) into the ABSENT WORK basket!	*Directions:* Fill in this form COMPLETELY! Staple this form to your late assignment(s). Put your late assignment(s) into the ABSENT WORK basket!
Date: _____ Class Period: _____	Date: _____Class Period: _____
Name: _____	Name: _____
Name of Assignment: _____	Name of Assignment: _____
This assignment was due on _____ [date].	This assignment was due on _____ [date].
Date of your absence: _____ [date]	Date of your absence: _____ [date]
Student Signature: _____	Student Signature: _____
Absent Work	Absent Work
Directions: Fill in this form COMPLETELY! Staple this form to your late assignment(s). Put your late assignment(s) into the ABSENT WORK basket!	*Directions:* Fill in this form COMPLETELY! Staple this form to your late assignment(s). Put your late assignment(s) into the ABSENT WORK basket!
Date: _____ Class Period: _____	Date: _____ Class Period: _____
Name: _____	Name: _____
Name of Assignment: _____	Name of Assignment: _____
This assignment was due on _____ [date].	This assignment was due on _____ [date].
Date of your absence: _____ [date]	Date of your absence: _____ [date]
Student Signature: _____	Student Signature: _____

Figure 4.7 Late Work Form

Late Work	Late Work
Directions: Fill in this form COMPLETELY! Staple this form to your late assignment(s). Put your late assignment(s) into the LATE WORK basket!	*Directions:* Fill in this form COMPLETELY! Staple this form to your late assignment(s). Put your late assignment(s) into the LATE WORK basket!
Date: _____ Class Period: _____	Date: _____ Class Period: _____
Name: _____	Name: _____
Name of Assignment: _____	Name of Assignment: _____
This assignment was due on _____ [date].	This assignment was due on _____ [date].
The reason this assignment is late: _____ _____	The reason this assignment is late: _____ _____
Student Signature: _____	Student Signature: _____
Late Work	Late Work
Directions: Fill in this form COMPLETELY! Staple this form to your late assignment(s). Put your late assignment(s) into the LATE WORK basket!	*Directions:* Fill in this form COMPLETELY! Staple this form to your late assignment(s). Put your late assignment(s) into the LATE WORK basket!
Date: _____ Class Period: _____	Date: _____ Class Period: _____
Name: _____	Name: _____
Name of Assignment: _____	Name of Assignment: _____
This assignment was due on _____ [date].	This assignment was due on _____ [date].
The reason this assignment is late: _____ _____	The reason this assignment is late: _____ _____
Student Signature: _____	Student Signature: _____

Grading papers is essential but can be time-consuming. The teacher must decide which papers to grade before instruction begins. Research has shown that student learning increases with timely feedback; students cannot increase their achievement if they are not informed of any errors they may have made on assignments. Not all papers need to be graded, but all must be corrected. Select for grading those papers that follow learning activities in which students engaged in concept attainment. Some teachers make copies of answer keys so that students can correct their own work.

Reducing the amount of paperwork also depends on using planning time effectively.

Applications

Following are some examples of routines established by teachers:

- At the beginning of each planning period, check e-mail and respond to those messages needing a reply.
- Keep a calendar that you can update on a daily basis with dates for parent conferences, committee meetings, and staff meetings. Using portable electronic devices enables you to have your daily schedule at hand at all times.
- Use one planning period each week for organizing materials, previewing media, checking mail, and ordering supplies.
- Clean off your desk each night and organize materials needed for the next day's lessons. Post instructions on the board for the next day.
- Select one planning time each workday for yourself that will be uninterrupted time. Post a sign outside the classroom indicating you do not want to be disturbed.
- Plan to stay late one day a week. This can eliminate taking work home on the weekends.
- Document on a regular basis student behavior issues, lesson successes and failures, and ways to improve instruction. Keeping a notebook on the desk for this purpose is useful.
- Establish times in which students can meet with you for extra help or makeup work.
- Set aside one planning time each week for communicating with parents. Document all conversations.

STUDENT RESPONSIBILITY

One expectation of teachers teaching in a block schedule is that students will take on increased responsibility. Responsible students take an active role in their learning when they recognize they are accountable for their academic achievement. They also make choices and take actions that direct them toward their educational goals. Once students take on responsibility for their own learning, classroom management can become easier. However, many students struggle with the concept of responsibility or have no intrinsic motivation to learn. These students often lack the necessary organization skills they need to keep track of homework, projects, and assignment due dates.

Responsible students

- complete all class assignments in a timely manner.
- complete all homework assignments and turn them in on time.
- demonstrate honesty and integrity.
- do not make excuses for their behavior.
- respect their teachers and peers.
- set educational goals.
- participate in class.
- manage their time to accommodate their activities and schoolwork.

Many teachers have expressed concern about whether students will complete and return assignments, especially if the school is on a schedule in which classes meet every other day. Turning in completed work and making up missed assignments due to absences is the responsibility of the student. Procedures for turning in late work and absent work were described above, and teachers should teach these procedures in the first weeks of class.

Homework assigned should be an extension of what is taught in the classroom; effective homework provides students with opportunities for additional rehearsal. Even when homework is directed at learning goals, however, students often fail to see the importance of completing it. Having students who fail to turn in homework complete a homework responsibility form can reinforce the importance of homework and may change negative behaviors. These forms also create an avenue for further communication with parents by requiring a parental signature. See Figure 4.8 as an example.

Figure 4.8 Homework Responsibility Slip

Homework Responsibility Slip	Homework Responsibility Slip
Please complete this slip if homework has not been turned in on the date due.	Please complete this slip if homework has not been turned in on the date due.
Date: _____ Class Period: _____	Date: _____ Class Period: _____
Name: _____	Name: _____
Was assigned homework on _____ [date].	Was assigned homework on _____ [date].
This homework was due on _____ [date].	This homework was due on _____ [date].
Assignment: _____	Assignment: _____
I know this was my responsibility and failing to do homework can affect my grade.	I know this was my responsibility and failing to do homework can affect my grade.
Student Signature: _____	Student Signature: _____
Parent Signature: _____	Parent Signature: _____
Homework Responsibility Slip	Homework Responsibility Slip
Please complete this slip if homework has not been turned in on the date due.	Please complete this slip if homework has not been turned in on the date due.
Date: _____ Class Period: _____	Date: _____ Class Period: _____
Name: _____	Name: _____
Was assigned homework on _____ [date].	Was assigned homework on _____ [date].
This homework was due on _____ [date].	This homework was due on _____ [date].
Assignment: _____	Assignment: _____
I know this was my responsibility and failing to do homework can affect my grade.	I know this was my responsibility and failing to do homework can affect my grade.
Student Signature: _____	Student Signature: _____
Parent Signature: _____	Parent Signature: _____

Applications

Here are further suggestions for enhancing homework return rates:

- Assign homework in class. Model what is expected and provide time for students to start work; monitor them for accuracy. If students have started and experienced success, they are more likely to finish. Only perfect practice makes perfect.
- Assign or have students choose study buddies so that each student has someone else in class to call.
- When working with groups, some teachers have assigned students the role of "caller" to remind other students in their groups to return homework.
- Use student self-monitoring devices, such as a chart that is colored in for homework completed.

Some school districts provide students with planners, which can be an effective tool if teachers provide instructions on how to use the planners and monitor their use. Teachers can provide students with other tools that will help them develop responsibility for learning. For example, student responsibility cards help students increase responsibility for their own learning. Students use the cards to monitor their on-time performance, their time on-task, whether they bring needed materials to class, and whether they complete assignments. These cards can be printed in different colors for different classes. The cards are given to students at the beginning of each quarter and should be placed close to the door so that students can pick them up as they enter the room. Another way to distribute the cards is to have students hand them out.

During the first week of school, time should be allocated to explain the importance of these cards and how students should use them. Rubrics can be developed collaboratively with the class to provide criteria for recording data on each section of the cards.

Students can complete the attendance and materials section while the teacher takes role. The teacher will pick up the cards for absent students and record the absence in the attendance box. The teacher can also attach any makeup work for absent students to their cards. Upon returning from an absence, students will not need to approach the teacher for their makeup work but can simply remove it from the card. See Figure 4.9 for an example.

Figure 4.9 Student Responsibility Card

Student Responsibility Card

Student Name: _____ Class: _____

Attendance/Tardiness					
Week	Mon.	Tues.	Wed.	Thu.	Fri.
1					
2					
3					
4					
5					
6					
7					
8					
9					
10					

Materials					
Week	Mon.	Tues.	Wed.	Thu.	Fri.
1					
2					
3					
4					
5					
6					
7					
8					
9					
10					

(Continued)

Figure 4.9 (Continued)

Task/Participation					
Week	Mon.	Tues.	Wed.	Thu.	Fri.
1					
2					
3					
4					
5					
6					
7					
8					
9					
10					

Assignments					
Week	Mon.	Tues.	Wed.	Thu.	Fri.
1					
2					
3					
4					
5					
6					
7					
8					
9					
10					

Comments	Times for Detentions/Extra Help

These cards can be useful for the classroom teacher in a number of ways:

- Quickly identifying students who have a habit of turning in work late or not at all
- Providing a quick tally of student attendance
- As noted, providing a place for absent students' make-up work
- In a parent conference, showing student attendance and punctuality
- Monitoring student time on-task during class

GUEST TEACHERS

Many teachers now use the term *guest teacher* rather than *substitute teacher.* The term *substitute* implies being replaced, whereas *guest teacher* implies someone in authority. Using the term *guest teacher* also indicates to students that they have a responsibility to treat this person as a respected guest. Teachers can get sick or need to be away from the classroom for some other reason. Preparing for a guest teacher can be very time consuming, but advanced planning can make the absence easier. For example, having a binder ready with all the necessary information specifically for the guest teacher can make the absence less stressful. The ideal situation is for the lesson to be on target with what is currently being taught, but sometimes a generic lesson plan may be necessary. Some school districts require emergency lesson plans be kept on file. Lesson plans can be e-mailed or faxed, or verbal instructions can be given over the phone. Some departments have an unwritten policy of teachers helping their peers in certain situations by providing guest teachers with lessons and instructions. Being a guest teacher can be a rewarding but challenging experience. The classroom teacher can take a number of steps to make the guest teacher's experience enjoyable and keep the students on-task:

- Provide a seating chart for each class.
- Provide a list of classroom expectations and discipline policy.
- Leave hall passes with directions for bathroom requests.
- Make sure to leave activities that will engage students for the entire class period.
- Leave detailed lesson plans.
- Provide a list of helpful students.
- Provide a feedback form for the guest teacher to complete (see Figure 4.10.).

Figure 4.10 Guest Teacher Response Form

Guest Teacher Response Form

Thank you for being my guest teacher. As a follow-up to your time spent in the classroom, it would be very much appreciated if you could complete this form and leave it in the guest teacher binder.

Guest Teacher Name: _____ Date: _____

Contact Information: E-mail: _____ Phone: _____

Today's Accomplishments	
Tasks Not Completed	
Uncooperative Students	
Absent Students	
Tardy Students	
Additional Information	

- Leave a list of any special instructions, such as for students who need to take medication.
- Make sure students are informed of the expectations in the presence of a guest teacher.
- Leave any necessary answer keys.
- Leave a thank-you note or card. It is always nice to be appreciated!

Classroom management in a block schedule often requires reviewing management strategies and techniques on a regular basis. As the school year progresses, effective teachers monitor their management for ways to change or improve. In addition, teachers who communicate frequently with their peers can obtain many new classroom management strategies. Each time a new school year begins, it becomes necessary for teachers to reflect upon previous school years to decide how they would like to organize their classrooms and manage student academics and behaviors. Those teachers who use effective classroom management strategies and consistently monitor for progress will reap the rewards of their efforts.

5 Brain-Based Learning

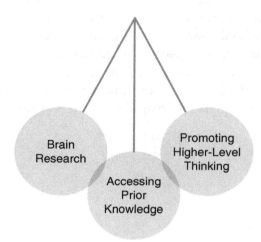

BRAIN RESEARCH

In Chapter 2, we discussed some features characteristic of the adolescent brain. Now we'll talk about the brain in general and how our understanding of this amazing organ can inform differentiating instruction for the learners in our classrooms.

We have learned more about the brain in the last 25 years than at any other point in history, mainly because of technological advances that allow us to look into the brain while it is processing information or doing a task. Positron emission tomography (PET) scans, which show glucose metabolism, and functional magnetic resonance imaging (fMRI), which shows changes in blood flow, reveal what areas of the brain are working. As educators, we need to pay attention to certain basic characteristics of the brain.

Fundamentally, six principles prevail:

1. *Learning involves the entire body and mind.* Learning is a natural process of the brain (Smilkstein, 2003). Neurons are located throughout the body. Auditory, visual, tactile, and kinesthetic experiences help to grow dendrites and make connections.

2. *The brain is social and appreciates collaboration.* Dialogue and other interaction are comforting and satisfying. All humans have the need to connect, associate, collaborate, and cooperate (Panksepp, 1998).

3. *Learning happens at many levels, both conscious and subconscious, in networks of association.* Parallel processing is going on constantly as the brain tries to make sense of both obvious and subtle stimuli. Learning naturally happens through curiosity and the perception of information's relevance and one's need to know.

4. *Emotions are key to the learning process.* Our emotions focus the brain's attention and promote the learning process through neurotransmitter releases (Ornstein & Sobel, 1988). A positive classroom climate is crucial for learning to take place.

5. *Patterns and schemas are necessary for the brain to make sense of new information.* The brain works on probability, calculated based on past experiences. Levine (1990) called this "horizontal threading." The brain checks the "files" to see if it knows anything similar to the new information. The brain tends to do better with "chunks" of information and looks for patterns to make sense of new ideas and concepts.

6. *The brain is unique and plastic.* Although each brain operates in basically the same way, we also know that heredity and environment play a large part in making each brain one of a kind. Thus, different brains prefer different modes of learning and have different prior knowledge, and one size does not fit all. *Plasticity* is the brain's ability to reconstruct and create new learning and understandings through the development of neural networks.

A Safe Learning Environment

The brain is on high alert to keep the person safe and alive. That is its primary focus. Although we are no longer out on the savannah with wild beasts, our brains are still constantly aware of potential dangers. In the school, schoolyard, and classrooms, these come in many forms:

- The bully
- The put-down
- The assignment that is beyond one's skill level
- The laugh when one speaks in class
- The fear of failure

For students to feel safe and concentrate on constructing meaning, the classroom has to allow for risk taking, experimentation, and trial and error with corrective feedback.

Figure 5.1 shows examples of features that make a classroom climate conducive or not conducive to learning.

Figure 5.1	Features of the Classroom Climate That Are Conducive and Not Conducive to Learning

Helpful and Safe	Obstructive and Negative
• Aesthetically pleasing surroundings • Displays of student work and successes • Lighting that is not stressful • Positive, can-do teacher • Variety and choice • Wait time • Think time • Positive, encouraging, and corrective feedback • Appropriate challenge based on skill level • Absence of threats • Respectful of diversity and learning styles	• Disorderly environment • Lack of visible student work and recognition • Harsh or inappropriate lighting • Insensitive teacher • Undue pressure and expectations • Limited or inappropriate feedback • Teaching to the middle or "one size fits all" approach • No recognition of diverse learning styles or student preferences

The Two-Hemisphere Brain

In 1968, Roger Sperry's research identified two different hemispheres of the brain and two different ways of processing information. One side seems dominant in each of us. Science has brought new revelations about gender and brain hemispheres as well.

Figures 5.2 and 5.3 show the processes that take place predominantly in each hemisphere and the preferences associated with each.

Gender Differences

Figures 5.4 and 5.5 show structural and performance differences between the male and female left and right hemispheres.

Figure 5.2 Brain Processes Linked to Left and Right Hemispheres

Left Hemisphere	Right Hemisphere
• Controls the right side of the body. • Uses information logically. • Responds to data analytically. • Is time-sensitive and aware. • Deals with life sequentially. • Organizes information. • Deals with information and materials in formal and systematic ways. • Processes from whole to parts and reorganizes the whole (sees the trees). • Responds to verbal communication, both receiving and expressing. • Music: Writes scientifically. • Is practical and factual. • Generates spoken language. • Control emotions, feelings. • Uses mathematics and computations. • Responds to abstract-oriented thinking. • Is concrete, explicit, and precise.	• Controls the left side of the body. • Reacts to information spontaneously and intuitively. • Takes a commonsense approach. • Does not consider time. • Deals with life randomly. • Diffuses information. • Deals with information and materials on the spur of the moment. • Sees the big picture or the whole (sees the forest). • Responds to body language, touch, and intonational pitch. • Music: Responds to sound and tone. • Focuses on ideas and theories and uses imagery. • Interprets language. • Freely expresses feelings and emotions. • Uses intuition to perceive and estimate. • Responds to sensory-oriented thinking. • Is symbolic and metaphorical.

Source: Adapted from Carter (1998), Gazzaniga (1998a, 1998b).

Figure 5.3 Preferences in the Classroom Related to the Dominant Hemisphere

Left Hemisphere Dominance	Right Hemisphere Dominance
• Prefers facts. • Relies on logical analysis and systemic solutions. • Likes repetition/rehearsal. • Makes traditional use of materials. • Values order and precision. • Learns well from models and demonstrations. • Values clear directions. • Wants instructions from teacher (auditory). • Expectations drive learning. • Relies on feedback for success. • Seeks approval. • Likes multiple-choice test questions.	• Prefers possibilities. • Relies on intuition and hunches to solve problems. • Likes inventive options. • Makes innovative use of materials. • Prefers randomness and haphazard organization. • Values spontaneity. • Elaborates on the original. • Expands on ideas given. • Suggests options. • Experiments with ideas. • Jumps into task without directions. • Curiosity drives learning. • Shows accomplishments to others. • Prefers essay questions on test.

Figure 5.4 Gender Differences: Structural

Males	Females
• Have a higher percentage of gray matter in left hemisphere. • Have more neurons in the cerebral cortex. • Left hemisphere has language areas for both males and females. • Have less blood flow in their brains. • Boys' brains "renew, recharge, and reorient" through the process of a "rest state." • More cortical area is devoted to spatial processing. • Have less serotonin and less oxytocin (human bonding chemical). Boys are thus more physically impulsive and sometimes less demonstrative of affection than girls.	• Have same amount of gray matter in both hemispheres. • Have more connections between the neurons in the same size space. • Have an active processor in their right brain as well. • Female corpus callosum (connecting the left and right hemispheres) is generally larger than in males (by almost 25% in adolescence). • Girls reorient without a "rest state." • Have more neural connectors than boys in the temporal lobes. Thus, they store more sensory details and often have a greater ability to listen and to pick up intonation clues while listening. • Generally have a larger hippocampus than boys, which processes memory storage. Girls thus have a learning advantage, especially in language arts. • Girls' prefrontal lobes are more active at an earlier age, and this decreases the impulsivity often apparent in boys. Girls also generally have higher levels of serotonin in the blood, making them less impulsive than boys.

Source: Based on information compiled from multiple sources, including the work of Baron-Cohen (2003); Blum (1997); Gurian, Henley, & Trueman (2001); Havers (1995); Moir & Jessel (1989); Rich (2000); Taylor (2002); Witelson (2004).

Figure 5.5 Gender Differences: Performance

Males	Females

• Use more cortical area for spatial and mechanical functioning.
• Perform better on spatial tasks such as
 	
  o three-dimensional rotation of objects,
  o motor skills,
  o noticing embedded shapes,
  o throwing accuracy, and
  o mathematical reasoning.
 	
• Lateralize and tend to more compartmentalize their learning.
	• Use generally more cortical area for emotive and verbal processing.
	• Perform better on
	
	  o perceptual speed tests,
	  o verbal fluency,
	  o memory sequence,
	  o identifying specific attributes of an object,
	  o precise manual tasks (finger dexterity), and
	  o mathematical calculations.
	
	• Are better at noticing a variety of emotions (temporal lobes) in others and use a greater amount of their limbic system to do so.
	• Tend to find multitasking easier. Make transitions more easily from one thing to another. Are more able to focus.

Source: Based on information compiled from multiple sources, including the work of Blum (1997), Moir & Jessel (1989), Rich (2000), and Witelson (2004).

In general, then, teaching can be differentiated by gender to facilitate the greatest possible learning opportunities for both boys and girls. Figure 5.6 lists suggestions for teaching with gender differences in mind.

Figure 5.6 Teaching to Gender Differences

Teaching Boys	Teaching Girls
• Offer as many kinesthetic, hands-on activities as possible: manipulatives, construction, projects, and experiments. • Provide tasks that require fine motor coordination (not as highly developed in males), as well as gross motor coordination (often preferred by males), such as that used in physical theater. • Keep oral instructions to a minimum and post instructions for reference. Boys will zone out with too many verbal directions or explanations. • Allow personalization of student's space to increase feelings of belonging (desk, locker, etc.). • Foster empathy and social interaction.	• Encourage physical activity to develop gross motor skills. • Use materials to promote sensory engagement and spatial development. • Celebrate successes in spatial tasks. • Offer dilemmas, puzzles, and problems that challenge perceptual learning. • Use team learning to foster social interaction and leadership skills. • Encourage participation and sharing from quieter female students.

Note: To read more about this, see Gurian and Stevens (2004).

This is not to say that we should do only one activity or the other based on gender. In fact, we should provide a full range of activities that develop both sides of the brain. Sometimes we can ask girls to engage in more activities that require manipulation with opportunities to build, construct, calculate, and design. And sometimes boys can be required to describe what they are doing verbally, as it is easier for them to vocalize when actively involved in a task. At that time, there is more blood flow to the cerebellum (the motor brain), and thus their vocabulary is greater. Offering opportunities for movement, hands-on manipulatives, and a variety of seating (chairs, rugs, cushions) also may help the brains of both girls and boys focus.

Applying Understanding of the Two Hemispheres in the Classroom

The inventory in Figure 5.7 may help students identify their dominant hemispheres. This information should not be used to label them but to help them be more aware of and knowledgeable about themselves.

Figure 5.7	Left Hemisphere + Right Hemisphere = Whole Brain

Circle the numbers that are most like you.

1. When I read about something new, I like pictures and diagrams.
2. I prefer step-by-step directions and to solve problems logically.
3. I get many ideas at once, like "brainstorming."
4. I like to learn by seeing and hearing.
5. I remember people's faces better than their names.
6. I can control my feelings.
7. I like to create new and unique things.
8. I can recall information quickly when I need it.
9. I like to learn by touching and doing.
10. I learn new words and vocabulary quickly.
11. People would say I'm emotional.
12. I can learn easily with patience and by noticing details.
13. I picture ideas and review things in "mental videos."
14. I like routines and have daily habits or rituals.
15. I rely on my intuition, and some people would call me spontaneous.
16. I can easily concentrate and focus when I need to.
17. I let a party "happen" and get involved with the people.
18. I plan a party down to the last detail.
19. I like to imagine new and interesting things.
20. I like true-and-false tests better than those where I have to write a lot.
21. I generally know what is going on and what everyone is doing.
22. I like to learn from the teacher.
23. I can see the whole jigsaw even though I have only a few pieces in place.
24. I can remember and describe details easily.
25. I sometimes lose track of time.
26. I usually manage time well.
27. I like group work and "catch" the mood of others.
28. I can concentrate well if I want to.
29. I like to learn by doing and touching.
30. I like to learn by listening and seeing.

_____ Number of odd numbers circled.

_____ Number of even numbers circled.

If you circled more odd numbers, you tend to be more right hemisphere oriented.

If you circled more even numbers, you tend to be more left hemisphere oriented.

Research from Key (1991) identified strategies that could be used specifically to engage the right and the left hemispheres in the learning process (see Figure 5.8).

Figure 5.8 Learning Activities That Strengthen Whole-Brain Processing

Respecting Left Hemisphere Preferences	*Respecting Right Hemisphere Preferences*
• Keep the classroom orderly and materials and bulletin boards neat and current. • Foster opportunities to read, write, and engage in numeracy activities. • Organize chalkboards and erase material that could be confounded with new material. • Provide agendas, expectations, and timelines. • Help students monitor their work, time, and successes. • Encourage logic and reasoning. Ask students to substantiate their thinking. • Encourage higher-order thinking.	• Provide multiple materials and resources. • Use hands-on experiences as well as role-playing and simulations. Allow options for reading and writing. • Use diagrams and illustrations as well as graphic organizers, charts, and timelines. • Include visual mapping of concepts and topics of study on agendas. • Allow students to interact, discuss, and articulate their ideas. • Use analogies and metaphors to help students make connections. • Bring lessons to closure and integrate new information with past learning.

Understanding Memory

In 40-minute classrooms, "stand and deliver" is sometimes all teachers can muster, as there is no time for group interaction, processing, and application. With extended periods of time available, however, teachers can structure learning to be more responsive to what we know about the brain. To support brain plasticity, or the opportunity for the brain to form and construct new neural networks (dendritic growth), time is required to move information and skills from sensory to short-term/working memory and ultimately to long-term storage (see Figure 5.9).

Sensory Memory or Focusing Attention

Sensory memory acts like a sieve, or filter, to screen out much of the input from our senses and internal organs. Without this filter, we would drown in a sea of information. Sensory memory decides which information should be passed on to short-term memory and which information should be discarded. These decisions are influenced by three additional processes: perception, expectation, and attention.

The structures in the brain related to sensory memory also determine whether we pay attention to incoming information. Our attention is

Figure 5.9 Information-Processing Model of the Memory System

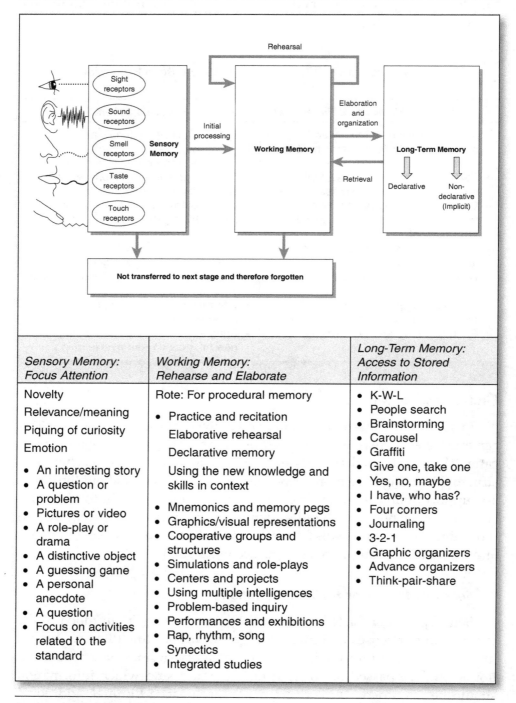

Sensory Memory: Focus Attention	Working Memory: Rehearse and Elaborate	Long-Term Memory: Access to Stored Information
Novelty Relevance/meaning Piquing of curiosity Emotion • An interesting story • A question or problem • Pictures or video • A role-play or drama • A distinctive object • A guessing game • A personal anecdote • A question • Focus on activities related to the standard	Rote: For procedural memory • Practice and recitation Elaborative rehearsal Declarative memory Using the new knowledge and skills in context • Mnemonics and memory pegs • Graphics/visual representations • Cooperative groups and structures • Simulations and role-plays • Centers and projects • Using multiple intelligences • Problem-based inquiry • Performances and exhibitions • Rap, rhythm, song • Synectics • Integrated studies	• K-W-L • People search • Brainstorming • Carousel • Graffiti • Give one, take one • Yes, no, maybe • I have, who has? • Four corners • Journaling • 3-2-1 • Graphic organizers • Advance organizers • Think-pair-share

Source: Parts of this illustration have been adapted with permission from *Building the Reading Brain, PreK–3* by Pat Wolfe and Pamela Nevills. Thousand Oaks, CA: Corwin, 2004.

focused by anything that the brain finds new, exciting, pleasurable, or threatening. Brain activation is the first step in the learning process. Our attention is initially captured through our senses, with the visual, auditory, and tactile senses being most efficient. Many stimuli are vying for our attention, but we usually give attention to what is interesting, relevant, novel, or engaging. In the classroom, we can capitalize on this by introducing information in new and exciting ways, making the learning experience enjoyable, and providing enough of a challenge to maintain the students' interest within a climate of low stress.

In addition, providing the students with a big-picture outline of what they will learn, how it relates to existing knowledge, and the goals of the lesson helps to capture and maintain their attention. Teachers often begin a lesson by providing students with an overview and the expected results:

- What is going to be covered
- Where it fits with previously learned information
- Why it is relevant to the student
- How it may be useful in the real world

Evidence of clear learning goals is important to the brain of the learner, as the mind needs to have a focus; an objective helps the brain stay on-task. As well, if the brain knows where it is headed, it consciously and unconsciously helps the process along. Some teachers have a standards board in their classroom where expectations are posted for the unit of study. This way the teacher can refer to them often during the course of the learning process, and students can relate the current learning activity to the ultimate outcome. Sharing the objective and purpose is a simple thing to do daily in the classroom, but research shows it is done only about 4 percent of the time (Learning 24/7, as cited in Schmoker, 2006, p. 18).

The beginning of a lesson or class should help students focus on the learning, connect it to prior knowledge or experience (open mental files related to the content or skill), and develop a rationale or compelling "need to know" related to the outcomes or expectations. We often assume that students will be interested in what we are teaching, but other pressing issues may be competing for their attention.

Short-Term and Long-Term Memory

The old adage "Tell them what you're going to tell them, tell them, and then tell them what you've told them," is useful to remember when designing a lesson or unit of study—with one exception. At the end of the lesson, students, rather than the teacher, should summarize learnings because it is the students who need to practice or rehearse the content. Students need to see the "big picture" as well as the pieces that will be examined.

Applications

Teachers in the block have offered the following additional tips for promoting and maintaining attention to leverage the way the brain processes memory. They note that in small ways we can make big differences in learning.

- *Provide advance organizers.* This strategy invites students to learn what they will be expected to do before they are asked to do it. Examples: "After watching this video clip, you will be expected to describe, in writing, key events leading up to the Iraq War," or "After reading the two stories, I would like you to use a Venn diagram to display their similarities and differences with respect to plot, character development, setting, and voice."
- *Use bracketing.* Bracketing invites students to put aside anything that is concerning them or might take them off-task. Example: "Jot down on an index card (or scrap of paper) anything that you are thinking or worrying about right now. Now put it in the desk! You may take it with you at the end of the period."
- *Eliminate distractors in the classroom.* Help students focus by removing clutter and objects that may vie for attention, distracting students from the presentation or task at hand.
- *Ask for expectations and questions.* When students realize that they have input into the how and why of learning, they are more likely to pay attention. For example, before a unit of study, ask students to peruse the materials and to generate a list of questions or to note areas of interest. Generate a class list of expectations (e.g., "If this unit is to meet my needs, I expect that we will address these subtopics. . . ."). Post their interests and refer to them as they are addressed.
- *Generate previous experiences that relate to the topic.* Most students love to share their experiences verbally, graphically, or in writing. When they are asked to do this, they focus attention on information stored in their neural networks of association that relate to the topic about to be taught.
- *Use stories.* Stories that have engaging characters and events appeal to all learners—visual, auditory, and kinesthetic. Stories focus attention because the words require the learner to create mental pictures of what is going on and because they usually create an emotional response.

- *Use novelty.* The mind is always seeking patterns. Anything that stands out from the ordinary focuses attention because it is novel and often unexpected. In some classes, for example, teachers dress up as literary or historical characters. In others, novelty may involve students in simulation; for instance, in one classroom, the teacher engaged students in a role-play of an assembly line so that they felt like the workers in factories during the Industrial Revolution.

Primacy-Recency Model

Something else to consider about how the brain learns is the notion of beginning, ending, and middle (BEM; Fitzgerald, 1996). As mentioned in Chapter 3 on planning for instruction, the brain pays more attention to what comes first in a sequence and remembers it best; it remembers next what comes last and remembers least of all what comes in the middle (see Figure 5.10).

Figure 5.10 Primacy-Recency Effect

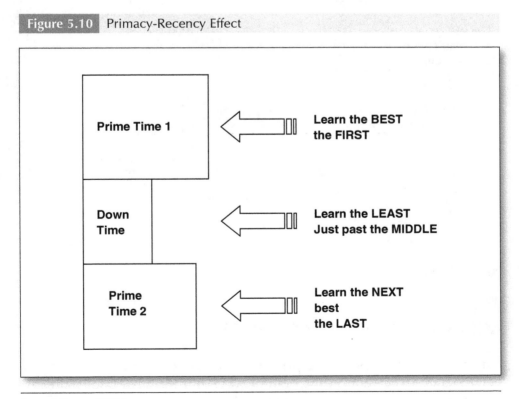

Source: Sousa (2006).

When learning episodes are divided into 20-minute segments, there are more firsts and lasts and, thus, proportionally more "prime time" to downtime (see Figure 5.11). Therefore, lessons divided into segments are more productive than one continuous lesson. New information and closure are best presented during the prime-time periods. Practice and hands-on lab activities are appropriate for the downtime. The digital natives do not have long attention spans and are used to "sound bites." Thus, in classrooms, we need to keep learning varied and appealing to the e-commerce crowd.

| Figure 5.11 | Features of the Classroom Climate That Are Conducive and Not Conducive to Learning |

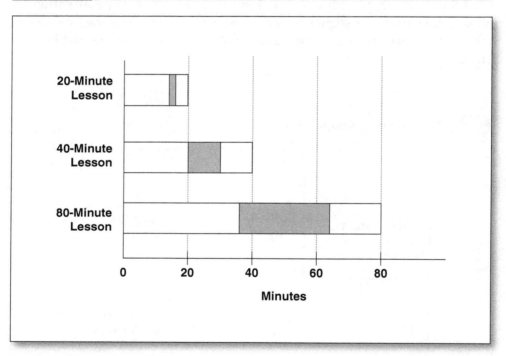

Source: Sousa (2006).

ACCESSING PRIOR KNOWLEDGE

Part of activation is accessing prior knowledge. All memory is stored in networks of association in the brain, and except for what one is already thinking about, all other information is unconscious. Thus, engaging students in thinking about their prior knowledge of or experience with a topic is crucial so that there are "hooks" for the new learning to connect to.

A week or so prior to beginning a new unit or topic, teachers can often survey students or use graffiti placemats, K-W-Ls, four corners, or anticipation guides to foreshadow the new topic and also gather pertinent information about students' prior knowledge, misconceptions, interests, and preferences.

Graffiti Placemat

This cooperative structure facilitates brainstorming. Students work individually to record their ideas, responses, or insights and then reach consensus with the group on common ideas. The graffiti placemat is particularly effective for activating prior learning at the beginning of a unit or lesson or for reviewing content/concepts at the end (Gibbs, 2001).

This exercise is often done on a large sheet of newspaper divided into enough sections for each person in the group. Students may draw or write in their space.

Directions for Students

1. Give the students a question, statement, or issue to which they will respond.

2. Each student takes a different-colored marker and writes for a short time (90 seconds).

3. The graffiti may be used in a number of ways. Here are two examples:

   • The teacher may call time and ask students to categorize or review the responses, looking for common ideas or themes.
   • Students can share their thoughts and write a summary statement in the center box.

4. Each group reads, discusses, summarizes, and presents its ideas. Here are some examples:

   • A math problem could be put on the overhead at the beginning of class, and each student would solve the problem in their space. Then students would share solutions with their group.
   • Students might brainstorm everything they know about a particular topic (e.g., Canada, ecosystems, Iraq). Then the group

could come up with a "big" question related to the topic in the center box. These questions could become part of the essential/personal questions in the unit.

- The graffiti placemat could serve as a homework check, with everyone jotting down what they read in the chapter last night.

The example in Figure 5.12 would accommodate four students, and the one shown in Figure 5.13 would serve three students.

The sample shown in Figure 5.14 could be one sheet of 8½ × 11-inch paper folded in four. Individually, the students, each on his or her own placemat, could write or draw what they know about four categories of a topic. For the topic Canada, for example, the four sections might be titled Economics, Geography, Historical, and Political.

K-W-L

This strategy (see Figure 5.15) was introduced by Donna Ogle (1986) to help students focus on a topic.

The *K* stands for *What do I Know or think I Know?* Asking this question opens mental "files" and pulls students' prior knowledge into their conscious minds.

The *W* stands for *What do I Want to know or Wonder about?* Asking this question helps students identify their areas of interest or passion so that teachers can tap into those areas and design learning to capitalize on them.

The *L* stands for *What has been Learned?* Asking this question facilitates reflection on the learning and its usefulness.

One middle school teacher found that his students did not respond well to K-W-L; they seemed too eager to "know" and "want to know" about a topic. So the teacher suggested that he wanted things to G-E-L for them (see Figure 5.16). He asked them to tell him what they have *Got right now,* what they *Expect,* and what they have *Learned.* This approach gave students more ownership of the assignment and appeared "cooler" to their classmates, thus not curbing their enthusiasm for learning.

As a prereading strategy, K-W-L or G-E-L can be useful to help students make sense out of print. It helps students focus on information that has meaning to them personally as well as interests and passions and learning that pique their curiosity. It also provides a vehicle for making predictions and facilitating critical thinking and reflection. More variations of K-W-L are K-I-C and K-P-C (see Figures Figure 5.17 and 5.18).

Figure 5.12 Graffiti Placemat: Five Sections

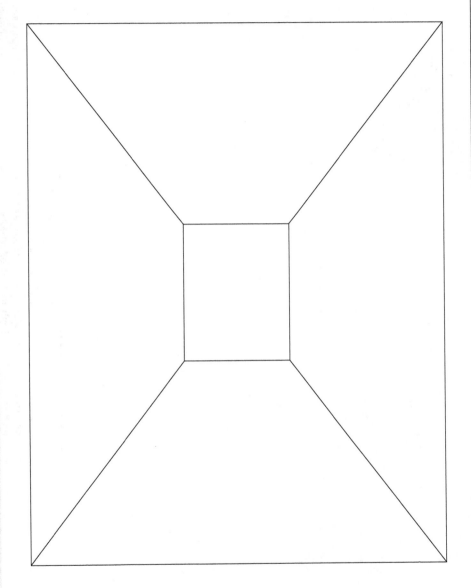

Figure 5.13 Graffiti Placemat: Three Sections

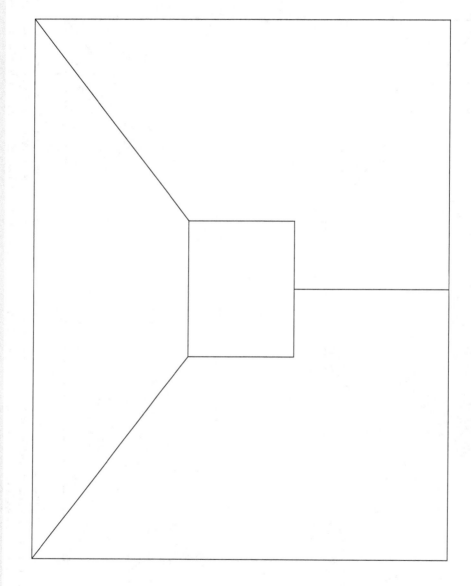

Figure 5.14 Graffiti Placemat for Individual Student: Four Sections

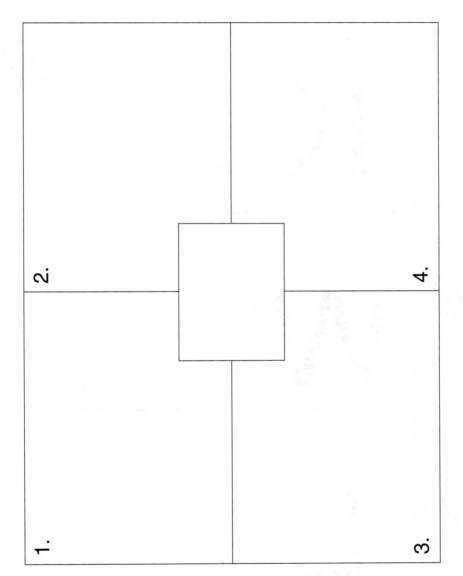

Figure 5.15 K-W-L

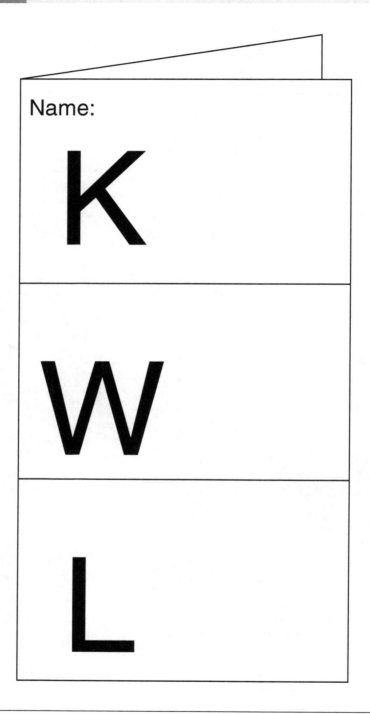

Figure 5.16 G-E-L

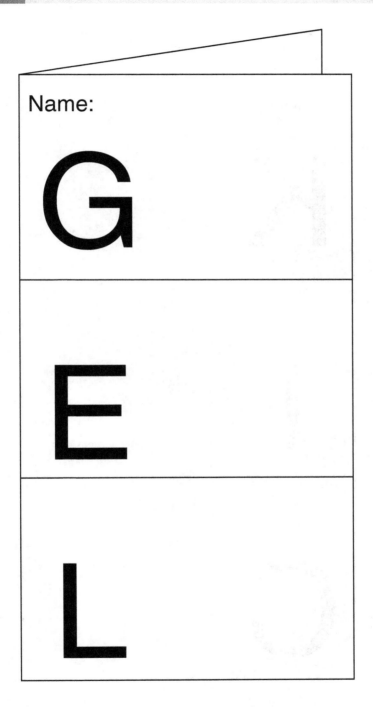

Figure 5.17 K-I-C

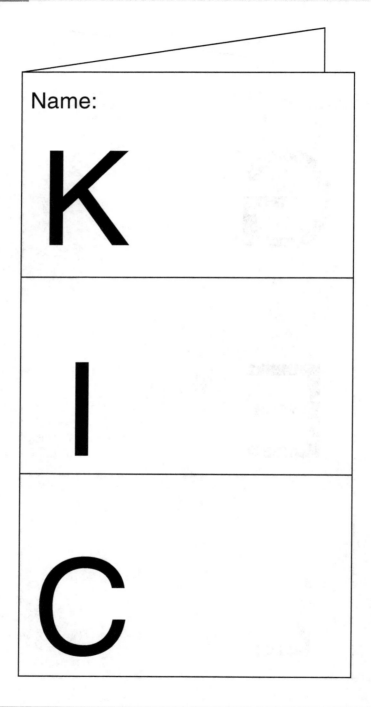

Figure 5.18 K-P-C

K-I-C

The *K* stands for *What I Know!*

The *I* stands for *What Interests me!*

The *C* stands for *Choice.*

- Whom might I like to work with?
- What might I like to explore in the content?
- How might I like to show what I learned?

K-P-C

The *K* stands for *What I Know!*

The *P* stands for *What I Predict!*

The *C* stands for *Check.*

- Whom could I ask?
- Where could I look?
- How was my thinking accurate or not?

Anticipation Guides

Before reading, students should have an opportunity to focus on the content in the chapter or unit of study and open their "mental files" to discuss and review what they already know or think they know. Doing so sets up curiosity about and anticipation of the learning to come. It also serves as a pre-assessment and identifies what students know (or have misconceptions about) and want to know (Head & Readence, 1992). Figures 5.19 and 5.20 show examples of what students may consider before reading a chapter or viewing a video about ecology or *Hamlet,* respectively. Figure 5.21 is a blank template.

Students may revisit the anticipation guide after the lesson to see if they have changed their minds and to add evidence that supported their original thoughts or caused them to change their minds.

ABC Brainstorming

Give students a chart like the one in Figure 5.22 and ask them to brainstorm all they know about the topic using the 26 letters of the alphabet to prompt them. This exercise opens formerly closed mental files and generates prior knowledge.

Figure 5.19 Anticipation Guide: Biology Example

Anticipation Guide: Biology Example

Before the Reading		Consider the Items	After the Reading		Evidence?
Agree	Disagree		Yes	No	
		A population is the same as a community.			
		Biospheres are composed of small units called ecosystems.			
		Abiotic factors include oxygen, water, temperature, and salinity.			
		Autotrophs include plants and animals.			
		Herbivores eat producers, and carnivores eat consumers.			
		A food chain is a single pathway of feeding relationships among organisms in an ecosystem that results in energy transfer.			

Figure 5.20 Anticipation Guide: *Hamlet* Example

Anticipation Guide: *Hamlet* Example

Before the Reading		Consider the Items	After the Reading		Evidence?
Agree	Disagree		Yes	No	
		The tragedy of *Hamlet* has a moral message.			
		Each of the main characters of the play lost a person important to them.			
		Hamlet kills four people in this play.			
		The main theme of this play was revenge.			
		Ophelia took revenge on Hamlet for her father's death.			
		Hamlet appears to be insane at times during the play.			

Figure 5.21 Anticipation Guide: Template

Anticipation Guide: Template

Before the Reading		Consider the Items	After the Reading		Evidence?
Agree	Disagree		Yes	No	

Figure 5.22 ABC Brainstorming

A	N
B	O
C	P
D	Q
E	R
F	S
G	T
H	U
I	V
J	W
K	X
L	Y
M	Z

PROMOTING HIGHER-LEVEL THINKING

Posing questions during lectures helps the brain pay attention and see a purpose for listening. It also helps students process the content and ask questions for clarification. Research shows that teachers ask 85 percent of the questions in the classroom, and most are at the recall level and do not invoke higher-level thinking (Goodlad, 1984/2004). Varying questions to challenge student thinking can increase student attention and the complexity of their interactions with what is being taught.

Figure 5.23 identifies Bloom's (1956) six levels of thinking and suggests verbs that can be used to direct student thinking at each level. The action words in the right-hand column offer enough variety so that visual, auditory, and kinesthetic learners can all find a level of comfort. The thinking levels also stimulate both the right and left brain hemispheres to support all students in using their dominant and nondominant sides. Teachers can vary questioning to pose questions that are challenging but not too difficult for each student, thus differentiating and including all learners.

Figure 5.23 Directing Verbs for the Six Levels of Bloom's Taxonomy

Thinking Level	Definition	Directing Verbs
Level 1: Knowledge Learn information.	Recall the facts and remember previously learned information.	Describe, list, identify, locate, and label
Level 2: Comprehension Understand information.	Understand the meaning of and the how and why of events.	Explain, give examples, paraphrase, summarize
Level 3: Application Use information.	Transfer the skill or knowledge to another situation or setting. Application tests knowledge and comprehension.	Infer, predict, deduce, adapt, modify, solve problems
Level 4: Analysis Examine parts.	Break down information into specific parts so that the whole can be understood. Understanding structure can help with comparisons.	Discriminate, classify, categorize, subdivide, delineate
Level 5: Synthesis Use differently.	Combine elements to create new and different ideas or models.	Induce, create, compose, generalize, combine, rearrange, design, plan
Level 6: Evaluation Judge the information.	Rank or rate the value of information using a set of criteria.	Judge, compare, criticize, contrast, justify, conclude

Figure 5.24 provides suggestions for questioning and potential activities at different levels of the taxonomy. This chart can help teachers think about options for formulating and asking questions to designing projects, assignments, and center activities in ways that tap into the levels of Bloom's taxonomy to invoke active processing. Not only do these offer a variety of levels of thinking, but they also appeal to the different multiple intelligences and learning styles.

During lectures, it is important to intersperse content with active processing time. Mary Budd Rowe (1987) suggested that a "10 and 2" rule be considered; that is, teachers give information for about 10 minutes and then allow students 2 to 3 minutes of processing time so that discussion and questions can emerge.

Figure 5.25, containing only the question prompts, is a resource that teachers can hold during a lecture. You can photocopy the page on colored paper and fold it in half. Holding it reminds you that you are asking levels of questions that students can handle and gives you a prompt if you need one.

Students can also use this page when reading new information so as to formulate good questions to discuss in class. A homework assignment might be to read the chapter and come back to class with one question at each level of the taxonomy ready to discuss with a partner. This assignment allows the teacher to monitor the conversations and pick up on who has completed the reading and which issues are clear and which need to be clarified. At this point, questions can be answered and concepts clarified before misconceptions develop and are remembered.

Students may use a variety of strategies to process the content and concepts introduced or reviewed in the lecture, such as pair partners, collaborative corners, double circle, or trio talk. Teachers can invite students to apply the information or concepts from the lecture to a real-world situation or a creative task that would facilitate deep understanding and long-term retention.

Using all levels of Bloom's will increase thinking. Likewise, incorporating Socratic questions will prompt students to think beyond the mere recall level of understanding. Try some of the following:

- Why do you think that?
- What do you really mean?
- Tell me more so that I understand.
- Are you saying . . . ?

Figure 5.24 Bloom's Taxonomy Question Starters

Question Starters	Potential Activities
Level 1: Knowledge (Recall)	
1. What is the definition of . . . ? 2. What happened after . . . ? 3. Recall the facts. 4. What were the characteristics of . . . ? 5. Which is true or false? 6. How many . . . ? 7. Who was the . . . ? 8. Tell in your words	1. Describe the . . . . 2. Make a timeline of the events. 3. Make a facts chart. 4. Write a list of . . . steps in . . . facts about . . . . 5. List all of the animals in the story . . . . 6. Make a chart showing . . . . 7. Make an acrostic. 8. Recite a poem.
Level 2: Comprehension	
1. Why are these ideas similar? 2. In your own words, retell the story of . . . . 3. What do you think could happen . . . ? 4. How are these ideas different? 5. Explain what happened after . . . ? 6. What are some examples? 7. Can you provide a definition of . . . ? 8. Who was the key character . . . ?	1. Cut out or draw pictures to show an event. 2. Illustrate what you think the main idea was. 3. Make a cartoon strip showing the sequence of . . . . 4. Write and perform a play based on the . . . . 5. Compare this . . . with . . . . 6. Construct a model of . . . . 7. Write a summary report of the event. 8. Prepare a flowchart to illustrate the sequence of . . . .
Level 3: Application	
Note: Applying without understanding is not effective application. 1. What is another instance of . . . ? 2. Demonstrate the way to . . . . 3. Which one is most like . . . ? 4. What questions would you ask . . . ? 5. Which factors would you change . . . ? 6. Could this have happened in . . . ? Why or why not? 7. How would you organize these ideas?	1. Construct a model to demonstrate using . . . . 2. Make a diorama to illustrate one event. 3. Make a scrapbook about the study. 4. Design a relief map to include relevant information about an event. 5. Produce a collection of photographs to illustrate a particular viewpoint. 6. Paint a mural expressing the theme . . . .

(Continued)

Figure 5.24 (Continued)

Question Starters	Potential Activities
Level 4: Analysis	
1. What are the component parts of . . . ? 2. What steps are important in the process of . . . ? 3. If . . . , then . . . ? 4. What other conclusions can you reach about . . . that have not been mentioned? 5. The difference between the fact and the hypothesis is . . . ? 6. The solution would be to . . . ? 7. What is the relationship between . . . and . . . ?	1. Design a questionnaire about . . . . 2. Conduct an investigation to produce . . . . 3. Make a flowchart to show . . . . 4. Construct a graph to show . . . . 5. Put on a play about . . . . 6. Review a work of art in terms of form, color, and texture. 7. Prepare a report about the area of study.
Level 5: Synthesis	
1. Can you design a . . . to . . . ? 2. Why not compose a song about . . . ? 3. Why don't you devise your own way to . . . ? 4. Can you create new and unusual uses for . . . ? 5. Can you develop a proposal for . . . ? 6. How would you deal with . . . ? 7. Invent a scheme that would	1. Create a model that shows your new ideas. 2. Devise an original plan or experiment for . . . . 3. Finish the incomplete . . . . 4. Make a hypothesis about . . . . 5. Change . . . so that it will . . . . 6. Propose a method to . . . . 7. Prescribe a new way to . . . . 8. Give the book a new title.
Level 6: Evaluation	
1. In your opinion, . . . ? 2. Appraise the chances for . . . . 3. Grade or rank the . . . . 4. What do you think will be the outcome? 5. What solution do you favor and why? 6. Which systems are best? Worst? 7. Rate the relative value of these ideas to . . . . 8. Which is the better bargain?	1. Prepare a list of criteria you would use to judge . . . . 2. Indicate the priority ratings you would give . . . . 3. Conduct a debate about an issue. 4. Make a booklist about five rules you see as important. Convince others. 5. Form a panel to discuss . . . . 6. Prepare a case to present your view about . . . . 7. List some common statements about . . . that people often make. Are they accurate?

Figure 5.25 Question Starters Template

Question Starters	Question Starters
Level 1: Knowledge (Recall)	**Level 4: Analysis**
1. What is the definition of . . . ? 2. What happened after . . . ? 3. Recall the facts. 4. What were the characteristics of . . . ? 5. Which is true or false? 6. How many . . . ? 7. Who was the . . . ? 8. Tell in your words	1. What are the component parts of . . . ? 2. What steps are important in the process of . . . ? 3. If . . . , then . . . ? 4. What other conclusions can you reach about . . . that have not been mentioned? 5. The difference between the fact and the hypothesis is . . . ? 6. The solution would be to . . . ? 7. What is the relationship between . . . and . . . ?
Level 2: Comprehension	**Level 5: Synthesis**
1. Why are these ideas similar? 2. In your own words, retell the story of . . . . 3. What do you think could happen . . . ? 4. How are these ideas different? 5. Explain what happened after . . . ? 6. What are some examples? 7. Can you provide a definition of . . . ? 8. Who was the key character . . . ?	1. Can you design a . . . to . . . ? 2. Why not compose a song about . . . ? 3. Why don't you devise your own way to . . . ? 4. Can you create new and unusual uses for . . . ? 5. Can you develop a proposal for . . . ? 6. How would you deal with . . . ? 7. Invent a scheme that would . . . .
Level 3: Application	**Level 6: Evaluation**
Note: Applying without understanding is not effective application. 1. What is another instance of . . . ? 2. Demonstrate the way to . . . . 3. Which one is most like . . . ? 4. What questions would you ask . . . ? 5. Which factors would you change . . . ? 6. Could this have happened in . . . ? Why or why not? 7. How would you organize these ideas?	1. In your opinion, . . . ? 2. Appraise the chances for . . . . 3. Grade or rank the . . . . 4. What do you think will be the outcome? 5. What solution do you favor and why? 6. Which systems are best? Worst? 7. Rate the relative value of these ideas to . . . . 8. Which is the better bargain?

- Is this the point you're making?
- Are you suggesting . . . ?
- Aren't you assuming . . . ?
- How else could that be interpreted?
- Who has a different point of view and why?

Think-Pair-Share

This strategy provides a simple structure that is easy to implement and has a positive impact on learners (McTighe & Lyman, 1988).

1. Students are given a question or problem (concept, idea, homework) and are asked to think about it.

2. They are then asked to pair with a partner and discuss the issue.

3. Then the pairs share with the whole class.

This is a great strategy to use for processing every 10 to 15 minutes throughout a lecture. It allows information to be discussed and questions to be answered before "cumulative ignorance" takes place or students are lost or confused by the end of the lecture. It is also a useful strategy to engage students in discussing homework, thereby deepening understanding through dialogue.

A Variation of Think-Pair-Share: Write-Draw-Make

This strategy invites students to write, draw (e.g., word webs, mind maps, graphic organizers), or create something (e.g., model, poster, collage, or diorama). It provides visual-kinesthetic learners with an active way of processing information and enhancing understanding.

Double Circles

This strategy is excellent for having students articulate their understanding, problem-solve, or rationalize their positions. It is useful for verbal/linguistic and bodily/kinesthetic learners who are able to clarify their thinking in an interpersonal and physical way. Students form two concentric circles, with the students in the inner circle facing out and those in the outer circle facing in (see Figure 5.26). Each facing pair responds to questions and issues and discusses them. Then each student in the outer circle moves to the next person in the inner circle, who becomes a new partner, and the conversation continues. This is a useful strategy for

Figure 5.26 Double Circles

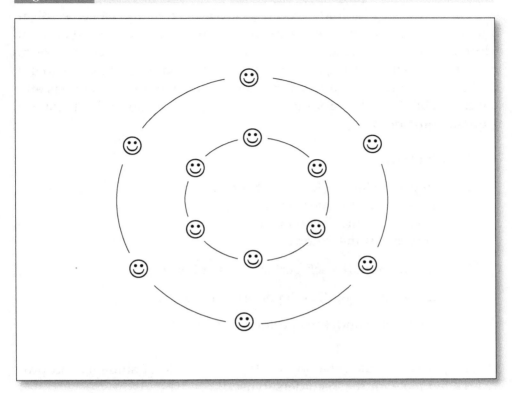

trust-building activities, as well as for mastering information. For example, it can be used as a review strategy in which the inner-circle students ask questions of the outer circle and then the process is reversed. Using strategies such as this one develops the expressive and receptive verbal language skills of students.

Interview Teams

Two pairs of students work together. Both partners in each pair interview each other. Then each of the four, in turn, shares with the group of four what he or she has heard from his or her partner. This activity can be used to access prior knowledge at the beginning of a lesson or unit, to check for understanding midway through a lesson, or to bring closure or consolidate new concepts. Interview teams can also be used as a strategy to facilitate review of previously taught content/skills. It helps students practice the skills of active listening and paraphrasing.

Trio Talk

This strategy gives students a chance to listen intently to one person at a time and offers the speaker a captive audience. It allows for a sharing of ideas or problem solving. It can be a good 5-minute process to use to clarify information during a lecture, and it is a good processing tool to use at the end of a session so that individuals can share their intentions and concerns about an idea or topic. It also works at the end of the lesson for summarizing ideas.

1. Form trios.

2. Each person takes a letter: A, B, or C.
   o Person A is the Interviewer.
   o Person B is the Respondent.
   o Person C is the Recorder.

3. In the first round, each performs his or her role.

4. In the second round, each performs a new role.

5. In the third round, each performs a new role.

Figure 5.27 shows the rotation of roles in each trio of students and provides a template for the Recorders to use.

Say Something

This strategy is similar to think-pair-share but more open-ended (Harste, Woodward, & Burke, 1984). After students have received some new information or experienced or observed a lecture, video, virtual experience, or reading, they form pairs and discuss their emotional and intellectual reactions to the material and any questions or misconceptions that need clarification. This exercise is an energizer, as students move and engage in discussion, and it also helps students process new learnings and ideas in a safe environment. The discussion can feel liberating, as there are no restrictions on the scope of the dialogue and no particular focus is given. Students may also debrief afterward by sharing their thoughts with the large group; doing so can help all students articulate their thinking and build on each other's ideas.

This chapter highlighted how the brain learns and how teachers can use this understanding of the brain to garner attention and open mental "files." Information on how the brain learns has many implications for teachers using a block schedule. The strategies here focused on how to

Figure 5.27 Trio Talk

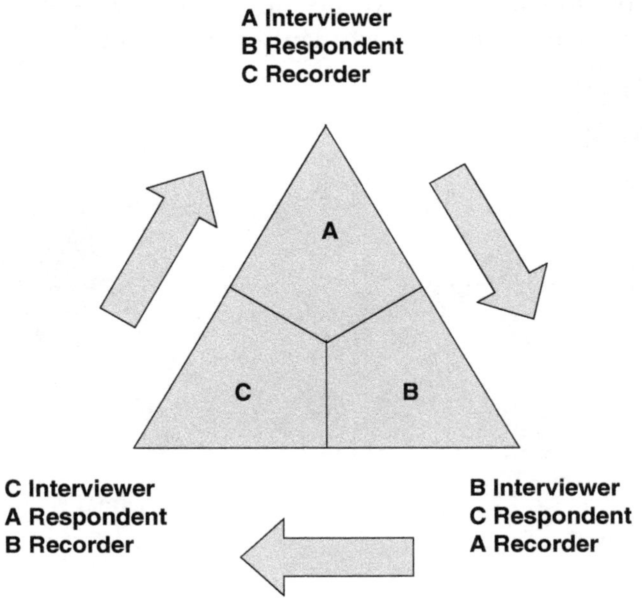

A Interviewer
B Respondent
C Recorder

A

C   B

C Interviewer
A Respondent
B Recorder

B Interviewer
C Respondent
A Recorder

Scribe Form

	Notes	Reflections
Person A: _____		
Person B: _____		
Person C: _____		

begin lessons and engage higher-level thinking, while taking into account current brain research and how students learn best.

Chapters 6 and 7 will provide the reader with more strategies that differentiate classroom instruction. Chapter 6 focuses on lecture and note taking and how to end lessons, while Chapter 7 focuses on strategies that research has shown can increase student achievement.

6 Lesson Plans in Action

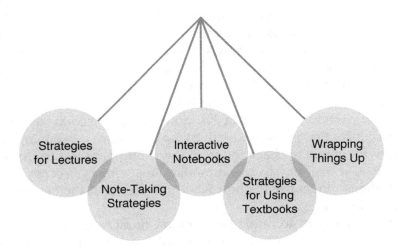

Strategies for Lectures

Interactive Notebooks

Wrapping Things Up

Note-Taking Strategies

Strategies for Using Textbooks

The previous chapter discussed the implications of brain research for structuring lessons and accessing students' prior knowledge. However, a written lesson plan is just a plan if it is not put into action. This chapter showcases numerous strategies that can be used to engage students actively in the lesson. For students to be successful, they must develop skills in extracting information from lectures and reading. The old formula of students taking notes, answering questions, and taking the test does not address the diverse learning styles of students. Fortunately, teachers can differentiate the way they lecture in many ways to engage students fully. Teachers can also provide students with options for taking notes and reading texts. In shorter time frames, teachers do not have the luxury of time to model numerous strategies. Block scheduling, however, provides teachers the opportunity to use several strategies to assist students in developing their note-taking, processing, and reading skills.

STRATEGIES FOR LECTURES

Direct instruction can be a meaningful way to disseminate information. Many teachers have experienced sitting through a lecture in which they were totally engaged—and have sat through lectures in which they had difficulty staying focused or even awake. The purpose of a lecture is to provide essential information about a topic. Research has shown that a typical student's attention span in minutes is their age plus or minus 2. Nonetheless, lectures can actively engage students if they are given opportunities to manipulate and work with the concept, both as individuals and in small groups.

In a block schedule, there can be a tendency to lecture too long. Following a 10 and 2 rule is one way to prevent students becoming passive learners; at the same time, this rule serves as an excellent pacing guide for the teacher. To follow this rule, teachers lecture for 10 minutes and then have the students work with the information for 2 minutes. In other words, the content needs to be chunked. The 2-minute activity can be in the form of discussion, working in interactive notebooks, reflection, questioning, drawing a concept map, pair-share thinking, summarizing, or simply sharing notes with others to check for accuracy. Using mini lectures in a block schedule is also one way to accommodate the primacy-recency effect, in which students remember the best what they heard at the beginning and end of a lecture.

Today's classroom technologies provide numerous ways to disseminate content so as to address individual student needs. Visuals are an essential component of a lecture. If using visuals, as with a PowerPoint presentation, for example, the instructor should keep the following in mind:

- Use keywords, not full sentences.
- Emphasize separate points by using bullets, numbers, or bold letters.
- Make sure there is adequate space between words.
- Maintain the same background, font, and general design during the presentation.
- If using colors, use no more than four per screen.
- To keep the students' attention, try to stand to the left of the screen. (Students read from left to right.)

Using different lecture formats can differentiate the dissemination of content. Whatever its format, however, for a lecture to be effective, it must have a clear introduction and summary. The lecture should also be well planned and clearly organized and should be accomplished in the time allotted.

Build in accountability by having students process the information from lecture by doing something. Providing choices for this portion of the instruction is one way to differentiate content. For example, students could be asked to construct a concept map from the information gathered, or an extension of the lesson could be assigned as homework. A social studies teacher might have students use the information gathered from a lecture to design a travel brochure to be shared with elementary students, middle school students, high school students, or even adults. Likewise, numerous strategies can be used during a lecture to engage learners and meet their individual needs. Many instructors use brainstorming techniques, discussions, problem-solving activities, case studies, and games to make lectures more interesting. Figure 6.1 shows a variety of lecture strategies that can be used.

Figure 6.1 Strategies for Lectures

Choose Passages/Fill In the Blank	Responsive Lecture
Students fill in the blanks of a written passage or lecture outline provided by the teacher. This can be an effective way to keep students engaged in the lecture. To create the worksheets, words can be deleted from PowerPoint handouts.	Combine class discussion with lecture by asking questions. • Ask good discussion questions; for example, how many of you agreed with _____? • Do not ask for recall questions unless you are going to do something with the responses.
Participatory Lecture	Intrapersonal/Reflection Lecture
Alternate mini lectures and discussion buzz groups, debates, simulations, and role-plays.	Students draw/write in their journals so that they can reflect on the content of the lesson. They can also silently reread their notes.
Demonstration Lecture	Think-Pair-Share Lecture
Giving a demonstration before, during, or after the lecture is an effective way to motivate student interest in the topic of the discussion.	• The teacher poses a question, prompt, or observation that students are to think about. • Students pair up to talk about the answer each came up with and identify the best answer. • Pairs then share their answers with the class.
Graphic Organizer Lecture	Windowpane Lecture
Use blank graphic organizers that can be filled in as the lecture unfolds. Students can fill in a blank graphic organizer along with the teacher.	Draw windowpanes or boxes that will be completed during the lecture. • Draw graphic representations, symbols, words, or other images in each windowpane that illustrate the point being made. • Students then try to re-create the images. • For closure, students can add content and pose questions.

NOTE-TAKING STRATEGIES

Note taking is an essential component of learning, yet some students struggle with it. In a differentiated classroom, students are taught several note-taking skills to allow them to choose which style best suits them. Regardless of which strategy students use, the importance of reviewing their notes and practicing what they have learned should be emphasized. Effective note taking can stimulate critical-thinking skills, help students remember what is said, and provide the tools for test preparation. Examples of note-taking strategies posted by the Student Academic Services at California Polytechnic State University (2010) follow.

The Cornell Method

This system was developed by Dr. Pauk, Cornell University, in 1949. This system provides a systemic format in which to condense and organize notes. The page is organized with a two-and-a-half-inch margin on the left used for processing. The Cornell Note template (Figure 6.2) shows the page is organized into three sections:

1. *Cue Column.* The cue column is kept empty while taking notes. Following the lecture, the notes are processed for the purpose of reviewing and reflecting.

2. *Note-Taking Area.* The lecture is recorded as fully and meaningfully as possible.

3. *Summaries.* The notes are summarized in a sentence or two.

Guided Notes

Teacher-prepared handouts, or notes templates, provide students with guides for note taking. This template (see Figure 6.3) contains a consistent set of clues to alert students to where and when to record concepts. When designing a template, the teacher needs to strike a balance between a fill-in-the-blank format and open-ended note taking.

The Outline Method

Students listen and write points in an organized pattern based on space indentation. Major points are farthest to the left, and more specific points are indented more to the right (see Figure 6.4).

Figure 6.2 Cornell Note Template

Template for Cornell Notes

Subject:_____Date:_____

A. Cue Column	B. Note-Taking Area
C. Summaries	

Figure 6.3 Note-Taking Template for an Event

Note-Taking Template for an Event

Event Description

When Did the Event Occur?   **Where Did the Event Occur?**

Why Did the Event Occur?   **How Did the Event Occur?**

Who Was Involved in the Event?

Figure 6.4 Outline Method for Lecture Notes

I. Topic

    A. Subtopic

       i. Detailed information
      ii. Detailed information

         1. More information
         2. More information

            a. Further information
            b. Further information

    B. Subtopic

II. Topic

    A. Subtopic

       i. Detailed information
      ii. Detailed information

         1. More information
         2. More information

            a. Further information
            b. Further information

    B. Subtopic

       i. Information
      ii. Information

III. Topic

The Mapping Method

Students record a graphic representation of the content of the lecture that relates each fact or idea to every other fact or idea (see Figure 6.5).

Figure 6.5 Map for Note Taking

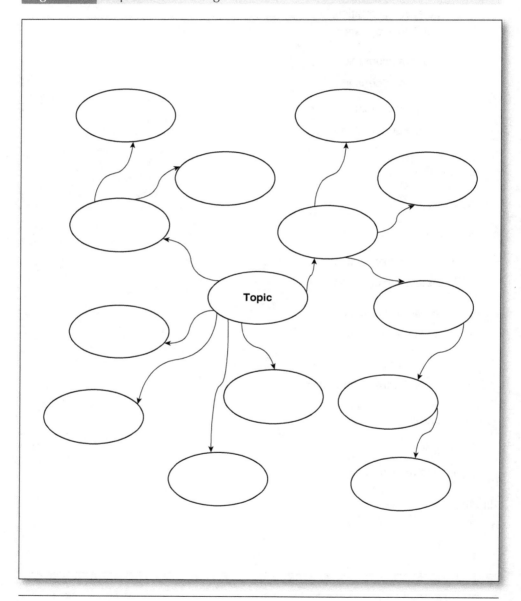

The Charting Method

Students set up paper in advance with columns and headings, or the teacher provides handouts set up in this way. This note-taking method is useful if the lecture format is distinct (see Figure 6.6 for a general template suggestion and Figure 6.7 for a social studies template example).

The Sentence Method

Students write every new thought, fact, or topic on a separate line.

INTERACTIVE NOTEBOOKS

Interactive notebooks began as a strategy in Addison-Wesley's program History Alive! Since then, many teachers have expanded on and added to the repertoire of ways in which the notebook is used. Why use interactive notebooks? Notebooks

- are a means of differentiating student processing of information.
- improve organizational skills.
- improve critical-thinking skills.
- express understanding and creativity.
- provide students with a resource to study for tests.
- record data.
- record progress.
- are a means of communicating what the student has learned.
- encourage students to be independent and reflective thinkers.
- serve as a reminder to teachers to give students time to absorb ideas as instruction unfolds.
- tell teachers, if there are blank pages, that they are providing too much information without giving students enough time to process the material.

Students will need a spiral-bound notebook or composition book and glue sticks or clear tape. The interactive part of the book is the left side, in which students react, reflect, organize, and interpret what is on the right side. This space creates an opportunity for students to reorganize new information in creative formats as well as express their opinions and

Figure 6.6 Charting Method Template: General

Lecture Main Topic/Date	Key Terms	Notes	Drawings/Diagrams
Topic A			
Topic B			
Topic C			
Topic D			
Topic E			

Figure 6.7 Charting Method Template: Social Studies

Lecture Main Topic/Date	Key Events/ Places/Dates	Key Players	Outcomes
Topic A			
Topic B			
Topic C			
Topic D			
Topic E			

feelings. They can explore their connections to what has been learned. Questions students may ask themselves include the following:

- What's my purpose for reading this?
- What do I already know about this topic?
- What information is important here?
- How can I paraphrase this information?
- How can I organize this information?
- What more do I need to know?
- What do I not understand?
- How does this relate to me?

The right side of the notebook is the input side, where students write down information they receive from listening to lectures, reading their text, watching videos, or listening to guest speakers. Figure 6.8 lists ideas for how students can interact with the information on the right side and what the information on the right side and their responses on the left side may look like. Also included is a chart that students can paste in their notebooks so they always have ideas for their work on the left side.

Teachers using interactive notebooks have found that students put more effort into their work and develop a sense of pride about their work, which in turn increases self-esteem. Notebooks need to be checked on a regular basis; collecting and grading all the notebooks at one time can make for extended grading sessions, so one might want to stagger the collection. However, reducing loose and lost papers and no longer dealing with messy binders is well worth the effort.

STRATEGIES FOR USING TEXTBOOKS

Marzano and collagues (Marzano, Norford, Paynter, Pickering, & Gaddy, 2001; Marzano, Pickering, & Pollock, 2001) reminded us that having students take notes and summarize, as well as providing them with advance organizers to help them do so, is an effective strategy for increasing student achievement. As students are introduced to new text or a new chapter in a text, we can orient them to the new material and thus increase the chances that they succeed in reading for information and comprehension.

Most texts are full of factual information, but they are not always organized in a way such that students can see the important information and the supporting details. Students often need to be taught strategies to extract information from texts and summarize their findings. The following are some strategies that can be used for summarizing.

Figure 6.8 Interactive Notebook Chart

Interactive Notebooks

Left Side	Right Side
• Concept maps • Tables/graphs • Mind maps • Venn diagrams • Pictures/drawings • Graphic organizers • Poems/limericks/raps • Songs • Cartoons • Comic strips • Advertisements • Summaries • Brainstorming • Timelines • Flowcharts • Word games • Personal responses • Pictowords/pictographs • Metaphors • Illustrated definitions • Mnemonic devices • Crossword puzzles • Foldables	• Lecture notes • Book notes • Goals • Homework • New vocabulary • In-class assignments • Research • Teacher questions • Practice problems • Videos • Presentations • Guest speaker notes • Informative handouts • Essays • Class discussion notes • Lab procedures • Lecture guides

1. Draw a picture for all the new vocabulary words.	2. Write a paragraph summarizing the information.	3. Write a reflection on the activity/ work. What did you like or dislike? What did you learn?	4. Create a crossword puzzle for all vocabulary.
5. Draw a cartoon with headlines demonstrating each new concept.	6. Create a concept map.	7. Write a poem using the information from the lecture notes.	8. Create a comic strip.
9. Write a story about using the information in your notes.	10. Draw a picture that will show the information in your notes.	11. Write a letter to a friend saying what you learned in class today.	12. Create a Venn diagram.

The Rule-Based Strategy

1. Delete trivial material that is unnecessary to understanding.

2. Delete redundant material.

3. Substitute superordinate terms for lists (e.g., *insects* for "bee, ants, etc.").

4. Select a topic sentence or invent one if it is missing.

Definition Frame

A definition frame is used to describe a particular concept and identify subordinate concepts.

1. *Term.* The subject to be defined

2. *Set.* The general category to which the term belongs

3. *Gross Characteristics.* Those characteristics that separate the term from other elements in the set

4. *Minute Differences.* Those different classes of objects that fall directly beneath the term

Argumentation Frame

The argumentation frame contains information designed to support a claim. Using an argumentation frame will lead to a persuasive piece of writing.

1. *Evidence.* Information that leads to a claim

2. *Claim.* The assertions that something is true; the claim that is the focal point of the argument

3. *Support.* Examples or explanations of the claim

4. *Qualifier.* A restriction on the claim or on the evidence for the claim

Symbol Notations With Self-Sticking Notes

Coding information (Davey, 1983) is a way students can make sense out of textbook information, increase their focus on the material, and analyze their own comprehension levels.

Set up codes for different types of responses to information, or students can invent their own codes. They may also jot down why that

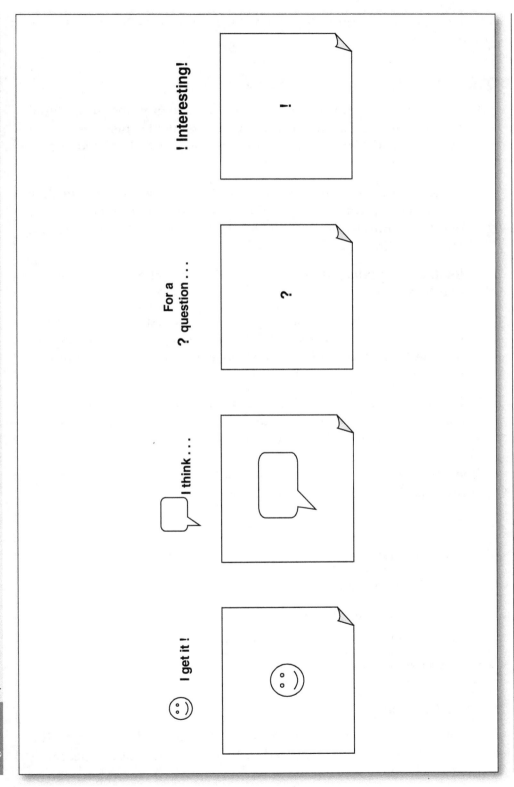

symbol was used, the question they have, why it is interesting, and so forth (see Figure 6.9).

SQ3R (Survey, Question, Read, Recite, Review)

1. *Survey.* This step gives the reader a chance to examine the material to check out the headings and skim the content. This provides an overview and helps students to access any prior knowledge connected to the reading.

2. *Question.* Students create a question for each section before they read it. The heading may give them a starting point for creating the question. Thus, students create for themselves a focus and purpose for the reading.

3. *Read.* Each student individually reads the section to answer the question.

4. *Recite.* After the reading, students are encouraged to recite the information that they have learned from the passage in order to answer the question. Students may choose to answer the question orally or in writing.

5. *Review.* After the reading is finished, students review the questions and try to recall the answers to each from memory. If they didn't take notes previously, now would be the time to write them.

Teachers may provide students with a note-taking or summarizing organizer to facilitate taking complete notes.

1. *Survey.* Look over the assignment.

2. *Question.* Make up questions for each heading.

3. *Read.* Read for information.

4 *Recite.* Tell the answers.

5. *Review.* Make notes to answer the questions.

Source: Anderson & Armbruster (1984b).

Reciprocal Teaching

Reciprocal teaching includes a dialogue that takes place between the teacher and students (or student leader) that results in students learning how to construct meaning when they are placed in must-read situations, taking tests, or doing assignments. Sometimes this approach is referred to as "study reading." It brings all aspects of literacy together, integrating speaking, listening, reading, and writing. It is a great strategy for the English-language learner, as it facilitates lots of dialogue in a safe and structured environment. The process of reciprocal teaching consists of the following four steps:

1. *Generating Questions.* Students generate questions that they share and answer individually and collectively with supporting material and rationales.

2. *Summarizing.* Students identify key points in and develop a summary of the information read.

3. *Clarifying.* Restating or paraphrasing deepens understanding because to restate, one must clearly comprehend the material. At this point, new language and terms need to be clarified.

4. *Predicting.* Students make assumptions, predictions, and generalizations from the information they have been considering. For example, if studying a piece of literature, they may predict what will happen in the next chapter. In social studies, they may generate a hypothesis about what will occur next, implications for the future, or next steps to take based on their new knowledge.

Question Swaps

Question swaps can focus the learner and facilitate reading with a purpose as well as help students construct personal questions about the new information. Students are directed to make up two questions to which they know the answer. For each of their questions, students will then

1. find one partner and swap their first questions;

2. answer their partner's question and include their own names; and

3. find a second partner with whom to swap the second question.

Figure 6.10 shows a template to use for this exercise.

Split-Page Notes

Split-page notes help the student actively process information through multiple verbal and written modes and then organize it into visual forms

Figure 6.10 Question Swaps

Name: _____

Topic
Question
Answer

Name: _____

Topic
Question
Answer

or graphic organizers. The dual processing engages both hemispheres of the brain and helps in comprehension and long-term memory. Figure 6.11 is an example template to use for this note-taking strategy.

Another example of a split-page note-taking format is the W5 organizer, shown in Figure 6.12, which can be used to take notes while reading a textbook. This organizer works well with social studies content. It also taps into the thinking skills of prediction. Chapter 2 described the learning styles of students, categorizing them as "beach balls," "clipboards," "puppies," and "microscopes." This organizer is great for students who are clipboards, as they love the clear, concrete organization of it. It helps beach balls be more organized. If puppies get to work with a partner, they enjoy the activity. Finally, the microscopes like the opportunity to be analytical and organize as well as to compare and contrast.

Cross-Classification Charts

Cross-classification charts, which show relationships and connections, help students to organize and record information in a way that facilitates active processing and can serve later for review. They can also be useful in organizing thoughts in the prewriting process. Cross-classification charts can be used in a variety of content areas; for example, when studying American authors in language arts class (see Figure 6.13), conflicts with U.S. involvement in social studies class (see Figure 6.14), and electricity in science class (see Figure 6.15).

Figure 6.16 is a blank cross-classification chart that can serve as a template adaptable to any unit of study.

Graphic Organizers

Graphic organizers can enhance student understanding. One teacher uses these to help students process content they have learned as a consequence of classroom experiences and homework. The matrix shown in Figure 6.17 is an example of an opening activity used to "connect" one class session with another, as well as to review homework. Students fill in the cells of the matrix to illustrate their understandings of the attributes of each of the shapes, as well as the qualities that distinguish the shapes from one another.

Four-Corner Graphic Summarizer for Organizing Information

A four-corner graphic can be an effective note-taking and summarizing tool. The following examples show how students can collect details about information while they are reading. Note taking can be done in a "dot/jot"

Figure 6.11 Split-Page Notes

Jot Down Key Words	Use a Graphic Organizer

Figure 6.12 W5 Organizer for Note Taking and Summarizing

Topic: _____

	Words	Pictures	What's Next?
Who?			
What?			
Where?			
When?			
Why?			
Summary			

Figure 6.13 Cross-Classification Chart for American Authors

Compare These	Period	Focus	Style	Features
Williams				
Miller				
Twain				
Hawthorne				

Figure 6.14 Cross-Classification Chart for Wars With U.S. Involvement

Compare These	Year	Issues	Allies	Outcomes
World War I				
World War II				
Korean War				
Vietnam				

Figure 6.15 Cross-Classification Chart for Electrical Properties

Compare These	Discovered By	Year	Effect	Principle
Resistance				
Volts				
Amps				
Ohms				

Figure 6.16 Cross-Classification Chart for Note Taking and Classifying

Compare These				

Figure 6.17 Sample Matrix for Geometric Shapes

Organizer	Edges	Vertices	Faces
Cylinder			
Cube			
Cone			
Sphere			
Square-based pyramid			
Rectangular prism			

fashion, in which students record just a few words beside a dot or bullet. It can even be done as a jigsaw with a group of four students, each completing one quadrant and then teaching the other group members. Students fill in the placemat and then write a paragraph summarizing the details from their full page.

Figures 6.18, 6.19, and 6.20 show three examples of how the four-corner summarizer could be used with content. There is also a blank figure (Figure 6.21) for your students' use.

WRAPPING THINGS UP

Primacy-recency theory suggests that the brain remembers best what comes first and next best what comes last. So if one wants to ensure students' enduring understanding of concepts, skills, and practices over time, it is essential to plan carefully the final moments of an instructional period and to structure experiences that will extend and enhance the quality of classroom learning.

Planning Review Strategies for Long-Term Retention

Most teachers find that key to students' ability to remember what they have learned over time is how many opportunities students have to rehearse, or practice, what has been taught. Effective teachers check for understanding frequently throughout the lesson/period to see if learning has taken place, to determine what further rehearsal or challenge is needed, and to assure themselves that no one is left behind. True differentiation depends on ongoing formative assessment to regroup and rehearse or extend and enrich content, depending on students' levels of learning and personal preferences, interests, and needs.

Teachers use many strategies to generate student "output" to accomplish this goal. For instance, as one teacher taught about the bones, muscles, ligaments, arteries, and nerves in the foot, he had students draw these on a blank picture of a foot. To "see" what students learned, he had them put aside their notes, draw around their own foot, and fill in the blanks. A math teacher gave groups of students colored streamers of different lengths, which they used to measure the heights of their group members. He then asked the groups to compute the mean and mode of the heights. Near the end of the period, he asked students to articulate what they had done to complete the task and then generate a "person on the street" definition of the terms. An industrial technology teacher had each student select something she or he had done in class and write a one-page summary of the steps to the process; the summaries were displayed on the shop wall.

Figure 6.18 Four-Corner Summary: Nutrition

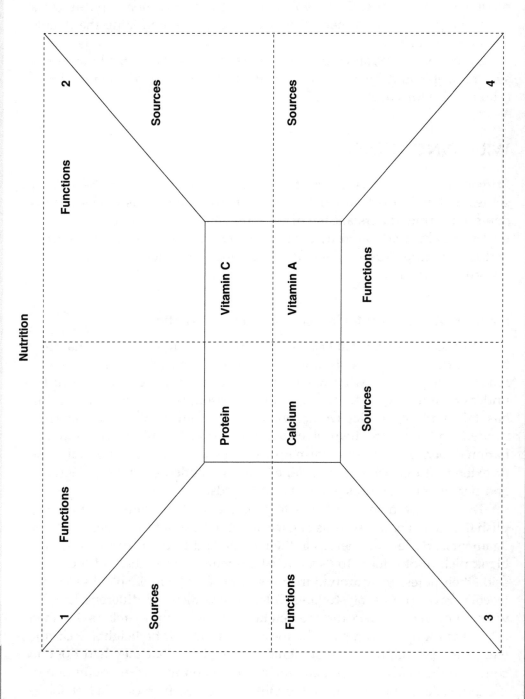

Nutrition

Functions

Sources

Vitamin C

Protein

1

Sources

Functions

Calcium

Vitamin A

Sources

Functions

3

2

Sources

Functions

Sources

4

Figure 6.19 Four-Corner Summary: Body Systems

Body Systems

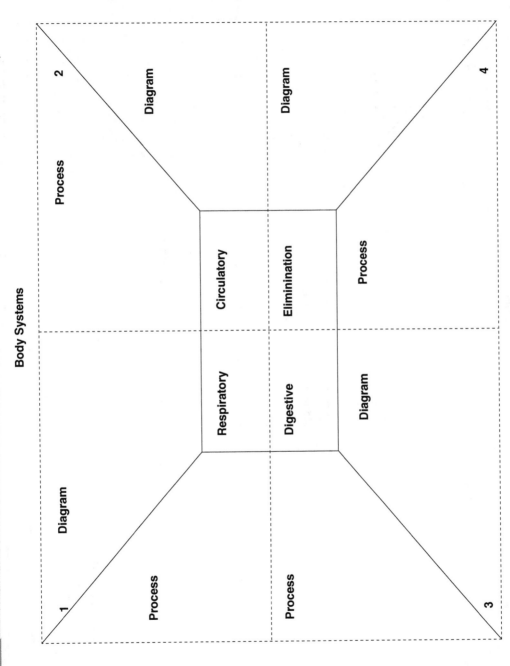

143

Figure 6.20 Four-Corner Summary: Fractions

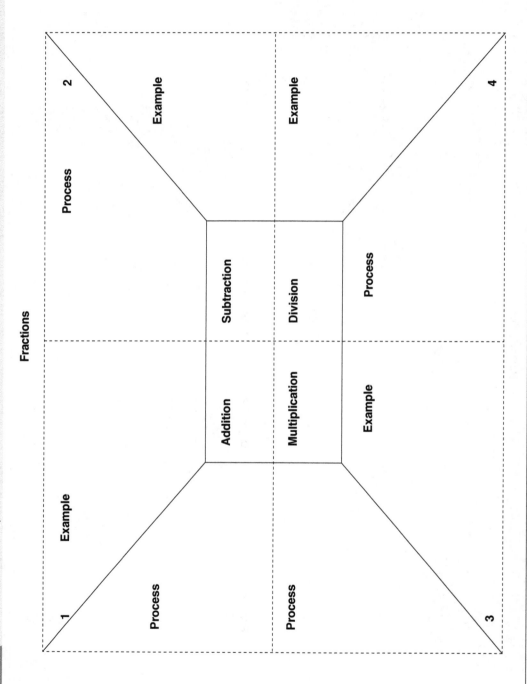

Fractions

1	2
Example	Process	Example
Process	Addition	Subtraction	
Process	Multiplication	Division	Process
Process	Example	Example
3	4

Figure 6.21 Four-Corner Summary: Blank Template

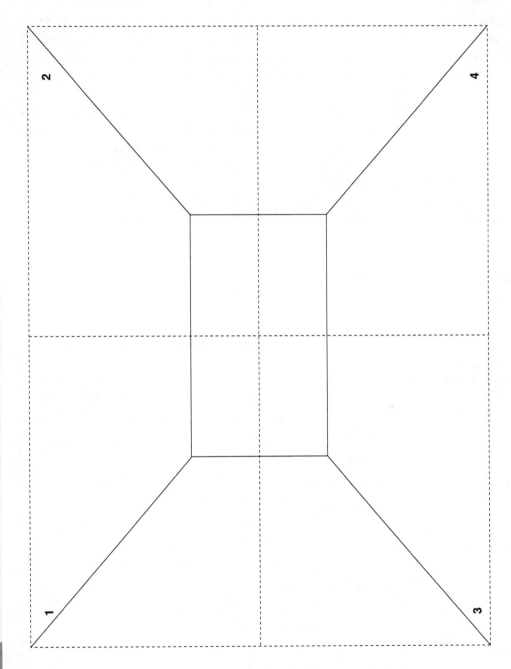

A social studies teacher handed each student a colored 3 × 5 card. Students had 10 minutes to write on their cards as much as they wanted about the lesson they had just experienced. They were able to use their cards during the exam. The teacher reflected, "Although some may perceive this as cheating, I think it is a simple way of inviting students to revisit content and highlight key points." Another teacher handed out strips of sticky dots and allowed 12 minutes for students to look through their notes and high-light, with the sticky dots, key points they wished to remember.

An art teacher and a music teacher both used a strategy called "reflec-tive pause," in which students were asked to stop what they were doing and analyze the piece they were currently working on. Students discussed their efforts and any difficult aspects of their performances, and the teacher collaborated in problem solving.

Figure 6.22 is a menu of options from which teachers and students may select when devising plans for vibrant class endings or for review.

Figure 6.22 Strategies for Review

Graffiti Placemat	Revisit the graffiti chart and cross off incorrect information and add new learning in another color.
ABC Brainstorming	Revisit ABC brainstorming sheet and cross off any incorrect information and add new items.
Jeopardy or Wheel of Fortune	These two games, based on the familiar television shows, provide an exciting medium for students to review key learnings from a lesson. Students in one classroom constructed a giant Wheel of Fortune in industrial technology class. Periodically, for different lessons, the teacher posted questions at each colored section of the wheel. Students formed teams. They spun the wheel and had to answer the question indicated by the arrow. Many review game templates are available for free download on the Internet.
Twenty Questions	Students form pairs. Each student writes 10 questions on a card, along with 10 correct answers to the questions. Student pairs take turns asking one another their collective 20 questions, prompting their partners to help them identify the correct answer and celebrating them when they do. Asking good questions helps clarify understanding and rehearse content.
Paper Pass	Each student develops two review questions and writes these on separate 5 × 8 cards. They autograph their cards and then pass their cards to one another as music is played in the background. They may sit or stand to do this. When the music stops, each class member must answer the question on the card in her or his hand. Then the card is returned to its author, who provides verbal or written feedback to the student who has answered the question.
Event Cards	The teacher prepares event cards from 5 × 8 cards with yarn attached to each of the top corners so that the cards can be worn around the neck. Each student is given a card. Without speaking to one another, students must line up in the same order as the events around their necks occurred. After the task is completed, each student must share one fact about the event she or he is wearing.

People Search or Find Someone Who Can

"Find Someone Who Can" or the "People Search" can be used as an icebreaker. It can be used with personal information or instructional material that students need to discuss, review, or check for clarification. Figure 6.23 is a sample of a People Search that could be used at the end of a lesson.

Steps and Directions

1. Give students a bingo grid or list of questions and/or tasks for which they need to find someone to answer or complete.

2. Each student takes his or her list and walks around the room, trying to find someone who is able to give an answer to a question on the sheet.

3. The student listens attentively to the answer that is given and jots down the name of the person who answered the question beside the answer.

4. When everyone has completed their grid, students can report out what they have heard and learned from others.

Give One and Get One

This strategy can be used to generate ideas, share ideas, or give the group an opportunity to transfer ideas learned in a class or discuss (see Figure 6.24; photocopy as many as needed for the class and cut the Give One, Get One worksheet into strips and pass one out to each student).

1 On your form, list two things you remember from today's class.

2. Meet with another person. Share one of your ideas. Record his or her idea on your form.

3. Continue meeting other classmates until you have 10 good ideas.

Wallpaper Poster

"Wallpaper poster" is a group comprehension strategy that supports summarizing and analysis for deeper understanding of complex concepts after students are introduced to the learning through articles, lecture, Internet, video, real-world documents, and/or text. This strategy allows

Figure 6.23 People Search or Find Someone Who Can

Name three new vocabulary words and their meaning.	Explain the major event in today's reading.	Describe one thing that helped your group be successful today.
What would be a good question related to today's material?	Explain to someone what you need to work on from today's class.	Tell three points of interest from today's class.
Suggest a way to remember some key material.	Suggest a symbol to represent key learning.	One thing you appreciated today . . .

Figure 6.24 Give One and Get One Template

1.	1.
2.	2.
3.	3.
4.	4.
5.	5.
6.	6.
7.	7.
8.	8.
9.	9.
10.	10.

teachers to pay attention to diverse learning styles, from verbal/linguistic to visual/spatial. This strategy also facilitates students' summarizing and clearly stating information in precise ways. This increases application of the concept, filing of information in long-term memory, and connection of new learning to prior learning (see Figure 6.25).

Steps and Directions

1. Have participants note the key points from the class. You could ask different groups to attend to different topics.

2. Have partners or small groups place the topic on the top of a piece of chart paper. (You can also use a mini poster and put the template on a piece of copy paper for pairs to use. An 8.5 × 14-inch piece of paper gives more room; construction paper simulates the idea of a concept poster.)

3. Students define the concept in their own words.

4. Create a symbol to represent the concept visually. Three students with colorful markers or pencils will do this work.

5. Give examples that support the idea and be able to rationalize them.

6. Add any questions that help increase relevance and application. This step helps students deepen understanding and increase memory.

7. Present to another small group (if template used as conventional graphic organizer) or entire group (if chart paper used).

I Have. . . . Who Has . . . ?

"I Have. . . . Who Has . . . ?" is a popular review strategy with some teachers. A science teacher played this game with her students. The teacher created playing cards and distributed these, one to a student (see Figure 6.26). A student timekeeper was appointed. Student 1 might read from her playing card, "I am a substance that provides energy for photosynthesis to take place." The student who has the name of this substance on his card responds. In this case, the student responded, "You are sunshine." Then the second student might read a prompt from his card, "I am a pigment found in the chloroplasts of plant cells." And the student who has the name of this substance on her card responds, "You are chlorophyll." The game continues until each class member has had a turn to respond. A technology teacher

Figure 6.25 Wallpaper Poster Instructions

Wallpaper Poster

1. Record the title on the paper.

2. Define the concept (key idea).

3. Create a symbol or visual to represent the concept.

4. Give examples of the concept and be prepared to give a rationale for your choices.

Figure 6.26 Sample "I Have. . . . Who Has . . . ?" Using Vocabulary for the Cell

I have a network of thin tubes and filaments. *Who has a plant cell?*	I have a cell with a cell wall. *Who has a mitochondrion?*
I have an organelle that produces energy. *Who has a chloroplast?*	I have an organelle where photosynthesis takes place. *Who has a ribosome?*
I have an organelle where protein is made. *Who has a cell membrane?*	I have a structure that is semipermeable. *Who has a lysosome?*
I have an organelle that contains digestive enzymes. *Who has a Golgi apparatus?*	I have an organelle that packages secretory materials. *Who has a nucleus?*
I have a structure that controls metabolism and protein synthesis. *Who has a nucleolus?*	I have a structure that synthesizes RNA. *Who has an endoplasmic reticulum?*
I have an organelle that provides intracellular storage and transport. *Who has any centrioles?*	I have two structures that separate during cell division. *Who has a chloroplast?*
I have an organelle where photosynthesis takes place. *Who has any cytoplasm?*	I have a liquid that contains organelles. *Who has a cytoskeleton?*

Figure 6.27 Template for "I Have. . . . Who Has . . . ?"

I have. . . . *Who has . . . ?*	I have. . . . *Who has . . . ?*
I have. . . . *Who has . . . ?*	I have. . . . *Who has . . . ?*
I have. . . . *Who has . . . ?*	I have. . . . *Who has . . . ?*
I have. . . . *Who has . . . ?*	I have. . . . *Who has . . . ?*
I have. . . . *Who has . . . ?*	I have. . . . *Who has . . . ?*
I have. . . . *Who has . . . ?*	I have. . . . *Who has . . . ?*
I have. . . . *Who has . . . ?*	I have. . . . *Who has . . . ?*

used this game to review computer terms and functions, and this game would work with any content in any subject area. Students practice active listening and declarative knowledge or skills, and they hear key vocabulary and connect definitions to the vocabulary. Figure 6.27 provides a blank template that can be adapted to any lesson.

Shaping Up a Review

"Shaping Up a Review" uses geometric shapes: a square, circle, and triangle. This exercise can be done as a review with partners or in small groups on a piece of newsprint or individually as a check for understanding. See Figure 6.28.

Learning Journals

Learning journals—that is, entries into journals or logs—are also a great way to summarize the learning, reflect on personal successes, and set goals.

Round-the-Room Brainstorming

When trying to generate multiple solutions, people can use "Round-the-Room Brainstorming." It energizes the group by showing evidence of the collective power of group problem solving and creative thought. Collectively, people have more and better ideas than one person working alone.

Steps and Directions

1. Divide into groups, one group for each chart.

2. Each group stands in front of a chart.

3. Choose a scribe in each group. Each group uses a different-colored marker. The marker goes with the group from chart to chart. (That way, if there are any questions about the suggestion, it's easy to ask the group using that color to clarify their ideas.)

4. Quickly brainstorm responses to the topic on the chart.

5. After a minute or two, when the signal is heard, move one chart to the right.

6. Quickly brainstorm at the new chart (1–2 minutes).

7. At the signal, move to the right and repeat.

Figure 6.28 Shaping Up a Review

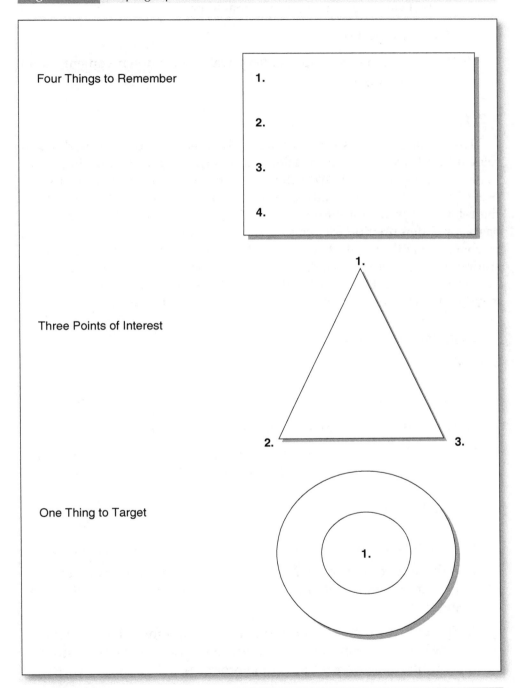

Four Things to Remember

1.

2.

3.

4.

Three Points of Interest

1.

2.   3.

One Thing to Target

1.

8. When the groups reach the charts where they started, analyze the data. Prioritize, cluster, or eliminate items.

9. Groups report out.

10. Students may then do a gallery walk to jot down content on an advanced organizer.

3-2-1

This strategy helps students solidify their learning by sorting through relevant and irrelevant information, summarizing, and connecting information (see Figure 6.29). With the right prompts, this strategy is a great prewriting tool and goal-setting template. It can even get students to see the relevant application of newer learning. 3-2-1 can also be an excellent basis for differentiation, depending on the grouping and peer work that teachers use with this strategy. When this is used with double circles, consulting line, or partners/triads, students can consult with peers and add to or refine their 3-2-1 card, foldable, or chart. Alternatively, students may engage in peer consultation prior to completing their 3-2-1 cards.

Steps and Directions

Basic Process

1. Give students a 3-2-1 card to fill out and share with a partner.

2. Students turn card in as an informal assessment or assignment.

3. Use for both closings and openings to check for understanding, reach application- or analysis-level responses, or practice summarizing.

Prewriting Process

1. Give students a 3-2-1 card to fill out and share with a small group.

2. Ask students to turn the 3-2-1 card into a short summary or analysis paragraph; they could put 3-2-1 at the top of the page and the paragraph at bottom.

3. Students turn in card and paragraph as an informal assessment of new learning connections and understanding or as a demonstration of application, depending on the prompt.

Figure 6.29 3-2-1 Cards

3	Things that interest me about . . .
2	Ways I could use . . .
1	Thing I wonder about . . .

3	Ways this is used in the real world . . .
2	Things this is similar to . . .
1	Question that this brings to mind . . .

3	Things I learned today . . .
2	Connections or "Ahas!"
1	Question I still have is . . .

3	Things I enjoyed during this class . . .
2	Suggestions I have . . .
1	Thing I'd like to discuss today . . .

3	Things I remember from last class . . .
2	Things I learned from homework . . .
1	Question I still have is . . .

Differentiation Process

1. Give partners or triads an opportunity to rehearse their thinking about 3-2-1 out loud. For older students, follow the next two steps.

2. Write your ideas on your 3-2-1 card or write with a partner.

3. Turn in the 3-2-1 card as a pre-assessment.

Students can also add to or refine their 3-2-1 based on the input of peers. If you want additional information about student thinking and understanding, you can have students add a final summary/analysis/ application paragraph to their cards. These also make great tickets out the door.

Planning Long-Range Assignment Using Products

The possible products listed in Figure 6.30 invite students to review and apply what they have learned. These products also allow teachers to assess how well students have learned and what was most significant to them.

Although this list is not exhaustive, it will provide a springboard for other ideas. The teacher must select differentiated tasks while considering learning styles, processing channels, multiple intelligences, and levels of thinking desired given the instructional context (e.g., students, time, setting) in which these will be played out.

Extending Learning Time Through Homework

In the block-schedule classroom, the teacher faces a challenge: how to sustain student interest and attention until the end of an extended period of instructional time. Beyond this is the additional challenge of how to inspire students to do homework to extend the potential impact of the initial classroom experience.

A synthesis of more than a dozen studies of the effects of homework in various subjects showed the assignment and completion of homework yield positive effects on academic achievement. The effects are almost tripled when teachers take time to grade the work, make corrections and specific comments on improvements that can be made, and discuss problems and remedies with individual students or the whole class. (Walberg & Paik, 2000, p. 9)

Figure 6.30 Products for Long-Range Assessments

• Make a game.	• Formulate a scientific theory.
• Write a book.	• Write a song.
• Create a slide show.	• Be a mentor.
• Develop a PowerPoint presentation.	• Make a timeline.
• Make a mural.	• Do something to make our world better.
• Draw a set of blueprints.	• Make a video presentation.
• Write a computer program.	• Draw a graph.
• Make a piece of art.	• Develop a new product.
• Keep a diary.	• Create a new leisure-time sport.
• Write an imaginary autobiography of a historical figure.	• Develop a collection of study prints.
• Write an opinion article.	• Design a simulation.
• Plan a journey.	• Compile a portfolio.
• Create a topographical map.	• Teach a lesson.
• Write a script and tape a conversation.	• Write and illustrate a children's story.
• Prepare a television program.	• Design and make a costume.
• Develop and use a questionnaire.	• Grow a plant and graph its growth.
• Create a newspaper.	• Write a biography.
• Make a political cartoon.	• Create a news report for television.
• Develop a poem.	• Do a pantomime.
• Design and construct a model.	• Write a new law.
• Present a mock trial.	• Create a bulletin board display.
• Conduct a debate.	• Create a dance.
• Create a recipe.	• Make a wall hanging.
• Develop a display.	• Give a demonstration.
	• Conduct an interview and summarize the results.

Applications

To be effective, homework should be

- explained and modeled effectively in class.
- stated explicitly with defined expectations for both students and parents.
- assigned for "perfect practice" of previously taught content. (Homework should *not* be assigned if content is unfamiliar; errors once practiced are difficult to undo.)
- monitored by parents. (Homework partnerships provide leverage points for developing positive home–school relationships.)
- related directly to the in-class lesson.
- appropriate to the student's level of achievement.

Some schools have embellished their homework programs and policies by creating homework hotlines, afterschool homework assistance centers, study groups, and study-buddy programs.

Realistically, teachers often find that because of the sheer volume, it is impossible to examine and offer specific feedback on every paper. If feedback is not provided, however, homework can be an idle exercise. Teachers therefore have created a variety of ways to address this dilemma so that homework is meaningful and extends learnings. Here are a few strategies used in classrooms operating on a block schedule:

- *Answer Keys.* Although this is not an optimal activity, some teachers provide students with answer keys to correct their work. Students have to analyze the nature of the mistakes they made in written form and hand papers in to the teacher.

- *Random Selection.* Some teachers use a scanning system in which, on certain days, only odd-numbered problems are checked and, on others, only even. Students don't know which will be checked. Some teachers call for homework from students whose last names begin with certain letters, as well as from any students who wish feedback from the teacher.

- *Processing Partners.* In some classrooms, students pair up and compare homework while the teacher monitors. This is a good way to check completion and eavesdrop on conversations that verify understanding. The teacher also discovers needs for clarification or reteaching.

- *Double Circles.* Students form two circles, one inside the other, with each circle facing the other. Students compare answers on two homework problems with the person whom they are facing. Those inside the circle rotate by one so that every third problem is discussed with a different partner.

- *Peer-Editing Groups.* Several writing classes use a peer-editing system wherein students who are familiar with scoring rubrics for writing samples analyze each other's writings and provide nonjudgmental but specific feedback.

In this chapter, we have presented numerous ways in which students acquire content knowledge from lectures and readings. Diverse learners appreciate differentiated ways to take notes and summarize information. The extended block of time allows for many opportunities to chunk tasks so that changes of state continually engage the many learners in each classroom. It is natural to experience a state of entropy, or "running out of steam," a bit more than halfway through an extended period of instructional time. Having a repertoire of strategies to review content, close a class session, and assign and check homework will contribute greatly to the goal of creating a classroom in which students remain positively engaged throughout a block.

7 Evidence-Based Best Practices

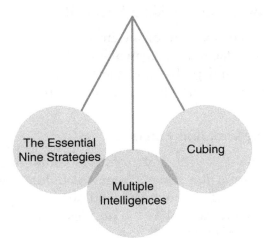

THE ESSENTIAL NINE STRATEGIES

Once information is in the short-term memory, we need the working memory to take over and process the content or skills multiple times to place them in long-term memory in the neocortex.

Marzano, Pickering, and Pollock (2001) carefully looked at the research from Mid-Continent Regional Educational Laboratory (McREL) throughout the 1990s. Their metacognitive study found nine strategies that resulted in increased performance for students by affixing skills and information in long-term memory.

1. Comparing, Contrasting, Classifying, Analogies, and Metaphor

Teachers can facilitate the examination of information for similarities and differences between and among things or ideas. The ability to classify in groups based on like attributes or the same themes or patterns can be explicitly demonstrated, supported, and encouraged. Venn diagrams, cross-classification charts, synectics, and metaphors help students connect new learning and ideas to past learning.

2. Summarizing and Note Taking

The ability to summarize, delete, distill, and analyze information in order to select what is important or relevant for learning is a skill all learners need. As discussed in Chapter 6, a variety of summary frames can help students accomplish this task.

3. Reinforcing Effort and Providing Recognition

Students are often unaware of the importance of effort in achieving success. Teachers can facilitate this awareness by using strategies such as recognition, rewards and praise, and metacognition as ways of demonstrating to students how extra effort can lead to growth.

4. Assigning Homework and Practice

Homework should be different from what students do in the classroom, not "just more of the same." Parents shouldn't be involved other than providing a place for homework and supporting the process. The purpose for homework, as well as the policies, outcomes, and feedback, should be clear to all involved.

5. Generating Nonlinguistic Representations

A variety of methods, such as graphics, models, mental pictures, drawing, and movement, should be used to elaborate and rehearse new learning.

6. Using Cooperative Learning

One of the most effective and well-documented instructional strategies is the formation of heterogeneous groups to accomplish academic tasks. This strategy uses higher-order thinking skills as well as focusing on the development of social skills.

7. Setting Objectives and Providing Feedback

Clear instructional goals that are stated in general terms and personalized by the individual learner help students focus. Continuous feedback from the student, teachers, and peers is important.

8. Generating and Testing Hypotheses

This can be done through the inductive or deductive process. Students should be able to articulate their hypothesis and, ultimately, the conclusions that they draw.

9. Providing Questions, Cues, and Advance Organizers

These tools help students open "mental files" to access prior knowledge before new learning takes place. This helps in pre-assessment of the knowledge and skills (related to standards) that a student possesses and gives a context for the learning experience to come.

Figure 7.1 relates the general strategies in the left-hand column from the Marzano, Pickering, and Pollock (2001) study to brain research and to specific tactics for the classroom.

Figure 7.1 Evidence-Based Best Practices and Brain Research

Instructional Strategies	Percentile Gain	Brain Research	Tactics
Similarities and differences, compare and contrast, classifying, analogies and metaphors	45	Brain seeks patterns, connections, and relationships between and among prior and new learning.	Classifying Comparing, contrasting Venn diagrams Synectics Concept attainment Concept formation
Note taking and summarizing	34	Brain pays attention to meaningful information and deletes that which is not relevant.	Mind maps Word webs Jigsaw
Reinforcing effort and providing recognition	29	Brain responds to challenge and not to threat; emotions enhance learning.	Stories of determination Celebration of successes
Assigning homework and practice	28	If you don't use it, you lose it; practice and rehearsal make learning "stick."	Create challenges in a variety of ways.
Generating nonlinguistic representations	27	Brain is a parallel processor; visual stimuli are recalled with 90% accuracy.	Mind maps Graphic organizers Models
Using cooperative group learning	27	Brain is social; collaboration facilitates understanding and higher-order thinking.	Think-Pair-Share Jigsaw PIGSF*

(Continued)

Figure 7.1 (Continued)

Instructional Strategies	Percentile Gain	Brain Research	Tactics
Setting objectives and providing feedback	23	Brain responds to high challenge and continues to strive based on feedback.	Helpful feedback Rubrics Criteria Expectations
Generating and testing hypotheses	23	Brain is curious and has an innate need to make meaning through patterns.	Problem-based inquiry Portfolios Case studies
Providing questions, cues, and advance organizers	22	Brain responds to wholes and parts; all learners need to open "mental files" into which new learning can be hooked.	Wait time Questioning techniques Agenda maps

Source: Designing Brain-Compatible Learning, 3rd ed., by Gayle H. Gregory and Terence Parry (2006). Thousand Oaks, CA: Corwin.

*Positive interdependence, Individual accountability, Group processing, Social skills, Face-to-face interaction

Similarities and Differences

The brain learns new information by processing similarities and differences. It relies on past experience and prior knowledge to make sense of new information, asking "How is this the same as or different from what I already know?"

There are many methods of having students look at similarities and differences, including the following:

- Classifying
- Comparing and contrasting
- Venn diagrams
- Metaphors and analogies or synectics
- Graphic organizers

The Venn diagram has long been used in mathematics; in fact, it originated with a British logician, John Venn. The diagram consists of two or more intersecting circles, each representing a set or sets (see Figures 7.2 and 7.3). Elements unique to a set are recorded in its corresponding circle, with elements shared by two sets recorded in the intersection of those circles. The problem sometimes with Venn diagrams is that the criteria are emergent and the process is not concrete; thus, some students have trouble handling the information.

Figure 7.2 TVenn Diagram: Icebreaker

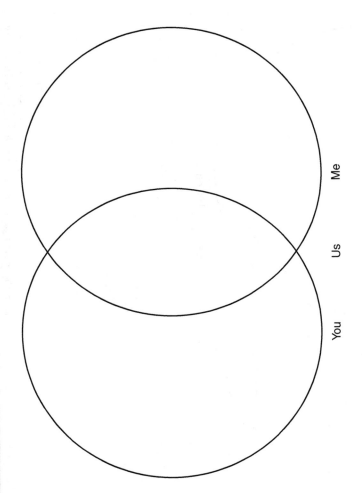

You   Us   Me

Appearance

Family

Hobbies

Sports

Foods

Pets

Figure 7.3 Venn Diagram: United States and Mexico

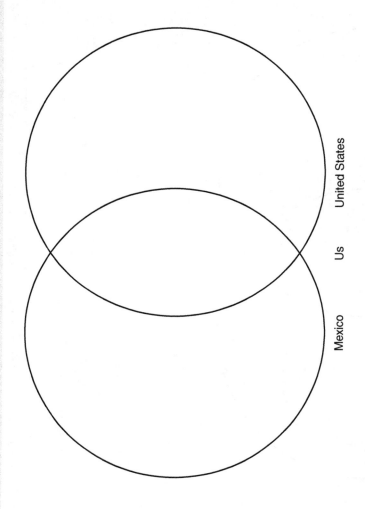

Mexico   Us   United States

Climate

Culture

Sports

Foods

Pets

Government

Figure 7.4 Triple Venn Diagram: Three Wars

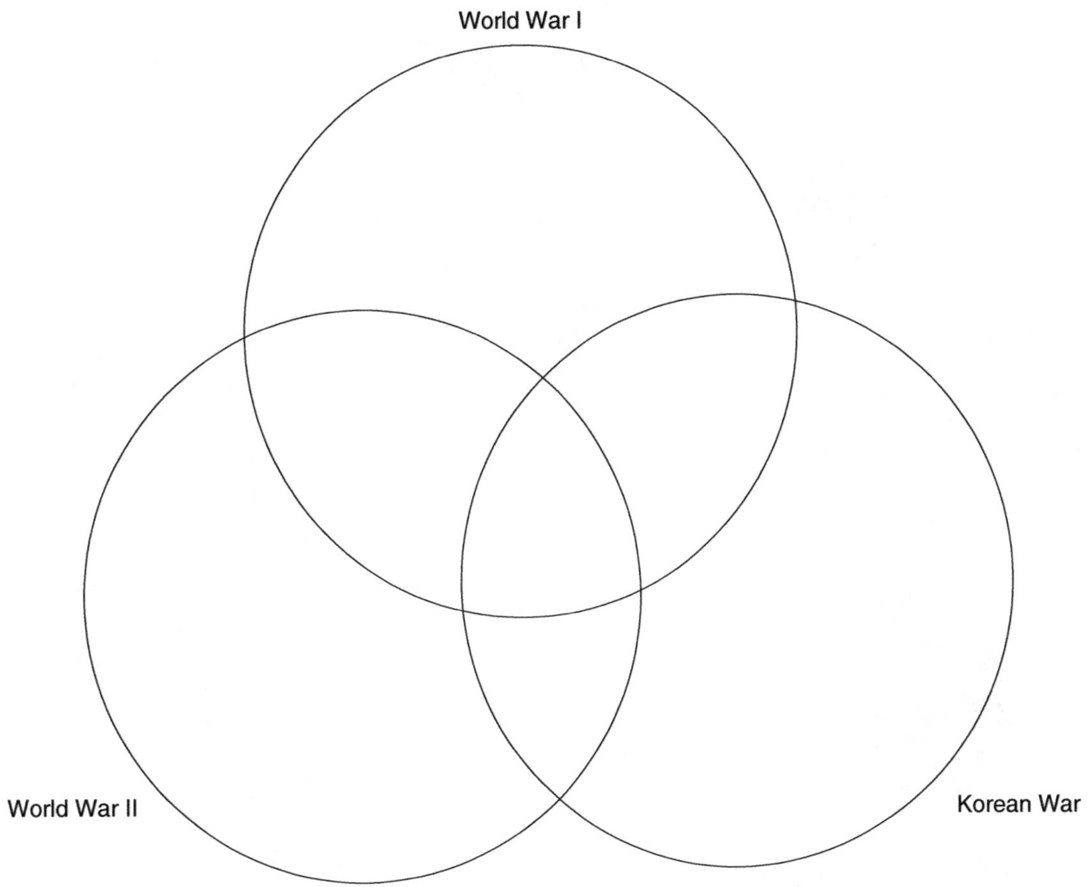

World War I

Korean War

World War II

169

Figure 7.5 Triple Venn Diagram: Template

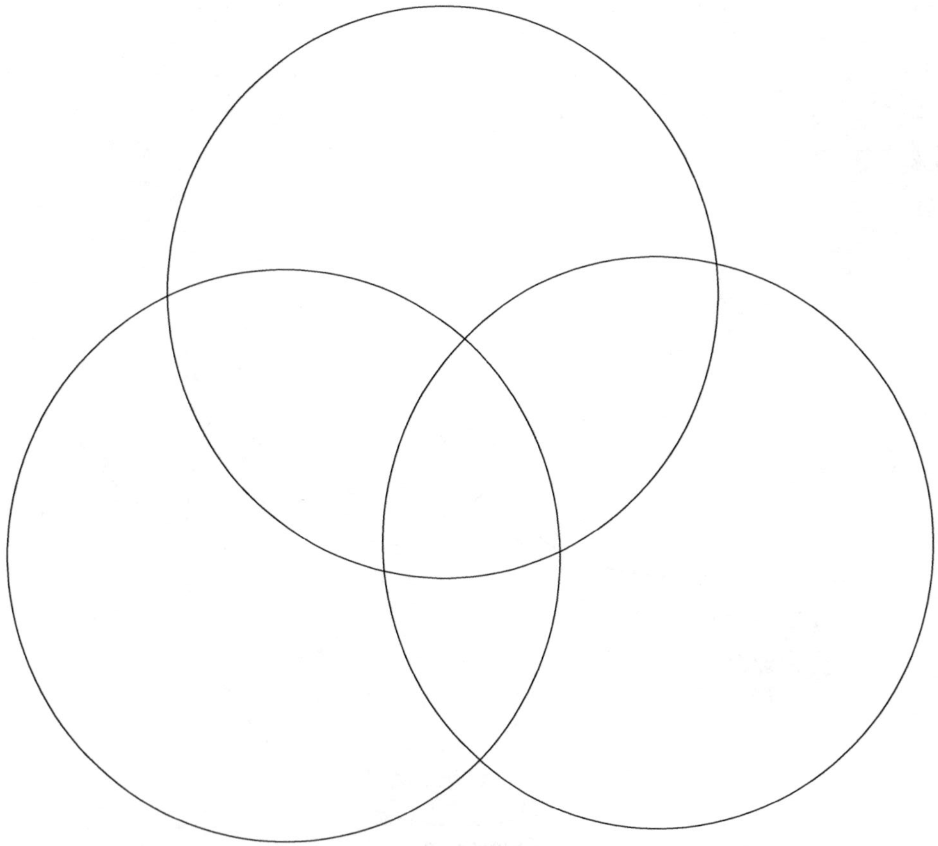

When three sets are being compared, the characteristics common to all three are recorded in the intersection of all three circles (see Figures 7.4 and 7.5). Triple Venn diagrams can be used to stimulate deeper thinking to extrapolate similarities among three concepts or topics.

Using organizers that are more linear, so that students can move down the page and do a section at a time, is also useful to provide variety, and student preference may prevail after several templates are shared with students. See two examples of this format in Figures 7.6, 7.7, and 7.8.

Direct Analogy

Direct analogy is a basic form of analogy. Students can be directed to select a topic they wish to explore in depth and then examine how it is similar to something that seems at first to be quite different. For example, the teacher could ask the class, "How is thinking like a video game," or, "How is democracy like a railway station?" In subject areas, the teacher might ask, "How is an election like a pizza?" "How is a test like snowboarding?" "How is sadness like a potato?" or "How is the Renaissance like a carousel?"

Direct analogy is useful for defining concepts and for checking understanding. It causes students to think deeply about a concept and its characteristics.

Personal Analogy

A personal analogy is often used to help students analyze and develop empathy and connections to identities outside themselves. They may identify with an animal, an inanimate object, a person, or something else. For example, to express feeling, students can describe themselves as a doormat or weasel. Personal analogies may give them a way to express emotions and help them develop empathy, resulting in a deeper understanding of themselves and other students.

Conflicting Analogies

Conflicting analogies are generated out of opposing opinions or viewpoints. They may almost be a "war of words" that helps people clarify their thinking, look at the upside and downside of ideas, and employ analytical thinking. This can include oxymorons such as "organized chaos," "focused meander," or "civilized hostility." Teachers can ask students to explore two opposite ideas, such as (a) How is the election an enabling hindrance? (b) How is isolation a blessing and a hazard? and (c) How is welfare necessary and a detriment? By looking at conflicting viewpoints, students develop a deeper understanding rather than getting just one point of view.

Figure 7.6 Compare and Contrast

Comparing Two Things

Similarities

Differences

Figure 7.7 Comparing Two Things With Criteria: Canada and the United States

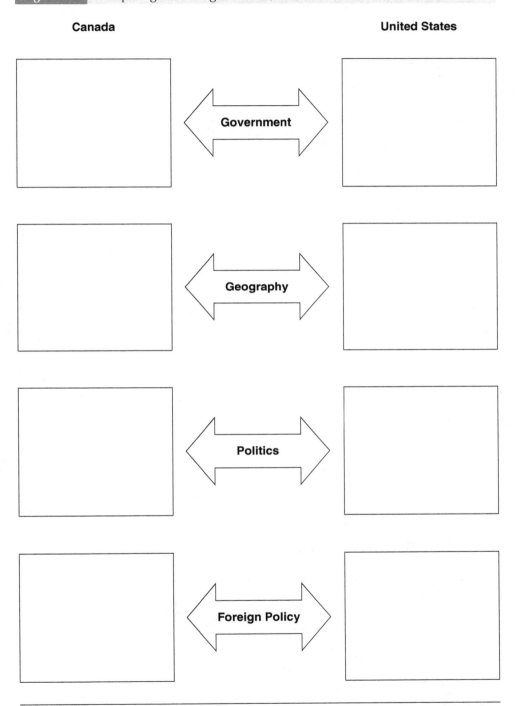

Figure 7.8 Comparing Two Things: Blank Template

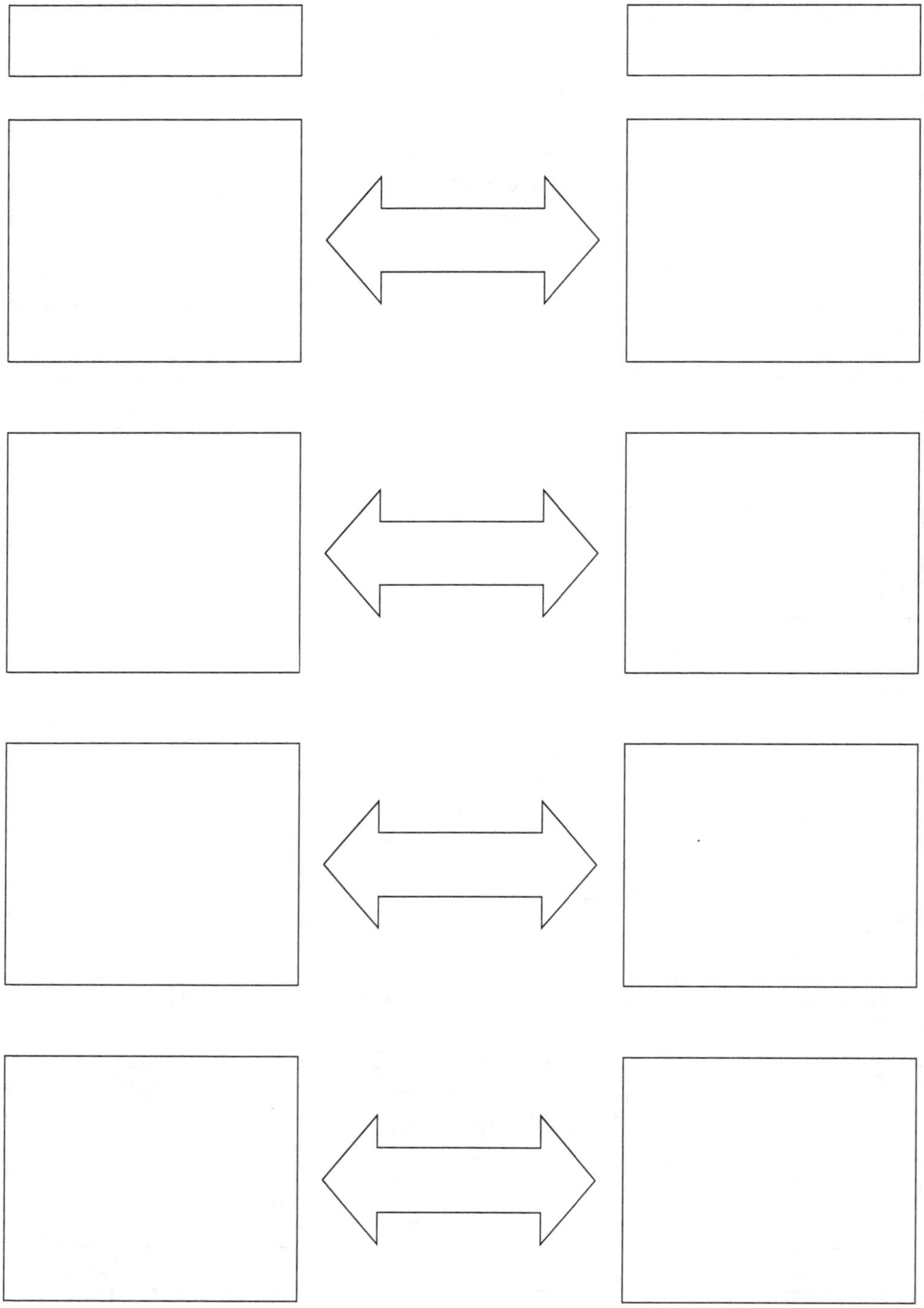

The PD360° website (www.pd360.com) is an excellent source of video clips that demonstrate the use of conflicting analogies in elementary and secondary classrooms.

Using Organizers

To maximize learning for students, teachers can use organizers to help students sort and classify information and make note taking meaningful, creative, and useful. The study by Marzano and colleagues (Marzano, Pickering, & Pollock, 2001) attributes a 27 percentile gain to the use of nonlinguistic visual representations, which include the use of graphic organizers. As discussed in depth in Chapter 6, students may use the organizers during the lecture or as a check for understanding after the lecture has concluded.

Graphic organizers have a number of attributes that enhance students' thinking skills. They allow students to make connections among pieces of information, making information easier to recall. They also allow students to break information into manageable chunks. Chunking information allows students to see the relationships among the separate pieces and is key to the formation of concepts, which leads to understanding. When this learning takes place in small groups, students have an opportunity to exchange and compare ideas, articulate their points of view, defend their own thinking, and probe the thinking of others. In these ways, true learning takes place.

Fishbone Diagram

This organizer, as its name implies, looks much like a fishbone. The problem, or the desired effect, is written in the box that forms the head of the fish. The possible causes are arranged along the bones, or ribs (see Figure 7.9).

Businesses and industries use this organizer when troubleshooting problems. They also use it when making business decisions or planning a course of action to bring about a desired effect. In business situations, most problems can be attributed to the following causes: personnel, procedure, equipment, and material. Brainstorming possible causes for a problem in terms of these four categories expands the scope of an inquiry and ensures that all the bases are covered.

Other categories may also be used for determining specific cause-effect relationships. For example, in using a fishbone diagram to determine the cause of a stock market crash, the categories could be world trends, current events, technology, and speculation. However, it can also be used as a summarizing graphic.

Figure 7.9 Fishbone Template

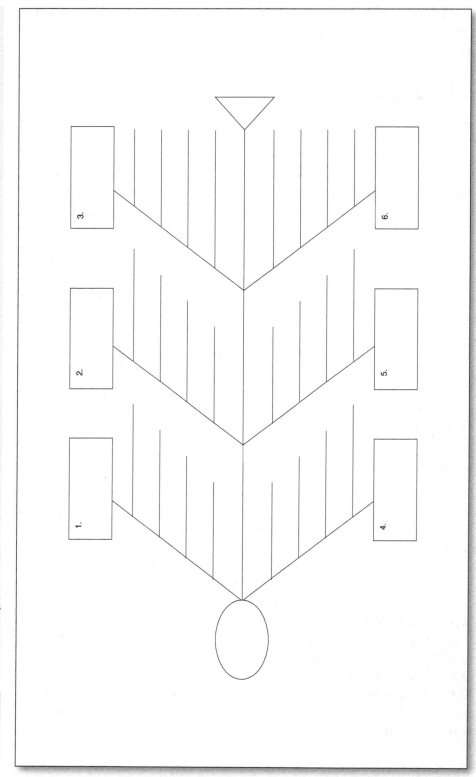

RAFT

RAFT (Role, Audience, Format, and Topic; see Figure 7.10) is a strategy developed by Santa (1988) that motivates and encourages creative writing as well as divergent thinking in students. It is also a check for understanding from another perspective as well as another elaborative rehearsal to solidify concepts and information.

It works this way:

1. Select content from any subject area that students need to process, review, and understand.

2. Consider the possible roles that students might take on in the writing as well as what the topic might be.

Figure 7.10 RAFT (Role, Audience, Format, and Topic)

Role	Audience	Format	Topic
Tree	Sun	Thank-you note	Sun's role in growth
Fraction	Percentage	Love letter	About their relationship
Heart	Fried chicken	Complaint	Effects on heart due to hydrogenated fat
Cucumber	Other vegetables	Travel log	Through digestive system
Sister (whose brother was killed)	Drinking drivers	Request	Don't drink and drive.
Magazine editor	National Rifle Association	Information	Need for rifle regulations
Taxpayer	President	Rationale	Why we need universal health care
Law officer	Parents	Advice	Effect of television and movie violence on teens
Health care workers	Public	Caution	Carbohydrates and type 2 diabetes
Teenager	Parent	Persuasive rationale	Allow another privilege
Juliet	Nurse	Thank you	Taking care of her
Bus driver	Students	Rationale	Bus safety
Rain forest	Society	Plea	Need for consideration

Simulations, Role-Plays

Simulations mimic real-world situations. These important learning approaches give students a context and vehicle to make sense of new concepts and information. They can be referred to as nonlinguistic representation. The process has four steps:

1. The teacher presents the topic and concepts to be explored, as well as a brief overview of what a simulation is.

2. The teacher gets students involved in the simulation by giving the procedures, rules, roles, scoring, or goals of the simulation.

3. Students work through the simulation, with the teacher as monitor and facilitator giving feedback. They stop periodically to evaluate and reflect on the process.

4. The teacher debriefs, and students apply learnings from the simulation.

Examples might include simulating a courtroom scene to explore an academic controversy or simulating a warehouse inventory situation to understand the law of supply and demand. In one parenting class, students were given lifelike dolls that cried and so forth. Students working in pairs (parents) were told that they must look after the "baby" for a week and record their interactions, the care given, and their feelings associated with caring for the child. The babies were to be fed, bathed, and played with appropriately. Students also had to provide babysitters when they could not care for the infant themselves. At the end of the week, students shared their journals and reflected on the commitment and patience needed to provide for helpless babies. This simulation was instrumental in showing students firsthand the responsibilities involved in caring for an infant that reading from a textbook could not possibly convey.

MULTIPLE INTELLIGENCES

A way to look at how we are smart is to examine Howard Gardner's multiple intelligences (1983). By no longer accepting the IQ score as the sole indicator of intelligence, Gardner broadened how we look at "being smart." According to Gardner, intelligent people are able to solve problems, handle crises, and create things of value in a particular culture using a variety of ways of accessing, processing, and applying information. He believes that we have many resources in our "thinking toolkit" and we can continue to increase those "tools" throughout life. We may have a predisposition for certain tools, but we can also grow more intelligent in all areas. The extended time of the block schedule is a perfect opportunity to allow students to rehearse in their areas of strength and to enhance their not-so-strong areas.

The following is a brief description of the eight intelligences.

The two communication intelligences are Verbal/Linguistic and Musical/Rhythmic:

1. Verbal/Linguistic

People with a high degree of this intelligence like to use words in different ways in communication and in thinking. They like to become involved in debates, storytelling, and poetry and enjoy the "lovely language" of metaphors, puns, analogies, and similes. They can read for hours and become lost in the language. They are often auditory learners and choose to listen, speak, read, and write. They love to communicate using a variety of tools such as letters, faxes, e-mails, and the like. Writers, actors, newscasters, and journalists generally have a high degree of this intelligence.

2. Musical/Rhythmic

People with a high degree of this intelligence have the ability to recognize and often produce melodies or rhythms and rhymes. They like music and are conscious of its impact. They appreciate and respond to a variety of music and rhythm sources. You often see these students beating out a rhythm that they pick up from their surroundings. They are highly responsive to many kinds of sounds. Musicians, songwriters, and vocalists have a high degree of this intelligence

The next four intelligences relate to objects in our world.

3. Visual/Spatial

People with a high degree of this intelligence are attuned to pictures, symbols, and drawings that appeal to the eye or the "mind's eye." They are able to see detail and appreciate graphs, charts, and representations to make sense of and develop an understanding of concepts and ideas. Artists, photographers, sculptors, and architects have perceptive powers of space and its relationships. These learners often think in pictures and have an innate sense of direction.

4. Bodily/Kinesthetic

People with a high degree of this intelligence have a keen sense of the tactile. They are aware of their own body and like to manipulate and handle materials to make sense of their world. They may excel in fine motor or gross motor skills. Their professions range from neurosurgeon to football quarterback to Broadway actor. They like their learning to involve motion, whether it be walking, building, or role-playing.

5. Logical/Mathematical

People with a high degree of this intelligence are at home with numbers and reasoning. They are attuned to identifying patterns, recognizing cause and effect, and sequencing. They love to solve problems and pose and answer questions. They appreciate opportunities to analyze, assess, use spreadsheets, and organize information. Accountants, lawyers, and scientists are logically mathematical.

6. Naturalist

People with a high degree of this intelligence are very in touch with the natural world of animals and plants. This includes the geography of our world, landscape, and weather. These people prefer to be outdoors and are observant of details in nature. They use patterns and attributes to classify and organize information. They have a deep appreciation for their environment.

The last two intelligences relate to the self.

7. Interpersonal

People with a high degree of this intelligence have a natural ability to interact with others. They are social beings who work well with others and are sensitive and intuitive to the feelings and moods of others. Often friendly and extroverted, they are attuned to the temperaments of those around them. They are valuable, appreciated members of the team.

8. Intrapersonal

These people have a high degree of self-awareness. They are cognizant of and can manage their own emotions and feelings as well as use this knowledge to guide themselves. They value self-reflection and goal setting. They are aware of their strengths and needs and act on that information. They are able to hold up "the mirror" to see themselves clearly and respond to the reflection.

Applications

How Are You Smart?

Circle the numbers of the statements that are most like you.

1. You love to read.

2. You sing along with music.

3. You love mysteries, puzzles, and games.

4. You like to go to new places and you do so easily.

5. You are well coordinated and move about easily.

6. You like collections and saving things.

7. You keep a diary or journal and write down your thoughts.

8. You know when someone is upset, angry, or depressed.

9. You like to tell and listen to jokes.

10. You'd like to play an instrument.

11. You like reading science fiction and learning about technological discoveries.

12. You notice other people's clothes and personal things.

13. You like to tinker with things and fix them.

14. You love being outdoors and enjoying the world.

15. You need quiet time by yourself.

16. You sometimes imagine how it would feel to be someone else.

17. You just know when things sound right.

18. You turn on music when it's quiet.

19. You think it's fun to work with numbers and problems.

20. You can find your way around cities and buildings.

21. You often move your hands and body while you talk.

22. You like to listen to the birds singing and the crickets chirping.

23. You like to do things by yourself.

24. You like to belong to a club or group.

25. You like words that are fun to say.

26. You like to sing, hum, whistle, or tap on the desk.

27. You like things organized in patterns and groups.

28. You are always doodling or drawing while thinking and listening.

29. You like games like charades and "hamming" it up.

(Continued)

(Continued)

30. You like to put things in categories and classify them.

31. You know what you like and what you are capable of.

32. You like to be with friends and just hang out.

33. You like to write stories and poems.

34. You get songs "stuck" in your head.

35. You like computers and working with them.

36. You enjoy TV, videos, and movies.

37. You have hobbies that let you build and make things.

38. You know a lot about animals and plants.

39. You like a challenge and set goals for yourself.

40. When you meet new people, you are interested to learn about them.

Using the Inventory Summary Table below, circle the numbers that are most like you. Then add the number of circles for each row and put the total number next to the appropriate color.

Multiple Intelligences Inventory Summary Table

Verbal/ Linguistic	1	9	17	25	33	Total: _____ Green
Musical/ Rhythmic	2	10	18	26	34	Total: _____ Red
Logical/ Mathematical	3	11	19	27	35	Total: _____ Black
Visual-Spatial	4	12	20	28	36	Total: _____ Yellow
Bodily/ Kinesthetic	5	13	21	29	37	Total: _____ Purple
Naturalist	6	14	22	30	38	Total: _____ Orange
Intrapersonal	7	15	23	31	39	Total: _____ White
Interpersonal	8	16	24	32	40	Total: _____ Blue

Some teachers have students put a number of beads of each color corresponding to the inventory on a shoelace or beading string or elastic thread. Younger students may want to wear the necklace or bracelet to remind them of "how they are smart."

The inventory in Figure 7.11 can also help students discover their strengths. Have students check off the statements that are most like them. They can count the number in each section and transfer that number to the blocks in the graph (Figure 7.12). The graph can then be cut out to show their unique profile. The students can compare their profile with those of other classmates and work with a partner who helps "fill up" their toolkit by adding complementary strengths.

Know Thyself

Let's face it: Most adolescents are most interested in themselves. However, they are constantly trying to fit in while at the same time being unique. That's a difficult challenge. It is important for teachers to be aware of the learning profiles of each student, and it is equally important for them to begin to recognize their own strengths and needs and take responsibility for using those strong areas and buoying up areas where they need growth. We want to offer a full range of choices so that sometimes students are working in an area of strength and sometimes in an area that needs strengthening.

Some teachers use the suggestions in Figures 7.13 and 7.14 to plan learning tasks so that all student strengths are included over the course of the lesson or the week.

Projects

Projects are an integral part of the differentiated block, as they allow for multiple creative rehearsals and, often, student choice. They can engage a full range of multiple intelligences and learning styles as well. Of course, they have to focus on the targeted standard and content. Too many projects can be time fillers or wasters that don't help students achieve the desired outcomes. It is disrespectful to ask that students spend their time that way. Also, the teacher and other classmates should monitor and support projects. Resources should be available to foster creativity; these are often the "hook" both to engage students and to foster commitment to the task. When choice is built in, students have a hard time not completing the assignment.

Figure 7.11 How Are You Smart?

Verbal/Linguistic	Intrapersonal
• I like to tell jokes, stories, or tales. • Books are important to me. • I like to read. • I often listen to radio, TV, tapes, or CDs. • I write easily and enjoy it. • I quote things I've read. • I like crosswords and word games.	• I know about my feelings, strengths, and weaknesses. • I like to learn more about myself. • I enjoy hobbies by myself. • I enjoy being alone sometimes. • I have confidence in myself. • I like to work alone.
Logical/Mathematical	**Visual/Spatial**
• I solve math problems easily. • I enjoy math and using computers. • I like strategy games. • I wonder how things work. • I reason things out. • I like using logic to solve problems. • I like to use data to measure, calculate, and analyze.	• I shut my eyes and see clear pictures. • I think in pictures. • I like color and interesting designs. • I can find my way around unfamiliar areas. • I draw and doodle. • I like books with pictures, maps, and charts. • I like videos, movies, and photographs.
Interpersonal	**Bodily/Kinesthetic**
• People ask me for advice. • I prefer team sports • I have many close friends. • I like working in groups. • I'm comfortable in a crowd. • I have empathy for others. • I can figure out what people are feeling.	• I get uncomfortable when I sit too long. • I like to touch or be touched when talking. • I use my hands when speaking. • I like using my hands for hobbies and crafts. • I touch things to learn more about them. • I think of myself as well coordinated. • I learn by doing rather than by watching.
Musical/Rhythmic	**Naturalist**
• I like to listen to musical selections. • I am sensitive to music and sounds. • I can remember tunes. • I listen to music when studying. • I enjoy singing. • I keep time to music. • I have a good sense of rhythm.	• I enjoy spending time in nature. • I like to classify things into categories. • I can hear animal and bird sounds clearly. • I see details when I look at plants, flowers, and trees. • I am happiest outdoors. • I like tending to plants and animals. • I know the names of plants and animals.

Figure 7.12 What Is Your Unique Multiple Intelligences Profile?

Word Smart							
Math Smart							
People Smart							
Music Smart							
Self Smart							
Picture Smart							
Body Smart							
Nature Smart							

Source: Adapted from *Integrating Curricula With Multiple Intelligences: Teams, Themes, and Threads,* 2008, by Robin Fogarty and Judy Stoehr, p. 57.

Figure 7.13 Suggestions for Tasks by Disciplines and Multiple Intelligences

	Social Studies	Science	Language Arts	Mathematics
Verbal/Linguistic	**Identify** the pros and cons of ...	**Explain** the function of ...	**Retell** the story in your own words.	**Prepare** an editorial to suggest how math is useful in a variety of careers.
Musical/Rhythmic	**Create** a song, poem, or rap to relate the events of ... Include appropriate background music during a presentation.	**Originate** a musical commercial for ...	**Write** a poem or ballad that tells the story.	**Compose** a jingle to remember geometric shapes.
Visual/Spatial	**Draw** a cartoon or storyboard to show the events of ...	**Diagram** the process of ...	**Create** symbols for the characters in the story that show their characterization.	**Design** patterns with a variety of shapes to create an interesting, artistic blanket.
Bodily/Kinesthetic	**Act out** the ... **Role-play** the ...	**Mime** the process of ... Create actions to show ...	**Plan** a charade game to test your knowledge of the character, setting, and plot.	**Model** shapes or processes and have other students guess ...
Logical/Mathematical	Follow the directions to **develop a position** for a debate ...	**Predict** what would happen if ...	**Construct** a logical argument for ...	**Design** a cross-classification chart to show ...
Naturalist	**Classify** the information ...	**Organize** the material into appropriate categories ...	**Analyze** the setting and how it contributes to the story.	**Categorize** and organize the processes.
Interpersonal	In a cooperative group, **build** a project that depicts ...	**Conduct** an interview with a noted scientist who discovered ...	**Describe** the relationships between the two main characters and why you believe they relate this way.	**Teach** others how you remember or use a formula.
Intrapersonal	In a journal, **relate** a day in the life of ...	Keep a personal diary to **show** what you know about ...	**Decide** on the character that you would like to be friends with and tell **why.**	**Reflect on** what method is most useful to you in mathematics.

Note: Please note the highlighted action-thinking words in the grid and the various levels of thinking.

Figure 7.14 Suggestions for Using the Eight Multiple Intelligences

Verbal/Linguistic	Musical/Rhythmic
• Brainstorm. • Organize thoughts. • Summarize. • Change the beginning or the end. • Describe it. • Write an advertisement. • Write an editorial. • Write a news flash. • Prepare a speech. • Develop a campaign platform. • Develop a challenging question. • Find evidence to support a claim or belief. • This is like _____ because _____. • Research the inventor or author. • Write a conclusion or summary. • Write main idea and supporting details. • Develop a book. • Record reading or writing. • Skim and scan. • Write the attributes. • Write adjectives or phrases to describe.	• Create a song. • Think of a theme song and explain your choice. • Write a poem. • Create a jingle or slogan. • Select sounds to fit the task. • Recognize pitch, tone, timbre. • Use background music. • Create a beat. • Make rhythmic movements. • Identify sounds. • Identify musical pieces. • Interpret a song. • Record music. • Develop an instrument. • Find appropriate background music.
Logical/Mathematical	Visual/Spatial
• Sequence it. • Design a game. • Develop a TV show. • Create a timeline. • Tell your process. • Categorize. • Find the missing piece or link. • Classify. • Rank ideas. • Use a matrix. • Design a graph. • Try a new idea against a model. • Design a survey. • Conduct an inventory. • Research and gather data. • Interpret data. • Explore the technology world. • Use a gadget. • Compute or calculate. • Use deductive thinking. • Use numbers.	• Draw a picture or graphic. • Make a flip book. • Create a photo essay. • Design a poster. • Design a puppet. • Depict the setting. • Make a collage. • Illustrate. • Plot on a graphic organizer. • Design or create. • Make associations using color; color code. • Use different art media. • Interpret art. • Design a book. • Sculpt it. • Draw a map and label sites of importance. • Develop a diorama. • Design a collage. • Highlight or create tabs. • Develop a character sketch. • Develop an editorial cartoon. • Write a cartoon strip with speech bubbles.

(Continued)

| Figure 7.14 | (Continued) |

Bodily/Kinesthetic	Interpersonal
• Name a thing's function. • Brainstorm. • Use your body to interpret meaning. • Play a game or sport. • Use manipulative. • Construct or build. • Role-play. • Perform. • Act it out. • Mime. • Put on a puppet show. • Show how you know. • Dramatize. • Create simulations. • Do an interpretive dance. • Do an experiment. • Invent or discover through trial and error.	• Work with others. • Empathize with others. • Work on a group project. • Conduct an interview. • Discuss with others. • Be involved in a conversation. • Come to a consensus. • Give or receive feedback. • Jigsaw information. • Be a team member.
Intrapersonal	**Naturalist**
• Select personal choice. • Work alone. • Apply metacognitive thinking. • Plan a way. • Develop a strategy. • Draw a conclusion about how it makes you feel. • Identify likes and dislikes. • Make choices. • Set goals. • Carry through a task. • Identify your personal preference. • Develop automaticity.	• Understand nature. • Use nature to work for you. • Study science. • Apply information to life. • Make a personal link between learning and your world. • Develop awareness of survival needs. • Identify scientific method and classifications. • Study land, sea, and air. • Make discoveries. • Invent. • Explore the world.

Source: *Differentiated Instructional Strategies in Practice: Training, Implementation, and Supervision* (2nd ed.), by Gayle H. Gregory (2008), pp. 55–56. Thousand Oaks, CA: Corwin.

For project work to be engaging and successful, it should

- try to tap into the student's passion.
- be seen as important work, worthy of the time spent.
- be real, hands-on, and all-consuming.
- apply new learning and practice skills in an interesting way.
- create a sense of relevant and real-world application.
- incorporate complex thinking skills in practical application.
- foster the development of collaborative social skills.
- be enjoyable—sneak the fun into real application.

Choice Boards

Teachers may use a choice board to enable students to tap into areas of strength and comfort and to prescribe opportunities to stretch in areas that need attention. Of course, clear outcomes or expectations must be considered when planning any instructional or rehearsal practice. The choice board in Figure 7.15 shows tasks that can be adapted to any lesson or content. Figures 7.16 and 7.17 are examples of choice boards as used to learn about *Romeo and Juliet* and U.S. presidents, respectively. Figure 7.18 provides a blank template.

The rubric in Figure 7.19 can guide students as they complete their choices. A generic rubric will suffice, as it is not necessary to create a rubric for each option on the choice board.

CUBING

Cubing is another technique that can help students think at different levels (Cowan & Cowan, 1980). Cubing is a technique for considering a subject from six points of view (Cowan & Cowan, 1980; Tomlinson, 2001). Cubing works well to break us loose from a particular way of thinking. Cubing also incorporates the multiple intelligences and attends to visual, auditory, and bodily/kinesthetic learners. The cube has six sides with a different prompt on each side.

One side of the cube may say: *Describe it.*

Another side: *Compare it.*

The third side: *Associate it.*

The fourth side: *Analyze it.*

The fifth side: *Apply it.*

And the sixth side says: *Argue for or against it.*

Cubes may vary with tasks or commands that are appropriate to the level of readiness of the group. Cubes may also be constructed with tasks that use a particular area of the multiple intelligences, such as verbal/linguistic, bodily/kinesthetic, or intrapersonal intelligence.

Why Do We Use Cubes?

Cubes, with their multiple sides, allow students to look at an issue or topic from a variety of angles and develop a multidimensional perspective. Cubes also offer a chance to differentiate learning by readiness (familiarity

Figure 7.15 Multiple Intelligence Choice Board

Multiple Intelligence Choice Board

Verbal/Linguistic	Musical/Rhythmic	Visual/Spatial
• Prepare a report. • Write a play or essay. • Give directions for . . . • Create a poem or recitation. • Listen to a tape or view a video. • Retell in your own words. • Create a word web.	• Create a rap, song, or ballad. • Write a jingle. • Write a poem. • Select music to enhance a story or event. • Create rhymes that . . .	• Create a mural, poster, or drawing. • Illustrate an event. • Draw a diagram. • Design a graphic organizer. • Use color to . . . • Create a comic strip to show . . . • Do a story board. • Create a collage with meaningful artifacts.
Logical/Mathematical		**Bodily/Kinesthetic**
• Create a pattern. • Describe a sequence or process. • Develop a rationale. • Analyze a situation. • Create a sequel. • Critically assess. • Classify, rank, or compare . . . • Interpret evidence. • Design a game to show . . .	**Free Choice**	• Create a role-play. • Construct a model or representation. • Develop a mime. • Create a tableau for . . . • Manipulate materials to . . . • Work through a simulation. • Create actions for . . .
Naturalist	**Interpersonal**	**Intrapersonal**
• Discover or experiment. • Categorize materials or ideas. • Look for ideas from nature. • Adapt materials to a new use. • Connect ideas to nature. • Examine materials to make generalizations. • Label and classify. • Draw conclusions based on information. • Predict . . .	• Work with a partner or group. • Discuss and come to a conclusion. • Solve a problem with others. • Survey or interview others. • Dialogue about a topic. • Use cooperative groups to . . . • Project a character's point of view.	• Think about and plan. • Write in a journal. • Keep track of . . . and comment on . . . • Review or visualize a way to . . . • Reflect on the character and express his/her feelings. • Imagine how it would feel if you . . .

Figure 7.16 *Romeo and Juliet Choice Board*

Choice Board: *Romeo and Juliet*

Verbal/Linguistic	Musical/Rhythmic	Visual/Spatial
Insert and act out a scene that you wrote for the play.	Create a photo essay or brochure to chronicle the sequence of events in the play.	With a partner, act out a scene from the play. You may videotape it if you wish.
Logical/Mathematical		Bodily/Kinesthetic
Create a theme song or rap with lyrics for Romeo and Juliet.	**Free Choice**	Design a map or paint/draw a picture of Verona.
Naturalist	Interpersonal	Intrapersonal
Write a journal from Juliet's, Romeo's, or the nurse's perspective on the course of events.	Analyze the rule of the monk. Was it in the best interests of the couple, or was it part of something more sinister?	The dilemma: Did they have to die? What else could have happened? Finish the story with a different ending.

| Figure 7.17 | Choice Board: American Presidents |

American Presidents Choice Board

Verbal/Linguistic	Musical/Rhythmic	Visual/Spatial
Chronicle the journey that the president took to the White House.	Write and sing a ballad that tells the story of the president's term in office.	Brainstorm the key events in this presidency and create a mind map to show them.
Logical/Mathematical Create a timeline of key events in this presidency.	**Free Choice**	Bodily/Kinesthetic Design a board game to show the events and critical events of this presidency.
Naturalist What was the music of the period, and how did it relate to historical events?	Interpersonal Create an interview with at least six questions that get at the essence of this president's philosophy or intentions.	Intrapersonal Write a news release that captures the influences this president had on world history.

Figure 7.18 Choice Board: Blank Template

Topic: _____

	Free Choice	

Figure 7.19 Rubric for Projects Engaging Multiple Intelligences

Name: _____

Theme: _____

Project Title: _____

Date: _____

Directions: Give yourself points: 5 is the highest score, and 1 is the lowest.				
Element	Criteria	Me	Other	Teacher
Presentation	Is it clear? Is it complete? Are all the key ideas explained?			
Quality	Is it interesting? Did it appeal to the audience? Did others learn from it?			
Uniqueness	Are a variety of intelligences used?			
Resources	Were a variety of materials and audiovisual content incorporated?			
Collaboration of group members	Was there equal participation? Did everyone contribute?			

These scores may be averaged.

Comments

A Plus or Cheer

A Suggestion

with content or level of skill), student interest, and/or learning profile (multiple intelligences). Cubes may vary in color and tasks, depending on the abilities and interest of the group. They add novelty and fun to learning. Cubing is a great strategy for bodily/kinesthetic learners, as cubes reinforce understanding and extend or demonstrate learning. See the examples in Figures 7.20, 7.21, and 7.22 and the template provided in Figure 7.23.

Applications

How Do We Use Cubes?

- Keep clear learning goals in mind when considering the use of cubing for different learners.
- Provide extended opportunities, materials, and learning situations that are appropriate for a wide range of readiness, interests, and learning styles.
- Make sure students understand the directions for the tasks, including the verbs used on the cube.
- Group students according to readiness, with different-colored cubes giving tasks or questions appropriate to their level of understanding of that topic and/or ability in that skill. Students assist one another in their learning.
- Ask students to share findings with the large group or to form groups of experts to share their tasks.

Figure 7.24 suggests verbs that may be used on the six sides of a cube.

Cubing may also be differentiated according to multiple intelligences. Cubes may be designed with a variety of activities to give students a chance to use their varied strengths. As an alternative, teachers can also use a die numbered 1 to 6 and provide students with activity cards at various levels of complexity related to the topic.

If students are studying the planets, for example, they might have a variety of cubes, each for a different one of the multiple intelligences, to process information for verbal/linguistic, musical/rhythmic, bodily/kinesthetic, visual/spatial, naturalist, logical/mathematical, interpersonal, or intrapersonal intelligence. Or in a class where students are reading *A Streetcar Named Desire*, cubes could be used that deal with visual/spatial intelligence as follows:

Figure 7.20 Cubing: Democracy

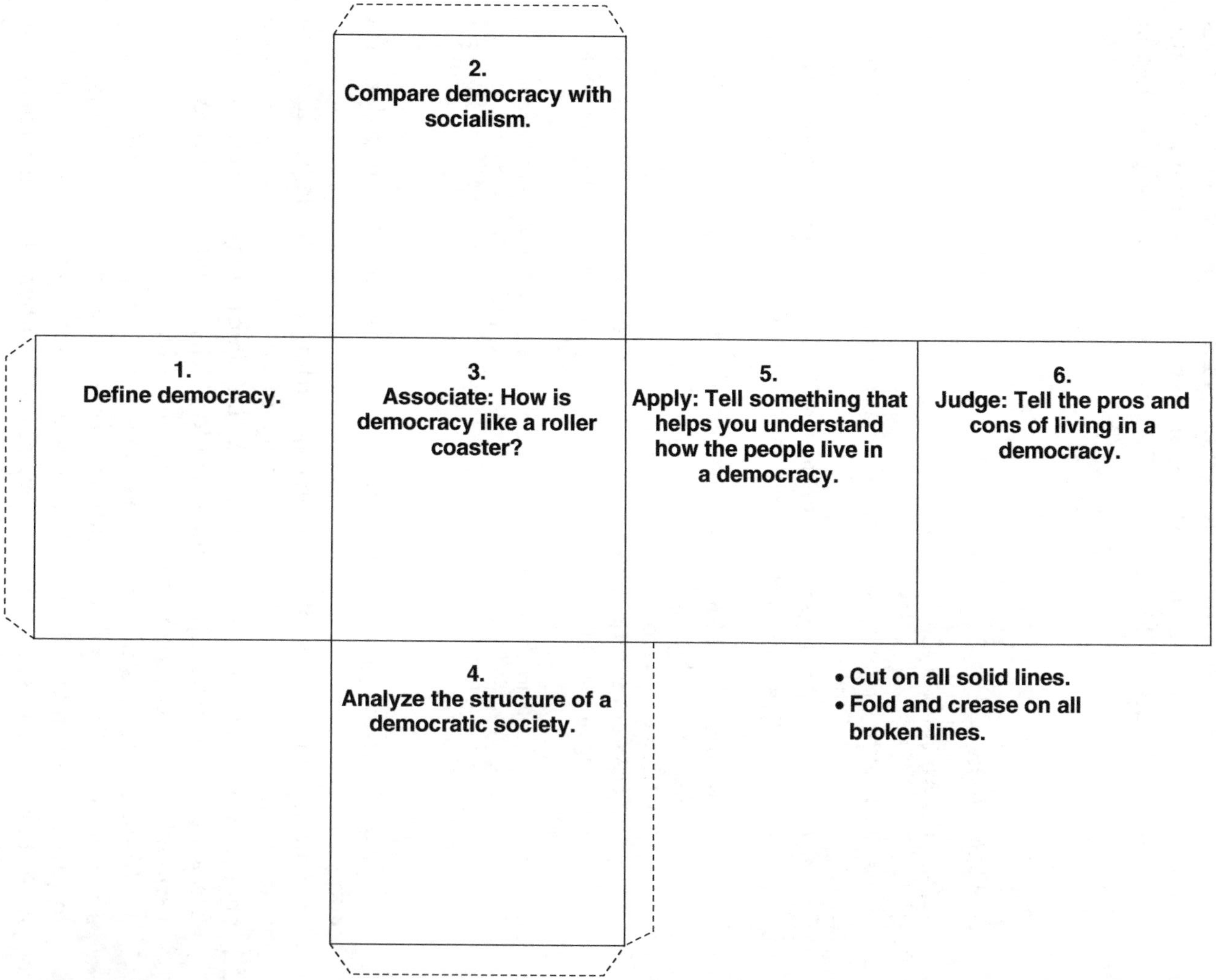

1.
Define democracy.

2.
Compare democracy with socialism.

3.
Associate: How is democracy like a roller coaster?

4.
Analyze the structure of a democratic society.

5.
Apply: Tell something that helps you understand how the people live in a democracy.

6.
Judge: Tell the pros and cons of living in a democracy.

• Cut on all solid lines.
• Fold and crease on all broken lines.

Figure 7.21 Cubing: Historical Science

2.

Compare how the work of this scientist was accepted to that of how scientists' work is accepted today.

3.

Associate: How has the work of this scientist affected people today?

4.

Analyze the concepts associated with the work of this scientist and discuss how it relates to what you have learned in class.

1.

Describe the major contribution this scientist made to society during his or her lifetime.

5.

Apply: How has the work of this scientist helped in your understanding of the concepts that have been presented in class?

6.

Judge: Argue for or against the theory or theories this scientist presented. Support your answer with evidence given by the scientists at that time.

- Cut on all solid lines.
- Fold and crease on all broken lines.

Figure 7.22 Cubing: *Romeo and Juliet*

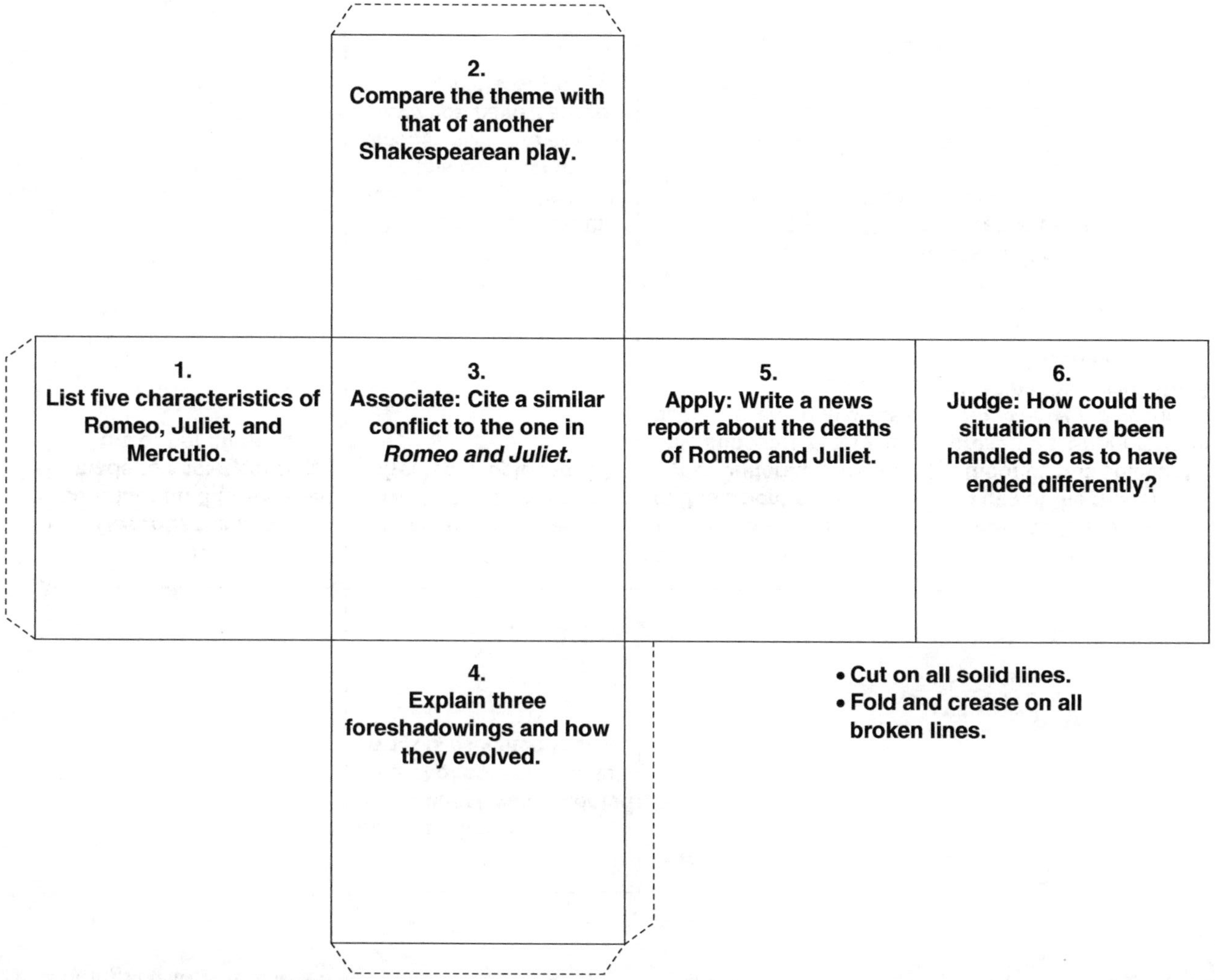

1.
List five characteristics of Romeo, Juliet, and Mercutio.

2.
Compare the theme with that of another Shakespearean play.

3.
Associate: Cite a similar conflict to the one in *Romeo and Juliet.*

4.
Explain three foreshadowings and how they evolved.

5.
Apply: Write a news report about the deaths of Romeo and Juliet.

6.
Judge: How could the situation have been handled so as to have ended differently?

- Cut on all solid lines.
- Fold and crease on all broken lines.

Figure 7.23 Cubing: Blank Template

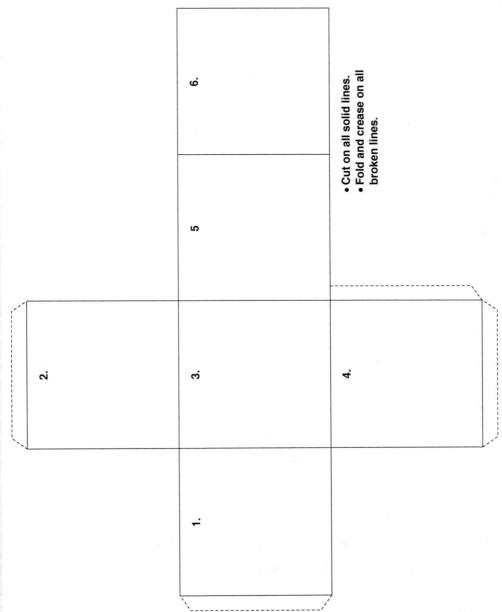

2.

1.

3.

5

4.

6.

- Cut on all solid lines.
- Fold and crease on all broken lines.

Figure 7.24 Verbs for Cubing

1.	4.
Tell Describe Recall Name Locate List	Review Discuss Prepare Diagram Cartoon
2.	5.
Compare Contrast Example Explain Define Write	Prepare Suggest Finish Prescribe Devise
3.	6.
Connect Make Design Produce Develop	Debate Formulate Choose Support In your opinion . . .

Green Cube

1. Draw Stella as you think she looks.

2. Use a Venn diagram and compare Stella and Blanche.

3. Use a comic strip to tell what happened in this chapter.

4. Shut your eyes and describe the setting. Jot down your ideas.

5. Predict what will happen in the next chapter. Use symbols.

6. In your opinion, is Stella a good sister?

Yellow Cube

1. Use a graphics program on the computer and create a character web for Stella.

2. Use symbols or a Venn diagram to compare Stella and Blanche.

3. Use a storyboard to show the progress of the plot to this point.

4. Draw the setting and label the items, people, and buildings.

5. What message do you think the writer wants people to remember?

6. Draw a symbol that illustrates your idea.

7. When you think of the title, do you agree or disagree that it is a good choice? Why or why not?

Both cubes are tapping into using visual/spatial intelligence, with the green cube working at a more basic level and the yellow cube stretching student thinking more toward the abstract, extending ideas and making connections.

Teaching diverse learners effectively in extended blocks of time requires all the previously mentioned strategies to provide variety and "fit" for unique learners in a differentiated classroom.

8 Cooperative Learning

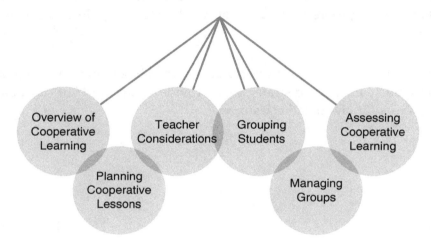

OVERVIEW OF COOPERATIVE LEARNING

Cooperative learning is a key strategy for the differentiated classroom that is using a block schedule. If students know how to work cooperatively, they will be self-monitoring and independent thinkers. This is a valuable skill for lifelong learning and for successful social and career interactions.

The social model of cooperative learning is one of the most researched strategies that improves student achievement. Many outstanding educators (e.g., Aronson, 1978; Bellanca & Fogarty, 1991; Bennett, Bennett-Rolheiser, & Stevhan, 1990; Cantelon, 1991a, 1991b; Clarke, Wideman, & Eadie, 1990; Johnson, Johnson, & Holubec, 1988; Kagan, 1992; Marzano, Pickering, & Pollock, 2001) have shared their expertise in cooperative learning with other educators. Students achieve mastery of content and skills and develop the thinking processes necessary for problem solving and higher-order reasoning. Cooperative learning is also reported to facilitate building positive relationships among students in class, which help students feel connected to and cared about in the classroom. Thus, cooperative learning increases their competencies in social and interactive skills, which help them get along with others in their families, the workplace, and the community.

Major studies in corporations show that the number one reason people lose their jobs is not what "they don't know and can't do" but interpersonal problems in the workplace (Johnson, Johnson, Holubec, & Roy, 1984). Processing information and ideas in a group helps students deepen their understanding through a mutual articulation of ideas and the variety of perspectives that group members share on the topic or problem. Dialogue, reasoning, and restating help participants make sense of ideas and help information "stick" in long-term memory through elaborative and rote rehearsal. In extended periods of instructional time, teachers identify cooperative learning as one of the most useful strategies to promote learning.

In differentiated classrooms, flexible grouping is a key tool in associating students by interest, readiness, and learning styles. TAPS is a way to remember the types of group structures and their uses in a differentiated block-learning environment (see also Gregory & Chapman, 2007; see Figure 8.1).

Results of Cooperative Learning

According to David and Roger Johnson (1991, 1994), when cooperative learning is implemented effectively, we can expect the following results:

- Higher self-esteem
- Higher achievement
- Increased retention
- Greater social support
- More on-task behavior
- Greater collaborative skills
- Greater intrinsic motivation
- Increased perspective taking
- Better attitudes toward school
- Better attitudes toward teachers
- Greater use of higher-level reasoning
- More positive psychological adjustment

Ekwall and Shanker (1988) reminded us that we learn

10 percent of what we read;

20 percent of what we see;

Figure 8.1 TAPS: Suggestions for Use

	Characteristics	Tasks
T **Total**	• Whole-class instruction • All students doing the same thing	• Pre-assessment • Presenting new information • Modeling new skills • Guest speaker • Viewing a video • Using a jigsaw strategy • Textbook(s) assignment
A **Alone**	• All students working alone • Student working on variety of tasks based on interest or readiness	• Pre-assessment • Journal entry • Portfolio assessment • Self-assessment • Independent study • Note taking and summarizing • Reflection • Tickets out
P **Paired**	• Students working with partners • Random selection of partners (card, color, etc.); teacher selection; or student choice • Task or interest oriented	• Brainstorming • Checking homework • Checking for understanding • Processing information • Peer editing • Peer evaluation • Researching • Interest in similar topic • Planning for homework
S **Small Groups**	• Homogeneous groups for skill development; heterogeneous groups for cooperative groups • Groups random or structured by teacher or students • Interest or task oriented	• Problem solving • Group projects • Learning centers • Cooperative group learning assignments • Portfolio conferences • Group investigation • Carousel brainstorming • Graffiti brainstorming

30 percent of what we hear;

50 percent of what we see and hear;

70 percent of what is discussed with others;

80 percent of what we experience personally; and

95 percent of what we teach to someone else.

Cooperative learning experiences increase students' abilities to retain what has been taught because it provides multiple opportunities to rehearse or practice content. Although cooperative group learning is a simple concept to grasp, it is more complex to implement than one might think.

Two Essential Elements of Successful Cooperative Learning

The first element of successful cooperative learning is a climate conducive to learning and thinking. Classrooms need to offer an atmosphere that is collaborative and supportive and that encourages risk taking and thinking.

The second element is the establishment of trust between and among students in the classroom. The teacher must consciously attend to building community with students so that students know one another better and understand each other's strengths and weaknesses. In groups, they will feel safe and supported while taking risks.

Trust building can be accomplished by teaching students simple structures that simultaneously help them process academic content and achieve standards in the curriculum. The following are examples of strategies that can be used both to foster trust and to address academic outcomes.

Collaborative Corners

Students select a corner, go there, and discuss a question, issue, or problem. Their selection may be based on a preference, an opinion, or a strongly held value. This can be used as a trust-building or icebreaking activity or to consolidate thoughts and develop a rationale for one's beliefs. For example, students could go to the corner to discuss a favorite location they would like to visit: Paris, Africa, Hong Kong, Egypt. In each corner, students would put their heads together and develop a rationale for their choice. Collaborative corners could also be used to signify a reaction to a statement that may be controversial; for example, "We should have universal health care." Students would go to the corner of choice: Agree, Strongly Agree, Disagree, or Strongly Disagree. Then they would develop a rationale with the group that assembles in their corner so as to articulate their position. Students could also choose a favorite character from a story and go to the corner and develop a character sketch with the group there. Collaborative corners can be used as a prewriting activity to generate ideas, vocabulary, and reasoning. This physical movement supports kinesthetic learners and raises all students' energy and oxygen levels while reducing stress.

Take a Stand

Another kinesthetic structure is having students take a stand on an issue. The teacher makes a statement and asks students to respond by standing in a row related to a particular response to the issue. The rows could be designated according to degrees of agreement and disagreement with a position, or students could stand in rows designated "I know a lot about the topic," "I'm not too sure about the topic," "I know one thing about the topic," "I know very little about the topic," and "I've never heard anything about this before." Students could also stand on a number from 1 to 10 according to how much they agree with a particular statement, such as "Every parent needs to take a parenting course." After the students have lined up, they can discuss with their linemates why they chose that particular row (i.e., what they know or why they agree or disagree). This makes a good anticipatory set at the beginning of a lesson. It can also be used at the end of a learning experience as a chance to discuss what has been learned.

Checkmate

Students pair up, and one partner answers the question or problem or practices the skill that has been taught. The other partner coaches and encourages. Then students reverse roles. After they are finished, they can meet with another pair to share their expertise. They show their appreciation of each other and celebrate their success. This activity works well with math problems and in reviewing homework in any subject.

Name Your Team

If students will work together over time or on a project, it can be a good idea to have them develop a name for their team or their base group. This helps them explore their commonalities and develop a group identity. It is a further opportunity to bond and develop trust. Students might come up with a name by looking at their personal multiple intelligences profiles, their hobbies and interests, and/or their personal characteristics. In the process, students often realize that they are more similar than different. In cooperative learning groups, students need to know each other at a deeper level than just what academic success they have had. Having personal knowledge of each other helps students realize that everyone is vulnerable in some areas and has strengths or talents in others. This realization enables tolerance and empathy to develop in the group so that while they are working, they will be more understanding of and able to make allowances for the diversity within the group.

Team Identity

To build trust and a spirit of inclusion, teachers may ask students to create a poster, collage, or banner for their team. Students can use symbols and pictures with a slogan to symbolize their unique team. Those students who like to use visual representations may prefer this form of expression.

Teachers with block classes comment that because students spend extended periods of time together, a variety of team-building and trust-building strategies is essential for classroom harmony and academic pursuits. In addition, these strategies provide vital opportunities for students to practice key skills needed in the workplace.

PLANNING COOPERATIVE LESSONS

As teachers work at implementing cooperative groups, they start small with simple structures, building trust and developing teamwork skills. This is a new process for teacher and students, and it takes time to master processes and work through problems and issues. The planner shown in Figure 8.2 may be used in thinking through the decisions that need to be made when planning cooperative group learning.

The charts in Figures 8.3 through 8.7 show cooperative tasks that may be used for assessing prior knowledge and skills, checking for understanding, actively processing information, and summarizing and note taking.

Figure 8.2 Planning a Lesson

This organizer may be helpful in helping teachers think about all the aspects of the cooperative lesson.

Standards		Content Objectives/Benchmarks	
Academic Activity		Social Behavior	
Assessment Tool		Data/Feedback	
Materials	Grouping	Roles	Accountability
Steps in Lesson (Directions, Expectations)			
Debriefing: Who? How?		Grading?	

Source: Robbins, P., Gregory, G., & Herndon, L. E. *Thinking inside the block schedule: Strategies for teaching in extended periods of time.* Copyright Corwin 2000.

Figure 8.3 Assessing Prior Knowledge and Skills

Knowledge of Canada (Neighboring Country)

Academic Goal: Brainstorm as many things as they can about Canada.

Social Goal/Skill: Accepting others' ideas

Materials: Life preserver with four sections, one for each student; marker for each student

Element	How I Will Incorporate/Teach
Positive Interdependence	*Goal:* Brainstorm as many things as they can about Canada. Share their ideas and check for accuracy. *Roles:* Timer, Checker, Timekeeper, Materials Manager *Resources*: Life preserver with four sections, one for each student; marker for each student.
Individual Accountability	Share their ideas with others and come to consensus about the accuracy of their information.
Social Skill	Accepting others' ideas
Group Processing	Say something positive to each other about what they have shared.
Face-to-Face Interaction	Students discuss and identify their information and explain it to the others.

Figure 8.4 Checking for Understandings

Math: Problem-Solving Strategies

Academic Goal: Students must solve a problem by collectively sharing ideas and strategies.

Social Goal/Skill: Building on the ideas of others

Materials: One piece of paper with problem and space to show their thinking as they solve it

Element	How I Will Incorporate/Teach
Positive Interdependence	*Goal:* Work through the problem together, talking out loud to share their thinking. *Roles:* Reader, Questioner, Checker (group of three) *Resources:* One sheet of newsprint and three markers
Individual Accountability	Each partner must be able to explain how to solve the problem.
Social Skill	Building on the ideas of others
Group Processing	Each student will write down one way the ideas of another student helped him or her.
Face-to-Face Interaction	Students discuss and identify key strategies to solve problems.

Figure 8.5 Acquiring Knowledge and Skills

Physical and Chemical Properties of Matter

Academic Goal: Students create a group portfolio.

Social Goal/Skill: Checking for accuracy

Materials: Materials and resources for each experiment; density lab, boiling point lab, distillation lab, and specific heat lab

Element	How I Will Incorporate/Teach
Positive Interdependence	*Goal:* Students create a group portfolio. *Roles:* Materials Manager, Scout, Project Manager, Recorder *Resources:* Materials and resources for each experiment; density lab, boiling point lab, distillation lab, and specific heat lab
Individual Accountability	Each student is responsible for one lab report in the portfolio.
Social Skill	Checking for accuracy
Group Processing	Discuss the data from each lab and question the process and content.
Face-to-Face Interaction	Students discuss and question processes and check for understanding.

Figure 8.6 Active Processing of Information

Persuasive Writing/Civics

Academic Goal: In trios, students write a persuasive letter advocating for something they see a need for in the nation.

Social Goal/Skill: Listening attentively

Materials: Paper and resource materials

Element	How I Will Incorporate/Teach
Positive Interdependence	*Goal:* In trios, students write a persuasive letter advocating for something they see a need for in the nation (e.g., gun control, overseas conflict, North Korean nuclear situation). Letter could be to a senator or state official. *Roles:* Persuasive Language Monitor, Argument Builder, Research Manager *Resources:* Paper and resource materials as needed
Individual Accountability	Each person is able to defend the group's position.
Social Skill	Listening with intent
Group Processing	Each student tells the other how well he or she listened and rates the partner on a scale of 1–5 (5 being a great listener).
Face-to-Face Interaction	Students discuss and build a rationale for their thinking in order to persuade.

Figure 8.7 Summarizing and Note Taking

Renaissance Explorers

Academic Goal: To create a synthesis of key accomplishments of each explorer

Social Goal/Skill: Working cooperatively

Materials: Placemat sectioned with four boxes; pictures of items in an envelope or a magazine that students may cut from

Element	How I Will Incorporate/Teach
Positive Interdependence	*Goal:* Create a newspaper article for each explorer and a cover sheet for the newspaper. *Roles:* Materials Manager, Copywriter, Technology Manager, Layout Manager *Resources:* Computer program for desktop publishing, resource materials, text and Internet access
Individual Accountability	Each student investigates one explorer, and together they will be responsible for all four. Any of them may be chosen as Reporter.
Social Skill	Working cooperatively. Use a T-chart (see examples in Figures 8.12 and 9.10).
Group Processing	Each student completes a ticket out telling how they contributed to the group goal and respected others.
Face-to-Face Interaction	Students discuss, clarify, and synthesize key information.

The acronym PIGSF (Johnson et al., 1988) may help with remembering these ideas (see Figure 8.8).

Positive interdependence is the process of designing group interactions so that all members are productive and engaged. We are all better if we put our heads together. Often teachers who do not build positive interdependence into their planning find that problems of equal performance and success arise related to the group task or goal. Although there are nine types of positive interdependence, usually only three or four are necessary to create a connectedness within the group. Without these, we sometimes will experience

- a student who takes over;
- a "social loafer";
- off-task behavior; and/or
- time wasted.

Each of the nine types of positive interdependence is described below.

Positive Interdependence Types

1. Goal Interdependence

The group has a common goal, and by working together, every member of the team is expected to achieve it.

2. Incentive Interdependence

Everyone receives the same reward but only if every member of the team succeeds. This may or may not be used depending on the level of independence and self-motivation of the individuals in the group.

3. Resource Interdependence

Resources, information, and material are limited so that students need to cooperate in sharing available resources. If everyone has the same materials, sometimes students will break away from the group, missing out on

Figure 8.8 PIGSF

Cooperative Learning: Five Elements

P	**Positive Interdependence**
	Students must feel that they need each other to complete the group's task. Roles, tasks, sequence, environment, common goal, incentive, simulation, identity, and outside forces must synergize to create positive interdependence.
I	**Individual Accountability**
	The group is not successful until each member has learned the material and helped with and understood the assignment.
G	**Group Processing**
	Students must be given time to analyze how well the group is functioning. Even a quick discussion is beneficial to skill growth and development.
S	**Social/Collaborate Skills**
	The teacher must ensure that skills in communication, leadership, trust, decision making, and conflict resolution are taught.
F	**Face-to-Face Interaction**
	The educational outcomes of oral summarizing, giving and receiving explanations, debating, and elaborating occur.

dialogue and questioning. To increase interdependence among the group members, the teacher can limit resources—such as texts, computer, scissors, readings, and paper—so that group members must share and rely on one another to make the learning experience successful.

4. Sequence Interdependence

The overall task is divided into a sequence of subtasks. Individual group members perform their particular tasks in a predetermined order. If each member of the group has an individual task to do within the group task, individuals feel needed and perceive that they are necessary members of the group. For example, there might be a Reader, Discussion Facilitator, and Recorder. Alternatively, tasks such as cutting, gluing, illustrating, researching, keyboarding, and editing may be assigned in the sequence they will occur during an activity. Students may rotate the tasks to give every member an opportunity to contribute with each step or role.

5. Role Interdependence

To increase the likelihood that students stay on-task, roles can be assigned so that each member of the group has a role that is necessary for the group to be successful and achieve the group goal. The following are some roles that can be assigned:

Encourager	Encourages each member of the group.
Questioner	Asks questions to help the work proceed.
Clarifier	Uses language to ensure clarity and understanding.
Summarize	Restates information for the group.
Prompter	Uses language to keep discussion moving.
Gatekeeper	Monitors the group process to include all members.

The bookmarks shown in Figure 8.9 may be given to students so that they have appropriate language to use when performing their roles. These bookmarks also allow students to simulate real-world "work roles."

Other roles that may be assigned are as follows:

Figure 8.9 Bookmarks for Student Roles

Encourager	**Questioner**	**Clarifier**
Helpful Language • Thanks for sharing. • Good idea. • What do you think? • Tell us more. • Right on . . . what else?	Helpful Language • What's a first step? • How could we . . . ? • What's the best plan? • When can we . . . ? • Who could . . . ?	Helpful Language • I think you said . . . • Tell me once more . . . • Is this what . . . ? • Explain to me . . . • Say again . . . • Did I hear . . . ?
Summarizer	**Facilitator**	**Gatekeeper**
Helpful Language • I think we agree that . . . • So far . . . • Some of us . . . • I think we said . . . • It seems to me . . .	Helpful Language • Another idea . . . • Perhaps . . . • I think . . . • My idea . . . • Suppose . . .	Helpful Language • Has everyone given an idea? • That's three done—we have ___ more to do. • Whose turn is it? • Let's check all the steps.

Recorder	Takes notes or records ideas. Completes necessary forms.
Reader	Reads all directions to the group or specific passage or section.
Reporter	Reports out to the large group after the group activity.
Materials Manager or "Go For"	Gets supplies and resources needed.
Timekeeper	Keeps track of time to make sure the task is completed.
Researcher	Carries out research necessary for the task and reports back to the group.
Liaison	Reports to the teacher on behalf of the group.
Observer	Keeps track of the group's activities and collects data on how well the group is functioning and using the skills expected.

The bookmarks shown in Figure 8.10 may be given to students as prompts and reminders of their roles.

Teachers need to know the students well enough to assign roles that will either capitalize on their strengths or provide practice in areas where they need to grow. For instance, one teacher assigned a student who often monopolized conversations an observer role, in which he focused on the group's interactions but did not speak. After playing this role for several class periods, he was assigned a new role. At one point, he began to blurt out a comment, realized what he was doing, and placed his own hand over his mouth and ceased speaking out of turn. Sometimes students can select their roles from those suggested by the teacher or group. This ensures a comfort level and further develops a commitment to the task.

6. Identity Interdependence

The group establishes a mutual identity through a name, flag, logo, or symbol. These can be augmented by a group song or cheer. If the group is going to work together on a major project over time, this can be a useful strategy.

Figure 8.10 Bookmarks for Keeping Students On-Task

Production Manager	Information Manager	Resource Manager
• Oversees the project. • Ensures everyone does his or her job. • Manages the process. • Keeps track of the project. • Communicates with the teacher when group needs direction.	• Ensures accuracy of materials. • Ensures quality of the product. • Listens and makes sure ideas are clear. • Follows written directions.	• Gathers and manages materials. • Properly stores materials. • Acquires and arranges materials so they are available.
Personnel Manager	**Technology Manager**	**Time Manager**
• Manages people and builds morale. • Encourages team members. • Helps resolve conflicts. • Helps solve problems. • Monitors effort and productivity.	• Assists with technology aspects. • Helps with computer needs. • Uses resources from Internet. • Helps with presentation techniques.	• Manages deadlines. • Helps team keep on track. • Communicates with production manager. • Negotiates time needed.

7. Outside Force Interdependence

The group competes against other groups or perhaps a time allotment. Sometimes giving students less time to begin with and adding time if they need more discourages students from wasting time at the beginning of the task.

8. Simulation Interdependence

The group members imagine that they are in a situation or role where they must collaborate to be successful. The brain loves novelty and intriguing situations. Sometimes the group task will lend itself to simulations in which students are asked to take on an identity as a "research team" or assume some other fantasy situation. Problem-solving situations that involve the roles of scientists or environmentalists can be enticing for students. For example, they could be a group of scientists researching a particular topic. Alternatively, they may take on the role of a real team that exists outside school. The simulation might include work in a real-world environment at the science or computer lab of a local business or industry. These simulations often give students an understanding of how the learning is relevant in the real world and helps them explore career options.

9. Environmental Interdependence

The group members work together within a specified physical space, such as an area of the classroom or within a specific table or desk configuration.

Individual Accountability Is Essential

In any cooperative learning task, students must achieve an academic goal to be successful. After any learning experience, students are assessed on what they know, what they can do, and how they function. They may be held accountable by a test or quiz, or they may be held accountable orally through randomly asked questions or in a large-group discussion. They could also be asked to model, demonstrate, or exhibit a new skill they have acquired.

Without accountability, students may become social loafers and let others do the work. If they know they are ultimately accountable, however, they tend to pay better attention to the discussion and process. Teachers might use a Reporter role without naming the reporter until the task is complete. In this way, all students are accountable potentially to be the Reporter.

Social Skills for Team Success

After building a positive, inclusive climate and developing trust, students must develop social skills to be successful in group work. Many students come to school with well-developed social skills that they have seen modeled in family situations and that they have practiced and received feedback on in their early and formative years. Their emotional intelligence is high. They are at ease with themselves. They manage their emotions and are self-motivated, seeking intrinsic rewards for learning. Not only are they self-aware, but they also are aware of others and can show empathy and can manage others and interact with others successfully (Goleman, 1995).

These abilities are not always present, however. If students have not had opportunities to encounter positive role models and learn from them, or if they have not been taught these skills, they may be lacking in this area of development. Although they have perhaps missed the optimal window of opportunity for developing these competencies, it is not too late if a focus is placed on social skills development and if situations are provided for practice and feedback.

Applications

Here are some fundamental social skills:

- Listening to others
- Taking turns
- Encouraging others
- Using positive statements
- Using quiet voices
- Participating equally
- Staying on-task
- Asking for help
- Using polite language

Here are some skills for maintaining group process:

- Checking for understanding
- Asking for clarification
- Following directions
- Disagreeing agreeably
- Resolving conflicts
- Accepting differences
- Encouraging one another

Teaching Social Skills

It is important that teachers help students learn the social skills needed to work successfully in collaborative groups and to accomplish their academic goals. Students need to be able to understand the following in relation to any social skill that has been targeted:

- Why the skill is needed
- What the skill is—what it looks, sounds, and feels like
- How to practice the skill
- The importance of practice
- The need for opportunities to debrief the learning process and reflect on the practice

Following are suggestions for teaching social skills.

Why the Skill Is Needed

Often at some point in group work, the need for a particular skill clearly presents itself. At this moment, it is ideal to analyze the situation to identify what is going on in the group and to identify the skill that will help the group function better. As the teacher or one group observes another, students can see a problem and suggest a skill that might be helpful for the group to learn and practice.

What the Skill Is

Any learning target must be clear and comprehensible to the learner. Often the teacher can facilitate the opportunity to highlight a particular positive social skill needed for successful collaboration. The use of the skill can be illustrated through a story, video, or current event. Students can role-play to get a sense of how the skill looks, sounds, and feels in action. Teachers can also facilitate the development of a two-column "T-chart" that looks at what the skill "Sounds Like" and "Looks Like." A third column—"Feels Like"—may be added (Hill & Hancock, 1993).

Thinking about feelings helps students develop the skill of self-awareness, and when they are able to identify personal feelings, they can be more empathetic to others. Students can generate these indicators as a class, contributing statements in their own words so that in group situations, the language is comfortable and familiar to use.

Figure 8.11 is an example of a chart that describes "using names." Students generated it during a discussion of the importance of calling one another by name.

Figure 8.11 Social Skill: Using Names

Sounds Like . . .	Looks Like . . .	Feels Like . . .
I hear my name.	Smiles	I'm important.
Names are said nicely.	Looking at the person	People care about me.
Everyone's name is heard.		

Students can show that they understand the skill by drawing about it, role-playing a situation in which the skill is used appropriately, using puppets to play out the skill in a particular scenario, or writing about themselves or others using the skill in real-life situations. Using a concept attainment lesson that gives attributes of the behavior may help students understand the skill and give them language to use as they practice.

Opportunities for Practice

When organizing group interactions, teachers need to identify the social skill that could be practiced appropriately during an activity. The skill to be practiced should fit the situation. For example, using names is important in activities where everyone needs to be involved, feel included, and participate equally. Likewise, equal participation is an important skill to use when the group is trying to share opinions and come to consensus.

Processing of Group Work

Group processing is an essential component of cooperative group learning, yet this step is often omitted due to lack of time at the end of an activity. Practicing social skills should result in improvement over time, but processing after the practice will improve the skills even more. The graph in Figure 8.12 shows three classes of students with their achievement level as well as their retention after three weeks. Class A was taught in a more teacher-directed way, Class B used cooperative group learning, and Class C used cooperative group learning and processed the social skill at the end of the group task (Gibbs, 2001).

Processing does not have to take inordinate amounts of time. It can be a two-minute discussion about how well the group worked together today or a student giving a peer a compliment for helping with a task. It is the

Figure 8.12 The Impact of Group Processing

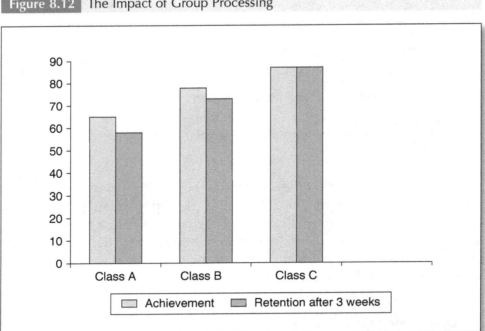

metacognitive aspect of the processing that highlights the social interactions of the group and raises awareness of collaborative work.

Checklists provide feedback to students on their growth in the area of social skills. Groups or individuals may dialogue about their use of social skills and fill in reflection forms. The following list of questions may be used two or three at a time for reflection and dialogue by group members:

What word would you like people to use to describe your group?

If they watched you today, what word would they use?

Did you listen to each other? What evidence do you have?

Did you respect ideas from other people? How did you do that?

Did you disagree in a "polite way"? What did you say?

Did you ask clarifying questions?

Did you extend other people's answers? What did that sound like?

Did you all participate equally? What evidence do you have?

Following are some personal reflection questions:

What were you being asked to do?

What information did you have?

Had you solved a problem like this before?

What strategies did you use?

What problems did you encounter?

What was your plan?

What can you predict?

How are you feeling about this experience?

What would you do differently next time?

Where can you get some help if you need it?

Students may also process their social skill growth and set goals by using a "pluses and wishes" format. Students list all the pluses, or positive aspects, of their working together and then all their wishes and plans for the next time they work together (see Figure 8.13).

Students might also be asked to reflect on their working relationships and to respond to questionnaires like the one shown in Figure 8.14.

Another resource for group processing is a team rubric (see Figure 8.15). Students can use the rubric to target an area of need and then process how well they did after the team task is completed. They might score themselves by circling the appropriate level related to the criteria.

Gathering Feedback and Debriefing the Skill

If students are practicing the social skill of "using names," one student acting as observer can use a checklist to check off each time names were used during the group activity. After the group has finished, the observer may share the data and discuss how well the group did. Students can then celebrate the progress they have made, if that is the case, or set realistic goals for the next time they work together. Figure 8.16 is a blackline master that can be used or adapted by groups to collect data and debrief the learning experience.

Face-to-Face Interaction

One of the greatest outcomes of using cooperative learning is that students dialogue, elaborate, debate, and see different perspectives from their peers. They learn to summarize, build on one another's ideas, and "wrestle" with challenges, projects, problems, and concepts. Educators are always looking for ways to build thinking skills into lessons and tasks. Cooperative learning is a wonderful strategy, as it lends itself to interactive thinking. Teachers can use concept formation or synectics (Gordon, 1961), Venn diagrams, or other graphic organizers to help students think together

Figure 8.13 Pluses and Wishes Worksheet

Pluses	Wishes	Plans for Next Time

Figure 8.14 Working Relationship Questionnaire

Working Relationship Questionnaire

Directions: How well did you work together on a scale of 1 to 5? What word describes how you feel about working together?

	Jake	Kenisha	Aron
We listened to each other.			
We helped each other.			
We got our work done.			
As a result of working together, I feel . . .			

Figure 8.15 Team Assessment Rubric

Criteria	1	2	3	4
Team uses time effectively.	Team wastes many minutes of class time.	Team uses about 50% of class time wisely.	Team makes class time useful.	Team uses all available time to complete activity.
Team uses appropriate research skills.	Team uses very few resources.	Team finds some resources and uses some skills.	Team uses appropriate number of resources and skills.	Team uses appropriate resources and skills and displays a high level of organization.
Team communicates ideas and shares information.	Team members rarely share ideas.	Team members share some ideas but do not engage in discussion.	Team members engage actively in communication and sharing of ideas.	Team members engage actively in dialogue, sharing, and mutually developing possible solutions.
Team members share the tasks.	Team members argue over work to be done.	Team members agree to share the tasks.	Team members share tasks and work diligently.	Team members are task driven, working toward excellence in their results.

in cooperative groups. Teachers can deliberately build in all levels of thinking by using Bloom's (1956) taxonomy so that students are exploring ideas and issues from all perspectives.

Figure 8.16 Reflecting on Our Group Work Together

Social skill we focused on:

We did a great job at . . .

Most of us . . .

We need to work on . . .

Personally, I need to work on . . .

In the space below, individuals print their names and indicate what skill they will work on the next time the group is together.

Name: _____   _____

Name: _____   _____

Name: _____   _____

Name: _____   _____

Each member signs to show agreement with the information on the form.

WE AGREE:

Name: _____

Name: _____

Name: _____

Name: _____

Jigsaw

This useful strategy includes the use of expert groups as part of the process. This strategy was introduced by Elliot Aronson in 1978 and elaborated on by Johnson et al. (1988) and Kagan (1992). Although this is an interesting and engaging as well as efficient technique for examining a large amount of content, it is a much more involved strategy than those previously outlined and should not be attempted until students have developed adequate social skills to cope with larger groups and complex tasks.

Initially, students are organized into groups of three or four members, often referred to as the "base group." Each group member is given a letter or number (e.g., 1, 2, 3, 4). The material to be examined is divided into the same number of pieces as there are members in the group (i.e., 3 or 4). Then the material is distributed to each member of the group. The next step is to form "expert groups" in which all the 1s meet together, all the 2s, and so on. In the expert groups, the members examine the material, information, or model; analyze the critical points (the what); and decide how to share that information back in their base group (the how). After the experts have finished their dialogue and have reached a level of understanding, they return to their base groups. Each group member, in turn, teaches teammates what he or she has learned.

This strategy is powerful in fostering interdependence, as each person has a key piece of the whole that is valuable for a shared understanding. Having to understand new information thoroughly enough to share it with others requires careful examination and critical-thinking skills. The ability to articulate, explain, or interpret helps the individual develop long-term and enduring understanding of the content.

For example, if students are studying the countries of Asia, they would be assigned areas such as geography, people, wildlife, and agriculture. The expert groups would meet and explore these four areas, and once their expertise was developed, they would return to their home or base groups and teach each other. Jigsaw can be used in any subject discipline with almost any content. It can serve as an advance organizer, as a strategy for presenting information (input phase), or as a closure activity to consolidate student learning.

Giving students a graphic organizer or summarizing chart can be very helpful to them as they record key ideas they read and discuss (see Figure 8.17). They can also record the information given to them from their expert team members on the organizer.

TEACHER CONSIDERATIONS

It is important that the teacher be cognizant of certain considerations when planning to use cooperative structures. Paying attention to these considerations will increase the chances that the groups will function well and achieve their academic goals, as well as develop the social skills and

Figure 8.17 Jigsaw

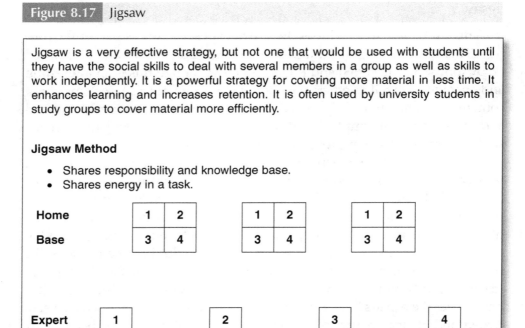

Jigsaw is a very effective strategy, but not one that would be used with students until they have the social skills to deal with several members in a group as well as skills to work independently. It is a powerful strategy for covering more material in less time. It enhances learning and increases retention. It is often used by university students in study groups to cover material more efficiently.

Jigsaw Method

- Shares responsibility and knowledge base.
- Shares energy in a task.

Home
Base

Expert

Home
Base
Share

Source: Aronson (1978) and Slavin (1980).

thinking skills they need for life. In a differentiated classroom, group interactions—with flexible grouping—are essential. The extended time periods of the block schedule allow for quality group work to occur if it is planned well.

Brainstorming

Brainstorming is often used to generate data and to problem-solve in cooperative learning. Brainstorming should FLOW (see Figure 8.18).

Figure 8.18 FLOW Brainstorming

F	Free flow of ideas.
L	Let all ideas come out, even off-the-wall ones.
O	Originality counts.
W	Weigh options later.

Applications

The following guidelines are helpful for group brainstorming:

- The teacher sets a quantity target to keep the group moving.
- The teacher stipulates a short time frame; this helps keep the group on-task.
- The teacher appoints a recorder.
- Each member thinks up a few items prior to group brainstorming. (This is referred to as "priming the pump.")
- The recorder jots down the group's ideas large enough for all to see.
- No criticism is allowed.
- No debate is allowed; just keep everyone's ideas flowing.

The following guidelines are helpful for round-the-room brainstorming:

- The teacher posts large sheets of chart paper around the room.
- The teacher writes a different topic, idea, or question on each one.
- In small groups at each sheet, students generate ideas for 45 seconds or so and then move to the next chart.

(Continued)

(Continued)

- When a group returns to the original chart, group members peruse, clarify, and summarize.
- Students can take out notebooks and record key ideas from the completed charts.

The "dot jot—paper pass" format is another way to structure brainstorming:

- Each group has a piece of butcher paper at its table.
- Each group brainstorms around a topic, issue, or question.
- Each idea is jotted down on the paper, following a dot.
- After a minute or two, each paper is passed to the next group so that those students can add more ideas.
- When the paper returns to the group where it started, the members organize a summary of ideas to be discussed and presented.

GROUPING STUDENTS

Students may be grouped for many reasons and in many ways. Sometimes for quick activities, students are grouped by asking them to get a partner of choice with whom they will work. Alternatively, the teacher can use a counting-off technique for random grouping. The following grouping techniques offer an array of options.

Counting Off

Divide the number of students by the number of members you want in each group. For example, 24 students divided by 3 is 8. Have the students count off 1 to 8. Then tell all the 1s, 2s, 3s, and so on to form groups of three and to move to a place to work together.

Cards

Some teachers use cards with different information or stickers on them and distribute these to the class. Students then need to find other students whose cards go with theirs. Here are some examples: (a) find the cards that have the same math answer (e.g., $2 + 3, 1 + 4, 6 - 1$); (b) find the cards that have the same color of dot, the same symbol, or the same geometric shape; (c) find the other three panels to form a complete comic strip; or (d) find the others who are singing or humming the same nursery rhyme, camp song, or popular tune.

Statistics

Another grouping strategy is to have students form a line around the room alphabetically or by birth dates. Students may also be grouped by similarities, such as having birthdays in the same month, being of the same age or height, having the same color of eyes or hair, having the same number of family members, having the same shoe size, or having the same astrology sign. This will take some preparation at the beginning of the semester; teachers will need to give students a questionnaire to fill out to gather the relevant information. Engaging students in analyzing the data they have generated can be instructive as well as fun.

Assignments

Teachers hand students the assignments with a number or symbol already on them. Students are asked to find classmates with the identical number or symbol. Another way of doing this is to print the assignments on colored paper and have students locate others with the same color of paper to form a group.

Name Tags

Place name tags on the tables where students are to be seated. Since some students are self-conscious about wearing name tags, names can be assigned that tie into the content of study. Examples include characters in a play or book, names of rocks and minerals, politicians, composers, artists, foods, muscles, bones, states, countries, theorems, greetings or statements in foreign languages, software names, and tools. Teachers who have used this approach suggest it is easiest and more affordable to use plastic name tag holders that can be reused.

Grouping Sticks

Some teachers use a wooden craft stick for each student. Each stick has a student's name and a different-colored square, circle, and triangle. When sticks are given out, teachers can ask students to find the other three with the same color of triangle and to form a group. Another day, it may be partners with the same color of circle. This activity facilitates the quick formation of random groups.

Caution: As much fun as grouping creatively can be, more energy should be put into the planning of the learning experience than into the grouping experience. Select approaches that take a minimum of time to orchestrate so that as much time as possible can be allocated to the learning task.

Heterogeneous Grouping Wheel

Planning heterogeneous groupings can be challenging for teachers. The team formation wheel, developed by Sheila Silversides (cited in Kagan, 1992), allows grouping students for a variety of purposeful heterogeneous activities.

To assemble the wheel, copy Figure 8.19 four times and cut out the concentric circles. Lay the four circles one on top of the other in a nesting fashion and fasten them with a brad.

Examples of Using the Team Formation Wheel

Group by Reading Levels

- Put the names of students who are expert readers in each section of the outside wheel, marked 1.
- Put names of "grade-level readers" in the sections of wheels 2 and 3.
- Put names of struggling readers in the sections of smallest wheel 4.

Group by Learning Styles

- Put the names of students who are more visual learners in each section of the outside wheel, marked 1.
- Put names of auditory learners in the sections of wheel 2.
- Put names of tactile learners in the sections of wheel 3.
- Put names of kinesthetic learners in the sections of smallest wheel 4.

Group by Multiple Intelligences

- Put the names of students who are more verbal/linguistic in each section of the outside wheel, marked 1.
- Put names of students who are more logical/mathematical in the sections of wheel 2.
- Put names of students who are more visual/spatial in the sections of wheel 3.
- Put names of more interpersonal learners in the sections of smallest wheel 4.

Group by Diversity

- Put the names of students who are English-language learners in each section of the outside wheel, marked 1.
- Put names of special education students in the sections of wheel 2.
- Put names of gifted or complex thinkers in the sections of wheel 3.
- Put the names of the remaining students in the sections of smallest wheel 4.

To group heterogeneously, form groups using one student from each concentric circle so that there is a variety of levels of expertise or interest in each group. To change the groups for another time just move each section of the wheel around one, two, or three sections.

How Do I Arrange the Room for Optimum Positive Interaction?

Students need to be "eye-to-eye" and "knee-to-knee" to facilitate dialogue when they are working in groups. It is much easier to make this happen if the

Figure 8.19 Grouping Wheel

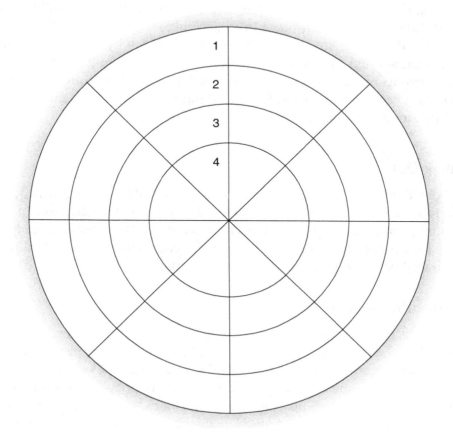

Source: "Wagon Wheel Teaming" is based on an idea developed by Sheila Silversides (cited in Kagan, 1992).

tables and chairs are moved into various formations as groups need to change. It may be a chore for teachers to set up the room by themselves; however, students can be a great help in reorganizing the classroom. The teacher can display a room design on the overhead, and students can organize the room as the initial task of the day. If only desks are available, then they need to be pulled together to get students in close proximity to complete a task successfully. To lessen the noise of rearranging, cut an X into tennis balls and slip them onto the legs of the desks like casters. In this way, desks can be slid into place quickly and quietly.

MANAGING GROUPS

A variety of problems can arise when students work in cooperative groups. Some of these are discussed below along with suggestions for resolving them.

Conflicts

When students work together, conflicts are inevitable. Building in social skills, such a "disagreeing in an agreeable way," may head off some conflicts. Providing students with insights about why conflicts usually occur—more often than not from differences in wants and needs of individual group members—can also be helpful. Formal training in conflict resolution can develop powerful social and emotional skills that will be valuable tools for a lifetime.

Tuning Out

Sometimes students seem not to be able to stay on-task. Giving them a specific role may be helpful. For example, giving the unfocused student the Encourager role may help that student stay included. Also, reminding students of their interdependence may entice other students to tell the individual who has strayed how important he or she is to the group.

Overbearing Student

The teacher could ask the overbearing student to be the observer and to collect data during the process; to observe others, the student must talk less. Using a "talking stick" may help because the student can talk only when he or she has the stick. Some teachers give each student five poker chips. Every time they speak, they must give up a poker chip. After all a student's chips are gone, the student must simply observe and let other students speak (Kagan, 1992).

Absent Student

The student who is absent may need a buddy to keep him or her informed of or on track with the work missed. A class and/or team folder with copies of work missed may also be a resource. As the availability of technology increases, students can use e-mail and team websites to keep connected. Some teachers have students, on a rotating basis, use a laptop computer to take notes. These notes are provided to students who have been absent or to students who have physical challenges that make note taking difficult.

Teacher Collaboration

No matter what the problem is, no one answer is guaranteed to work. Each collaborative situation and each student is unique. Therefore, problem solving will involve trial and error. Other teachers who teach a particular student may be a good resource, having found strategies that work for that individual. Many teachers who are implementing cooperative group learning post their problems in faculty lounges or workrooms, and other teachers can brainstorm and make suggestions or share strategies that have worked for them in similar situations. As a faculty, this activity reinforces that "we are in this together," working for student success.

Coaching Students to Successful Group Interaction

Cooperative group learning is a simple concept with a complex implementation. We need to start small by teaching students social skills and using simple strategies such as these:

- Think-pair-share
- Turn and talk
- Say and switch
- Say something

It takes time for group work to evolve into a successful enterprise. We must persist longer than they resist. It will take multiple rehearsals, sometimes 7–20 practice trials, to develop a skill to the automatic level.

Applications

Consider the following strategies to build successful group interaction:

- Continue to reinforce social skills through practice, reflection, and group processing. Have students ask, *How did we do today?*
- Get clear about the objective and purpose of the group task and make sure students are clear, too.
- Reinforce positive interdependence so there are no "social loafers" or "takers over."
- Make sure the task is worthy of interaction. Examples include brainstorming, consensus building, debating, and using creativity.
- Model for and coach those students who need help working with others.
- Circulate, assess, interject, and monitor the groups to head off problems and keep students on track.
- Provide a "sponge activity" so groups that finish sooner have a meaningful next step. You might post an extension activity or have a list available of activities that students can pursue in extra time.

Managing Gifted Students

Gifted students may sometimes balk at working in groups, as they feel they are quite capable alone. Nonetheless, Lou et al. (cited in Marzano, Pickering & Pollock, 2001) assured us that gifted students do well in cooperative groups; just like other students, they deepen their understanding through dialogue and debating ideas. Sometimes in heterogeneous groups, however, they take over or become impatient with others. Putting gifted students in a group together with other students at a high level of readiness raises the complexity of their thinking through challenging one another's rationales and building on others' ideas during discussions.

There should be a difference in the activities of a heterogeneous group and a homogeneous group. If readiness levels are an issue, then the level of challenge should be appropriate; that is, just beyond the skill level. Gifted groups should be sufficiently challenged beyond the regular tasks at grade level.

ASSESSING COOPERATIVE LEARNING

To grade or not to grade: that is the question! Again, no one answer or rule about assigning grades applies when one uses cooperative group learning. Often teachers can use cooperative group learning as the vehicle for accomplishing standards and then assess individually with more traditional methods of evaluation, such as by administering tests and quizzes or by assessing each student's individual portion of a group project.

Experience has taught many teachers that moving too quickly to group grading before groups are functioning well or students and parents understand and appreciate the value of cooperative group learning can be a disaster that may cause resentment toward the strategy. Here are some questions teachers should ask themselves:

- Is there one group product?
- Is there an individual portion of the task?
- Is there a social skill that can be given a grade?

It may not be necessary or even fair to assign a grade if the groups are just beginning to work together. Also, evaluation may not be necessary if the activity is simple and short-lived. Checklists, observation forms, and reflections may be more appropriate tools to encourage students to set personal and team goals and plan strategies for improvement. In time, sharing grades will become more acceptable, and they will reinforce the concept of collaboration when the product is a collective one and a true spirit of collaboration exists. Teachers may decide to use a combination of grading practices based on the standards targeted in the learning experience and the social skills students are working on. Whatever method of grading is used, clear criteria and an understanding of how grades will be given must be explained up front.

Chapter 9 discusses assessment for the differentiated block classroom in depth, including how having extended class time allows for integrating feedback into the cycle of learning.

Applications

Following are various ways to grade that can be used alone or in combination:

Grade for . . .

- Group product
- Individual part of the product
- Test or quiz mark
- Demonstration
- Presentation

Grade for . . .

- Academic product
- Use of social skill
- Individual role

Grade . . .

- 30 percent for participation;
- 35 percent for group academic product; and
- 35 percent for individual academic product.

Your own combination:

- _____
- _____
- _____

Cooperative group learning is well worth pursuing in any classroom, as it has great promise for academic achievement as well as for developing interpersonal skills that transfer beyond the classroom to life. It is necessary that teachers persist longer than students resist in order to implement a quality group learning effort in the differentiated block schedule classroom. Start small! Use simple strategies. Teach social skills and take time to debrief. Cooperative group learning will be a great asset to student learning as well as classroom management.

9 Assessing Student Learning

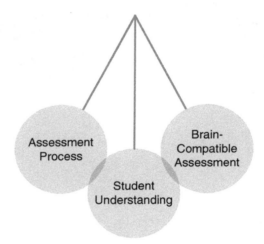

ASSESSMENT PROCESS

In classrooms, teachers and students cannot rely on personal opinions to assess the performances and achievement of learners. One opinion at one point in time is also not valid. Students need continuous feedback during the learning process so that they have an indication of how they are doing based on clear criteria and indicators. This is the *assessment* process—from the Latin *assessus*, "to sit beside." Students are graded at particular intervals based on the quality and/or quantity of their work and how close they are to the standard. This is *evaluation*, placing a value on growth.

The assessment process informs the learner and the teacher. The brain naturally seeks feedback. As students receive the data, they can analyze and reflect on the information so that their progress can act as a motivator and they can set goals in areas that still have room for improvement. Feedback or assessment data can also inform the teacher about what is working, how students are doing, next steps to plan for the learners, and what in the program needs to be changed. Assessment data also inform the school, parents, and community.

When educators clearly identify and share standards with criteria and indicators that describe success, they enable students to internalize the "target" and thus make it more likely that the students will succeed. Richard Stiggins, founder of the Assessment Training Institute, reminded us that most students can hit any target that is clear and holds still long enough. In his book *Student-Centered Classroom Assessment* (1997), Stiggins discussed seven guiding principles of assessment:

1. Assessments require clear thinking and effective communication.

2. Classroom assessment is key.

3. Students are assessment users.

4. Clear and appropriate targets are essential.

5. High-quality assessment is a must.

6. Understand personal implications.

7. Assessment involves teaching and learning.

The block schedule allows more time for building in and facilitating teacher, peer, and self-assessments that let students know how they are progressing in relationship to the standards.

With continuous feedback, support, time, choice, and an enriched environment, learners can continue to improve and to master standards. The learning cycle keeps the learning process moving forward. Feedback offered with support helps students achieve a state of *relaxed alertness,* a term used to describe the condition of an appropriate level of challenge in a safe environment. As teachers strive to enable learners to reach standards and expectations that are meaningful and worthwhile, they need to begin with the end in mind.

STUDENT UNDERSTANDING

Educators have long tried to get students to understand concepts and acquire knowledge. The definitions of *understand* (*Merriam-Webster's Collegiate Dictionary,* 2003) include "to grasp the meaning of," "to have thorough or technical acquaintance with or expertness in the practice of," and "to be thoroughly familiar with. . . ." Here are some realities of acquiring understanding:

- It is not superficial but conscious.
- It is not shallow but deep.
- It is not instantaneous but developmental.

People show their understanding through their ability to explain, apply, empathize, interpret, define a perspective, and thus create an awareness of self-knowledge. In planning curriculum, teachers need to consider various learning experiences and assessment tools that will enable their students to develop understanding that endures. The planning model shown in Figure 9.1 is a series of thoughtful questions for teachers to consider when planning with standards in mind.

Figure 9.1 Planning Model for the Learning Cycle

Questions to consider: How will we know if they know?

Describe criteria and indicators for judging success.

What will students *know* (facts, knowledge)?

What will students *understand* (concepts, big ideas)?

What will students be able to *do* (skills, processes)?

What *attitudes or behaviors* will be developed?

Rubrics and targets may be used at this point to show students the expectations.

What assessment tools will be used to collect data?

What learning strategies will enable students to develop these competencies? (Remember, one size doesn't fit all.)

How will feedback be built into the process?

How will metacognition and goal setting be addressed?

Extended periods of instructional time can provide students with an opportunity to explore content in depth with the goal of long-lasting understanding (Wiggins & McTighe, 1998). Larger blocks of time help us move from misconceptions to essentials necessary in the learning process (see Figure 9.2).

To collect data on student growth and achievement, teachers can use any of the many assessment tools now available. Some assessment tools and strategies are shown in Figure 9.3.

Figure 9.2 Misconceptions Versus Essentials

Misconceptions	Essentials
One assessment is enough.	Many assessment tools validate data.
Personal judgment alone is enough.	Clear criteria and indicators are needed.
Teachers do assessments to students.	Students are partners in the assessment process.

Figure 9.3 Assessment Tools and Strategies

Getting to Know Them	Pre-Assessments	Check for Understanding
• Surveys • Inventories • Style preferences • Environment • Interests: topics or subjects • Multiple intelligences • PMI	• Concept webs • Graphic organizers • T-charts • Alphabet brainstorm • K-W-L • People search • W5 • Anticipation guides • Rubric • Quick writes • Tickets out • 4 Corners • Questioning • Graffiti • T/F tests	• Questioning • Homework • Tickets out • Journaling • Give one, get one • Quizzes • Conferences • Partner dialogue and eavesdropping • Carousel brainstorming • Demonstrations • Whiteboards • SMART board • Observations • 3-2-1 • Fist of 5 • Thumbs-up

BRAIN-COMPATIBLE ASSESSMENT

Current available cognitive research on how humans learn questions, as well as informs, educational practice in terms of assessment. The acronym BRAIN can help teachers focus on issues concerning assessment (see Figure 9.4).

Let's take a closer look at each component of brain-compatible assessment in a differentiated block schedule.

B: Brains Need a Safe, Risk-Free Environment in Which to Flourish

A state of relaxed alertness is required in which learners are challenged by tasks just beyond their skill level in a safe, nurturing, supportive environment that embodies the concept of FLOW. The environment should be enriched with manipulatives and other resources that facilitate the growth of dendrites (neural connections). Clear criteria and a variety of ways to demonstrate competencies must be provided so that students can approach learning with confidence and optimism. Developing rubrics and clear targets with students helps them internalize expectations and enhances their understanding of the learning tasks.

Clear Expectations

Athletes who compete are accustomed to being scored on a rubric. The criteria and indicators for the task are well defined and shared prior to the performance. Armed with this knowledge and comfortable that no "got-chas" will crop up toward the end, students are more able to tackle the challenge and confidently achieve the goal.

Figure 9.5 is an example of a scoring rubric that may be used to share expectations of quality performance with students prior to the task of designing an oral presentation. In this case, the rubric acts as a clear target. It may be developed by the teacher or in collaboration with students, who are often able to articulate criteria for a quality performance. When students generate the rubric, they internalize the expectations and proceed more enlightened toward a quality presentation. The rubric is valuable not only for understanding the target but also as a coaching tool that students can use to give peer feedback as they practice their presentations. Finally, it can serve as an evaluation when students are ready to give their practiced and polished delivery. If a grade is required, the teacher may weight each criterion to arrive at a final grade. For example, the organization and coherency score may be multiplied by 3, whereas the eye contact may be weighted by only 1.

Figure 9.4 Brain-Compatible Assessment

B	*Build* environments that are safe and where students feel confident and encouraged to practice and take risks in the learning process.
R	*Relevancy* and meaningful tasks are essential to captivate learners.
A	*Adequate* time to learn is necessary. We don't all learn on the same day in the same way. Multiple ways to practice, understand, and apply new learnings and receive ongoing feedback are necessary to continue to set goals and meet standards.
I	*Intelligence* is unique to each student. Each person learns and demonstrates understanding in personal and different ways as each brain is hardwired differently due to both nature and nurture.
N	*Negotiation*, or transfer to long-term memory, takes time, continuous rehearsal, and conscious planning with feedback, including reflection and metacognition.

Figure 9.6 is another example of a rubric, this one for scoring laboratory reports. This rubric would guide the learner to be more successful in the task and serve as a scoring device.

R: Relevant and Meaningful Tasks and Assessments Engage the Learner

Real-world applications, useful information, and skills applied in a meaningful context are more likely to capture and focus student attention, which in turn has the potential to facilitate learning. Authentic assessments include projects, products, performances and exhibitions, dioramas, maps, research, video productions, models, portfolios, speeches, presentations, and demonstrations in which standards are embedded in real-world situations. These assessments are engaging and bring relevance to learning. They also provide an opportunity for elaborative rehearsal so that new information and concepts can be more deeply explored; thus, the student fosters new connections in the brain and retains the information in long-term memory. Such assessments also appeal to particular interests

Figure 9.5 Rubric for Student Presentations

Criteria	1	2	3	4
Content	• Does not seem to understand the topic very well.	• Shows a good understanding of parts of the topic.	• Shows a good understanding of the entire topic.	• Shows a full understanding of the topic.
Preparedness	• Student does not seem at all prepared to present.	• The student is somewhat prepared, though it is clear that rehearsal was lacking.	• Student seems pretty prepared but might have needed a couple more rehearsals.	• Student is completely prepared and has obviously rehearsed.
Eye Contact	• Slouches and/or does not look at people during the presentation.	• Sometimes stands up straight and establishes eye contact.	• Stands up straight and establishes eye contact with everyone in the room during the presentation.	• Stands up straight and looks relaxed and confident. Establishes eye contact with everyone in the room.
Volume	• Volume often too soft to be heard by all audience members.	• Volume is loud enough to be heard by all audience members at least 80% of the time.	• Volume is loud enough to be heard by all audience members at least 90% of the time.	• Volume is loud enough to be heard by all audience members throughout the presentation.
Visual Aids	• No visual aid used in presentation or it is illegible.	• Visual aid distracts from content or is illegible.	• Visual aid helps presentation but contains one distracting element or is difficult to read in some places.	• Visual aid used enhances presentation, keeps audience's attention, and is legible.
Organization	• No organization is apparent. • Thoughts do not flow logically. • Presentation is confusing.	• Presentation goes off track in places. • Gaps may exist. • Some of presentation is logical and organized.	• Most of presentation has good organization, is logical, and demonstrates a clear plan.	• Entire presentation is well organized, logical, and demonstrates a clear and complete plan.
Coherency and Flow	• Need to connect ideas to have a flow.	• Most ideas are linked, though some links flawed; pauses may be distracting.	• Presentation flows from one idea to another. • Ideas are linked well.	• Presentation is extremely clear with purpose and logical flow.

Figure 9.6 Science Scoring Rubric: Laboratory Reports

Criteria	1	2	3	4
Question/ Purpose	The purpose of the lab or the question to be answered is not stated or is irrelevant to the investigation.	The purpose of the lab or the question to be answered is partially identified, but it is not stated in a clear manner.	The purpose of the lab or the question to be answered is fully identified, but it is not stated in a clear manner.	The purpose of the lab or the question to be answered is clearly identified and stated.
Experimental Hypothesis	No hypothesis is stated.	Hypothesized relationship between the variables and the predicted results has been stated but is not very reasonable.	Hypothesized relationship between the variables and the predicted results is reasonable.	Hypothesized relationship between the variables and the predicted results is clear and reasonable.
Experimental Design	Experimental design is not relevant to the hypothesis.	Experimental design is relevant to the hypothesis but is not a complete test.	Experimental design is adequate to test the hypothesis but leaves some unanswered questions.	Experimental design is a well-constructed test of the stated hypothesis.
Variables	Variables are not described and lack relevant detail.	Most variables are clearly described with most relevant detail.	All variables are clearly described with most relevant detail.	All variables are clearly described with all relevant detail.
Data	Data are not shown or are inaccurate.	Data are accurately represented in written form, but no graphs or tables are presented.	Data in tables and/or graphs are accurately represented. Graphs and tables are labeled and titled.	Data are represented in professional-looking and accurate tables and/or graphs. Graphs and tables are labeled and titled.
Conclusion	No conclusion is included in the report, or it shows little effort and reflection.	Conclusion includes some of what was learned from the experiment.	Conclusion includes most of the findings that support or do not support the hypothesis and what was learned from the experiment.	Conclusion includes all of the findings that support or do not support the hypothesis and what was learned from the experiment.

and preferences. Wiggins (1992) described authentic assessment this way: "One must please a real audience, make a design work, or achieve an aesthetic effect that causes pride or dismay in the result" (p. 27).

Authentic assessments generally tap into higher levels of thinking and problem-solving abilities. These authentic tasks engage teachers and students in new roles as they plan and learn together. In these more authentic assessments, teachers should consider the following:

- Standards are selected and embedded in the tasks.
- Data collection tools are designed to track progress.
- Students learn processes to gather, analyze, manage, and synthesize information.
- A variety of levels of thinking (per Bloom's taxonomy or others) are tapped.
- Time management and persistence strategies are built in.
- Opportunities to work collaboratively and/or independently are considered.
- Some choice is allowed to accommodate individual interests and preferences.

When designing authentic tasks, students need guidance in planning and managing the process. Figure 9.7 is an example of an organizer that students can use to plan an exhibition. See also Figures 9.8 and 9.9, which are other tools for students to use to get started and plan an authentic project.

A: Adequate Time Is Needed to Practice, Reassess, Try Again, and Ultimately Master Concepts and Skills as Needed

It takes time to rehearse and/or elaborate to achieve long-term retention, whether the rehearsal be declarative or procedural. The brain naturally seeks feedback. All people soon lose interest in a game or other task if they do not see progress from their efforts. Feedback is necessary to encourage continued effort and to adjust behavior and plans. It has been said that a person cannot "fatten a pig by weighing it." Students who have received continuous feedback and coaching from a variety of sources, whether from others or through self-reflection, tend to do better and reach mastery.

Observation

With short instructional periods, teachers get little chance to interact and observe students as they problem-solve and work together. If teachers believe that all learners need feedback, then building in time to give

Figure 9.7 Organizer for Planning an Exhibition

Topic: _____

Expectations

Essential Questions

Secondary Questions I'd Like to Investigate

Figure 9.8 Getting Started: Brainstorm

What Do I Know or Think I Know?	What Do I Want or Need to Know?	Where? How? When Will I Learn It?

Figure 9.9 Planning Guide

Plan	Time Schedule	Notes

How Will I Share?	Resources/Materials

Source: Adapted from Ogle (1986) and Stephen, Gallagher, & Workman (1993).

it is important. Longer class periods allow application time during which teachers can work with individual students on enrichment or remedial tasks. Using sticky notes, teachers can jot down observations during the period and transfer them later to student files. Teachers can also use checklists and observation forms. It is unrealistic, however, to think that one teacher can give adequate feedback to all students in the class, each period. That is why it is so important for teachers to help students develop observation and feedback skills that they can use with others or themselves.

Teachers might use a matrix with students' names across the top and skills listed down one side to track the frequency with which students use particular skills. Teachers can easily observe student skills such as listening attentively, taking turns, using polite voices, and sharing tasks. They can also observe student skill development in areas such as computer use, coordination in physical activities, and organizational procedures.

Cautions in Observation

Be sure that

- skills are carefully identified.
- expectations are clear.
- the observation is not too complex; observe one or two behaviors and only one or two students at a time.
- you get data through two or three observations, as one may not be accurate.
- feedback is nonevaluative; that is, only the facts are given, not a judgment. Judgments should be made by the individual or group, as a response to the feedback, through self-reflection and dialogue.
- rubrics used as tools for giving feedback are clear and understandable.

Figure 9.10 is an example of an observation chart that can be used for data gathering.

I: Intelligence Is Unique to Each Individual

People acquire knowledge, develop competencies, and display or demonstrate understanding in different ways, depending on their unique, individual ways of "knowing." Therefore, teachers should consider the

Figure 9.10 Looks Like, Sounds Like

Skill: _____

Directions: Fill in the "Looks Like" and "Sounds Like" columns with criteria describing the skill to be observed.

Observer: Check off the behaviors you see or hear as you observe the group work together. Note the names of group members who used those behaviors.

Looks Like	Sounds Like

multiple intelligences in designing both learning activities and assessment strategies.

Contracts

To personalize instructional and assessment tasks further and capitalize on students' multiple intelligences, teachers may design contracts to facilitate individualized approaches to learning. The authentic tasks mentioned previously are excellent vehicles to honor students' diverse multiple intelligences profiles and to create options in a contract. Contracts give students choice in the learning process and ownership of designing their own learning. This is highly motivating and tends to generate commitment from students. It allows for creativity, an emotional hook, and elaboration of content for long-term retention.

Teachers have been using forms of contracts for many years. It is one way to work with students who are accomplishing behavioral objectives in an individualized program (Berte, 1975; Knowles, 1986; Tomlinson, 1999; Winebrenner, 1992). A *contract* is a brain-compatible tool used to set goals for student learning. Students vary in interests and abilities, and often a contract can help the learner do the following:

- Have realistic expectations.
- Stretch him- or herself.
- Outline basics required.
- Self-empower.
- Deal with multiple intelligences.
- Capitalize on strengths.
- Ensure success.
- Manage time effectively and efficiently.

In a contract, a basic *core set* of expectations based on standards for all learners is clearly delineated at the onset of the unit. To do this, a teacher must

- outline clearly the content and skills involved in the unit.
- develop criteria for success.
- design the assessment process.
- identify timelines.
- share grading guidelines with students.
- delineate clear expectations.

A contract may include optional topics and activities, such as the following:

- Research or inquiry questions to further extend learning
- Activities for multiple intelligences
  - ○ Presentation in an area of interest
  - ○ Exhibition
  - ○ Project
  - ○ Debate/academic controversy
  - ○ Community outreach/interview
  - ○ Song or rap
  - ○ Narrative or short story
  - ○ Skit or dramatization
  - ○ Role-play or talk show

A contract is clearly mapped out for the student or group of students. Timelines and the core expectations are outlined for all, and students have opportunities to increase success through time management and planning. Opportunity is also provided for negotiation and development of flow—that state in which the learner has a sense of control, feels challenged at an appropriate skill level, receives ongoing feedback, is unconscious of time, and feels intrinsic motivation (Csikszentmihalyi, 1990). Contracts and the negotiation of choice in assessment lessen the chances of students "downshifting," emotionally hijacking the project, or developing a sense of helplessness and anxiety. Figure 9.11 is an example of a contract, and a blackline master of a blank contract form is provided in Figure 9.12.

N: Negotiate Long-Term Retention

Varied learning experiences provide students with memorable moments. Pat Wolfe, an educational consultant noted for her insights into the implications of brain research for classroom practice, reminded teachers that real learning takes place when long-term memory is altered (Wolfe & Sorgen, 1990). The more vivid the experience, the more vivid the memory. Also, location of the learning experience, emotions associated with the learning, and contexts in which the learning occurred all contribute greatly to developing memories. Dialogue, reflection, and metacognition help solidify learnings and facilitate transfer to long-term memory. The use of logs, journals, and portfolios likewise contributes.

Figure 9.11 Contract: War in Iraq

Iraq War Contract

Directions: To help you improve your understanding of the causes of and reactions to the war in Iraq, you may complete the core activities and then choose any optional activities that, when included, will total at least 40 points.

Complete the following contract and hand in by _____

Core Activities That Everyone Will Do	Points
1. Read the chapter in the text and view the documentary video. Fill in the questionnaire. (10)	
2. Using the computer program, create a timeline of events that led to U.S. involvement in the war. (5)	
3. Select one key political leader and chronicle his or her involvement with the war. Present your findings. (10)	
Optional Selections	*Points*
4. Create a photo essay depicting the events that led to U.S. involvement in the war. (10)	
5. Draw a story map or mind map illustrating the contributing factors. (10)	
6. Write a letter to the president and share your views on why you think the United States should or should not be involved in the war. (5)	
7. Compare the music that was popular during three major conflicts in American history and that describe the sentiment of the populace. (5).	
8. Using a Venn diagram, compare and contrast the causes of the Persian Gulf War with the Iraq War. (10)	
Total Points	

_____

Student Signature

_____

Teacher Signature

Figure 9.12 Blank Blackline Master Contract

_____ **Contract**

Directions: To help you improve your understanding of _____, you may complete the core activities and then choose any optional activities that, when included, will total at least _____ points.

Complete the following contract and hand in by _____.

Core Activities That Everyone Will Do	Points
1.	
2.	
3.	
Optional Selections	Points
4.	
5.	
6.	
7.	
8.	
Total Points	

_____

Student Signature

_____

Teacher Signature

Metacognition

Metacognition, the thinking about one's thinking, is a key to being able to access previously used strategies and information and use it in new situations. Teachers may give students the opportunity during the lesson (e.g., 10 minutes of lecture and 2 minutes of reflection and partner talk) or at the conclusion of the lesson to reflect on process, content, or how the new information or skill can be used in the real life of the learner. Strategies such as "Plus, Negative, Interesting" (PNI; de Bono, 1976, 1985) are useful in helping students focus on specific aspects of the material (see Figure 9.13). If students have viewed a video, read an article, or experienced any other learning experience, PNI may be used to reflect and project individual or group ideas.

De Bono (1985) also created the "six thinking hats" activity; students wear the hats metaphorically, or in primary grades, students may wear actual hats as they react to new information or experiences. Individual students or small groups may choose a colored hat, or in a small group, each member may wear a different hat to ensure that all aspects of the topic are explained.

- The *white hat* examines the material or topic to gather data. This is a rational, neutral viewpoint. *(Crystal clear)*
- The *gray hat* examines from the downside and identifies cautions, flaws, errors, risks, and other negative aspects, somewhat like playing the devil's advocate. *(Dark side)*
- The *green hat* examines the situation with an eye to creative opportunities. What are the possibilities, connections, and new approaches? *(Green growth)*
- The *red hat* examines the information and explores the feelings and emotions involved. What intuition or gut feelings surface? *(Heart)*
- The *yellow hat* examines the situation looking for all the positive things associated with this topic. How is this optimistic and beneficial? *(Sunshine)*
- The *blue hat* is the reflective perspective. Those who wear it examine and summarize and draw conclusions from the material. *(Reflective pool)*

In extended blocks, teachers and students have time to reflect on and discuss issues beyond learning them at just enough depth to recall for the

Figure 9.13 Plus, Negative- Interesting (PNI)

P Plus	These are the things that are important . . . This is the upside of . . . This explains . . . Now I know . . . Now I can . . .
N Negative	The downside of this is . . . I'm concerned about . . . What worries me is . . . I'd like to explore . . . further because . . .
I Interesting	That is an interesting idea . . . I never thought of things in that way . . . This is a different way of looking at . . .

test. Time to relate, connect, and reflect is valuable in the learning process so that new information and skills are internalized through metacognitive strategies.

Logs and Journals

These reflective tools have long been used in language arts classrooms to connect learning and clarify the learner's thoughts about a character or idea. Keeping a log or journal also enhances writing skills. In recent times, other subject disciplines have realized the power of logs and journals in the assessment process. Entries may be written, audiotaped, videotaped, put onto a disk, or illustrated with graphic organizers or other visual representations according to individual student interests and preferences. The power of logs and journals is in the reflection and goal setting completed by the individual or group.

Applications

For journal writing, sentence stems are often given to help generate idea flow:

- What really interested me was . . .
- It makes me wonder . . .
- It was puzzling to me . . .
- I enjoyed . . .
- I was not comfortable with . . .
- I'm confused about . . .
- I want to know more about . . .
- The next step for me is . . .
- Other issues I would like to pursue . . .
- I continue to wonder about . . .

PNI or six thinking hats may also serve as a springboard for journal writing. Students can use PNI to reflect in their journals, or they can choose a particular hat (or the teacher can assign one) and wear it as they reflect. For those students who find it difficult to focus, this may be a guide as well as a creative way to stimulate metacognition. Logs generally capture information and track events (see Figure 9.14). Journals are more reflective in relationship to the facts or events. These two activities can be done simultaneously for, respectively, time management and reflection by individuals or small groups while working on a cooperative task.

The prompts for writing in journals/logs may be used with a ticket out (Burz & Marshall, 1998). Students complete tickets out individually at the end of the period to feed back reactions and reflections to the teacher. Students might respond to a question or jot down two things they learned and one question they still have. This allows students to give the teacher valuable information in a "safe" manner, and the teacher can respond to it at the beginning of the next class. Teachers can also use this information when planning next steps in response to students and their needs. If, for example, some students seem to have a firm grasp of the concepts or skill, the teacher may give them a challenging or enriching activity to extend their understanding. Students who are still a little vague may need more rehearsal or more specific instruction or coaching.

Portfolio Reflection

Portfolios are invaluable reflection and goal-setting assessment tools. Initially, the teacher must decide how to manage and store them, what to

Figure 9.14 Combination Journal/Log

Log Entry		Journal Reflections	
Date	Process	Reactions	Tomorrow I will . . .

include, and how to assess or evaluate them. Teachers who have used portfolios as assessment tools realize, however, that the power of the portfolio is in the reflection time.

Students can use graphic organizers to facilitate reflection (see Figure 9.15). Other visual organizers include a Venn diagram, which students use to compare a previous piece of work with a more recent example; a sequence chart students use to track processes so that they can replicate them in other situations; and a mind map on which students can draw symbols and representations of things that were significant in the learning.

> If we expect our children to make the transition to the highest level of learning, their environment and their role models must view downtime, or quiet time, as a positive experience and a welcome respite from the world's increasing deluge of sensory stimulation. (Burns, 1992, p. 73)

In longer periods or blocks, students and teachers have more time to slow down and not just cover the content but come to understand it deeply. They share ongoing feedback, which can propel the learner into the next phase of the learning process. More time also allows students and teachers to build a relationship. Relationships provide valuable connections that are often lacking in some students' lives. Relationships also influence students' perceptions of content.

Because learners have different interests and strengths and thus prefer a variety of ways to learn as well as to demonstrate their achievement, longer periods of time enable teachers and students to dialogue and set goals through reflection and metacognition. Assessment is not "teach, test, and hope for the best" in a frantic time frame but rather is an ongoing process of practice, feedback, and goal setting. Unlike the movie critic who judges and awards symbols such as stars or thumbs-up based on just his or her personal judgment or preference, classrooms should provide fertile ground for differentiated student growth and continuous improvement. In safe environments with a variety of engaging tasks and constructive, thoughtful feedback, students can take risks and practice and develop competencies they can take with them for life.

Figure 9.15 Graphic Organizer to Facilitate Reflection

Log Entry

Date	Process	Reflections and Next Steps	

Strategies

Stems for reflection:
- What I learned from this project is . . .
- What I want to focus on next is . . .
- I included this because . . .
- I would change . . . if I did this again.
- I now know that . . .

This _____ made sense to me because _____.

The next time I try a _____, I will _____.

10 Using Assessment to Adjust, Compact, and Group

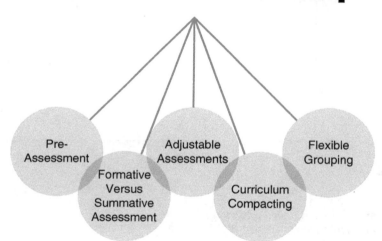

Pre-Assessment

Formative Versus Summative Assessment

Adjustable Assessments

Curriculum Compacting

Flexible Grouping

We used to plan a lesson by choosing the content and standard that students should *know*, *understand*, or be able to *do* (KUDOs). However, even though students are at the same grade level, they do not have the same degree of mastery of knowledge and skills from the previous year of learning. Also, not every student has the same background and experience and so is not necessarily as knowledgeable or able in every topic or skill as other students. We also know that students have been socialized in the digital age and thus have many different interests and attention spans. Despite all this, we often force them to endure the same lesson (in the same format) whether they already know the content or have no idea what is going on. This is why we need to make adjustments in our lesson planning. Assessment is a key tool that informs us how to adjust.

PRE-ASSESSMENT

Assessing student knowledge prior to the learning experience helps the teacher find out

- the prior knowledge of students;
- their level of understanding related to the standards, objectives, concepts, and skills;
- what needs to be included in the unit of study;
- what needs to be reviewed, retaught, or extended;
- what interests and preferences they have; and
- what kinds of flexible groups to set up (T: *total*, A: *alone*, P: *partner*, S: *small* group).

When teaching with high achievement as a goal, it is important to assess learners to find out what they already know from their prior learning and experiences. By doing a pre-assessment of knowledge, teachers can plan curriculum and design instruction with more precision.

Some teachers claim that pre-assessment takes too much time to prepare, administer, and analyze, taking time from the learning process. However, using formative assessment prior to teaching allows us to use the learning time more efficiently.

Written tests/quizzes are one form of pre-assessment. Others include the following:

- Four corners
- Graffiti placemat
- ABC assessments
- Graphic organizers
- Word web
- Fishbones
- Tickets out
- Quick writes
- Anticipation guides
- Surveys
- Individual K-W-L or G-E-L
- 3-2-1
- SMART boards
- Whiteboards

- Clicker technology
- Effective questioning
- Conferences
- Portfolios

FORMATIVE VERSUS SUMMATIVE ASSESSMENT

Most of the last century we focused on summative (evaluative) assessment, grading and ranking students with reference to criteria or norms. However, we have learned that formative assessment shows more promise for student growth and improvement. "Formative assessment is a planned process in which teachers or students use assessment-elicited evidence of students' status to adjust their ongoing instructional procedures or by students to adjust their current learning tactics" (Popham, 2008, p. 6). Figure 10.1 compares formative and summative assessment.

We have learned that feedback is the "breakfast of champions." Athletes get better at their skills and ultimately the game when coaches

Figure 10.1 Comparing Formative and Summative Assessment

Assessment for Learning (Formative Assessment)	Assessment of Learning (Summative Assessment)
Check to see which knowledge and skills have been learned or need further rehearsal so as to target what to do next.	Check to see what has been learned at the end of the learning time or unit of study.
Provides information to the teacher and students about what progress has been made.	In the form of grades or marks, reports to the broader community as required.
Provides data regularly, which can be used to set goals and make adjustments in the learning cycle.	Is presented periodically.
Specific descriptive feedback, rather than grades, targets successes and identifies improvement needed.	Given in the form of grades, scores, and/or marks.
Focuses on growth from previous trials.	Usually criterion-referenced with respect to standards or expectations or norm-referenced, comparing student to student.
Students are actively involved.	Often done to students without their involvement; students are usually passive recipients of the assessment.

give them specific descriptive feedback on what they are doing well, what areas need attention, and specific suggestions for improvement. Olympians get a score at the final event, not in the practice and coaching phase.

Formative assessments allow teacher and students to change or modify their learning tactics in order to understand concepts or develop skills better. We long ago learned that "saying it louder and slower" does not work as a second choice. Fortunately, we have in our repertoire multiple ways of rehearsing information and skills, including the tactics in Figure 7.1. Some learners need only a few rehearsals to grasp ideas or develop skills, whereas some may need many practice trials and interactions with the material.

Another important consideration is that the classroom be a climate conducive to trial and error for all students. Recall the principle: fair isn't always equal, and equal isn't always fair. Students know that they differ in strengths, abilities, interests, and preferences, and as "coaches" we want to help them accept that we are all different in how, when, and what we learn. Building a collaborative learning community in the classroom helps all learners feel safe and be able to take risks. They will understand and become more accepting of different levels of complexity or challenge across tasks and assignments and different choices of ways to learn and rehearse new material and skills.

ADJUSTABLE ASSIGNMENTS

Adjustable assignments that are based on formative assessment data allow teachers to help students focus on essential skills and key concepts while recognizing that they may be at different levels of readiness. Different learners may handle different levels of complexity or abstraction. Although an assignment is adjusted for different groups of learners, the standards, concepts, and content of the assignment have the same focus for all students, and each student has the opportunity to develop essential skills and understanding at his or her appropriate level of challenge. Flexible activities ensure that students explore ideas at their level, while building on prior knowledge and experiencing incremental growth.

Levels may be adjusted by readiness so that same-readiness-level students work together or do the same task at the appropriate level of complexity. Alternatively, the tasks may be adjusted by multiple intelligences choices, and students choose their tasks. Or students may be grouped heterogeneously by readiness so that each group has some "spark plugs" to ignite those students at a lower readiness level.

The Need for Adjustable Assignments

Using adjusted assignments allows students to begin learning where they are and to work on challenging and worthwhile tasks. If we were growing flowers and some of the seeds had sprouted and were ready to flower, we would not pull them out by the roots and make them start again from seed. We, of course, would give the plants that were advanced in their growth the appropriate amount of light, water, and food that they needed to flower, and we would nurture the seedlings that were just sprouting to accelerate their growth. Adjusting assignments allows for reinforcement or extension of concepts based on student readiness, learning styles, and/or multiple intelligences preferences.

Teachers need to consider the degree of complexity of learning tasks so that they will be challenging but not overwhelming. Doing so establishes the state of "flow" (Csikszentmihalyi, 1990), the condition that exists when learners are so engaged, excited about learning, challenged, and nurtured by appropriate feedback that they are oblivious to anything else. Students are at their most productive and most creative in this state:

> People seem to concentrate best when the demands on them are a bit greater than usual, and they are able to give more than usual. If there is too little demand on them, people are bored. If there is too much for them to handle, they get anxious. Flow occurs in that delicate zone between boredom and anxiety. (Goleman cited in Csikszentmihalyi, 1990, p. 4)

Adjusting assignments to the level of the student also increases the chances of success for each learner because that success is within reach, and ultimately success will be highly motivating. Adjusting assignments also decreases the chances of "downshifting" and the sense of helplessness that students feel when a challenge is beyond their capabilities.

Implementing Adjustable Assignments

Initially, as in any planning process, the concepts, skills, and content that will be the focus of the activity are identified and aligned with targeted standards and expectations. Methods of pre-assessment (quizzes, journal entries, class discussions, learning profiles, etc.) allow teachers to gather data to determine the prior knowledge of students about the new content or the skill that is targeted for learning. The pre-assessment data are compiled. Then the key standards and concepts to be taught during the unit are determined. The teacher decides what should be taught to the total class and how it will be presented. The appropriate places to teach these concepts and/or skills are determined. Finally, assignments are adjusted to meet the needs of learners based on their present knowledge or skill levels. The teacher will answer the following questions when making decisions about these assignments:

- What content does each of the groups already know?
- What does each group need to learn?
- What strategies should be used to facilitate the learning of each portion of the content?
- What is the most effective way to group for each activity?
- What assessment tools will be used so that students will be accountable?
- Is the plan meeting the individual needs of students?

Figure 10.2 shows a worksheet the teacher can use to plan flexible assignments. After giving the pre-assessment, the teacher analyzes the data and plots them on the chart in Section A. Then the teacher considers what the students still need to know and be able to do to extend their learning. The teacher fills in the B part of the grid with a learning that is suitably challenging and engaging in order to bring those learners to the next level. It may be a lesson, activity, task, or assignment. Students may do different assignments independently or in pairs or in small groups, thus leaving the teacher free to interact and facilitate new content or processes with other groups of students. The teacher may choose from a variety of curriculum approaches, such as projects, centers, integration, or problem-based learning.

Here is an example that is typical of what teachers face every time they start planning for all of their students.

Example: Spanish Class

The teacher gave a variety of instructions to students during the previous week and noted which students had an extensive vocabulary of directional language, who had some, and who had very little (see Figure 10.3). Section A shows what the three groups of students knew and were able to do in relation to the standard and content. Section B shows what needed to be done to extend the learning for that group.

The High Degree of Mastery group (only four students) went online and found street maps of Buenos Aires and Madrid. They wrote directions to areas or points of interest and produced posters advertising the attributes of that location.

The Approaching Mastery group designed a board game that used the vocabulary of giving directions. They produced interesting adaptations of board games with which they were familiar and wrote task cards for the games using vocabulary beyond what they had used in the past.

Figure 10.2 Using Adjustable Assignment Grids

Adjustable Assignment

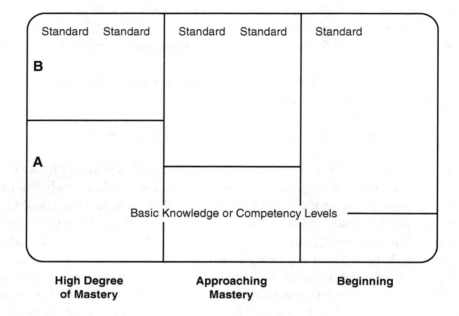

This is not the number of students but the level of competency related to the standard.

Standards

Content

The Beginners group worked in pairs to give one another directions to various areas in the school. They drew task cards and were able to direct one another to the cafeteria, office, or computer lab using Spanish. They then participated in a game similar to Twister, in which they spun a wheel and followed the directions given.

More levels of readiness may be identified and adjusted if needed, but when beginning this process, three levels may be complicated enough for the teacher to manage.

Figure 10.3 Adjustable Assignments: Spanish Class

Standard Standard **B**	Standard Standard	Standard
A Students have a mastery of terms including *right, left, turning, crossing, across from, go back, behind, in front of,* and *next to* . . .	Students have an ability to give an understanding of the basic terms *forward, backward, right,* and *left.*	These students are able to give simple commands such as *go, stop, left,* and *right.*
High Degree of Mastery	**Approaching Mastery**	**Beginning**

Standards

To be able to communicate in daily situations

Content

Giving and following directions

Example: Social Science Class

Figure 10.4 shows a grid used in a social science class. As a pre-assessment, the teacher used a ticket out on which each student did a quick write to explain what he or she knew about the Bill of Rights. Section A shows what the students already know, and section B is the plan to fill the gap.

A blank grid in Figure 10.5 is provided for your use in adjusting levels of readiness based on pre-assessment.

CURRICULUM COMPACTING

Curriculum compacting is a strategy first shared by Joe Renzulli (1992) of the University of Connecticut (see also Tomlinson, 1999, 2001). It facilitates extended learning for the student who is very capable and knowledgeable in a particular topic in a subject area, maximizing the effective use of time for this learner.

Many students, because of prior experience, interests, and opportunities, may bring to the topic existing knowledge and skills. These may have been acquired through reading, travel, or personal interest about a topic or from a mentor or role model who has had an influence on the learner. For these students, compacting may be used on occasion in order to enrich their curriculum, enhance and stretch their thinking, and help them develop into more self-directed learners. In many classrooms, where teaching to the middle is the norm, some learners are bored as they "repeat history." Compacting/enriching may be used with high-end or advanced learners identified through pre-assessment.

How to Plan for Compacting

Phase 1

In this phase, after an exploratory session in which students are able to access prior knowledge and discuss their initial concepts, a pre-assessment is given.

This may be in the form of a

- pretest;
- conference where the learner shares knowledge and understanding about the topic; and/or
- portfolio presentation in which students show evidence of their comprehension and skill levels.

Phase 2

After the pre-assessment, the teacher analyzes the data and identifies what the student already has mastered and what the student still needs to learn.

This additional knowledge or skill may be acquired by

- joining the total class group for that concept or information;
- independent study;
- homework assignments;

Figure 10.4 Adjustable Assignments: Social Science Class With Part B Completed

Standard Standard **B** Impact	Standard Standard Historical foundation Personal relevance	Standard What is it? Basic elements How might it help us today?
A Are knowledgeable about the Declaration of Independence, Constitiution, and the Bill of Rights.	Know some aspects of the Bill but not its significance.	Are aware of the term *Bill of Rights* but not its impact or content.
High Degree of Mastery	**Approaching Mastery**	**Beginning**

Standards

Students are able to describe the basic ideas set forth in the Declaration of Independence, Constitution, and Bill of Rights.

Content

The Fourth Amendment

- collaborating with a mentor or learning buddy in or outside school; and/or
- online learning.

Phase 3

Once the missing pieces have been added, the student may choose or be offered one or several in combination of the following:

Figure 10.5 Adjustable Assignments: Blank Template

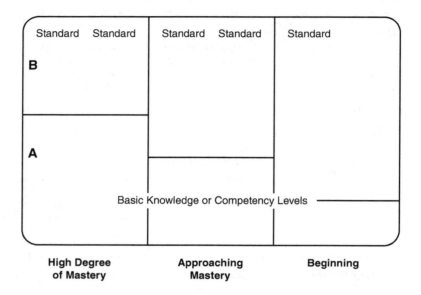

Standards

Content

- An investigation or research project
- A complex problem to solve
- A service-learning opportunity
- A project
- A negotiated contract
- A special assignment

These assignments facilitate the challenge of applying knowledge and skill in a practical and/or creative way. Robert Sternberg (1996), a noted psychologist, defined *successful intelligence* as including the aspects of being analytical, practical, and creative, not just as knowing.

Sternberg says successfull intelligent people

- are self-motivated, independent, and reasonably self-confident.
- can control their impulses and delay gratification.
- initiate things, complete tasks, and follow through.
- don't procrastinate and know when to persevere.
- translate their thoughts into effective products and actions.
- know and make the most of their abilities.
- are not afraid to risk failure and accept fair blame.
- seek to surmount any personal difficulties.
- can focus on both the large problem and the minute details.
- balance creative, analytical, and practical thinking.

The grid in Figure 10.6 may be helpful in planning an enrichment task. This chart shows how students can become more practical, analytical, and creative with a concept to deepen their thinking. In this way, learners enhance their understanding and obtain an added perspective on the subject matter.

Compacting/enrichment is a strategy often used with academically gifted or talented students to enhance their curriculum. It may be done in a pullout or partial-pullout model or orchestrated in the classroom with the subject teacher. If students are pulled out, they should not miss other subject areas of study that they have not mastered. Also, teachers must be sure that students really do have full mastery of the concept, not just surface-level knowledge. Students should not be required to complete the regular classroom assignments in the subject for which they have completed the compacted curriculum.

What Does It Look Like?

Some forms of compacting/enrichment take into consideration that some students have ample prior knowledge or experience to warrant a full semester or grade-level subject advancement. Examples are the Spanish student who skips first-year Spanish because she is fluent in the language, the ninth grader who joins the tenth grade for Spanish each day, and the student who has demonstrated such proficiency in Pre-Algebra that he skips Algebra 1 to start Algebra 2.

Agendas

The teacher may want to have students develop an agenda to keep track of time and tasks (see Figure 10.7). Students fill in the date and the

Figure 10.6 Chart for Planning Enrichment Tasks

Standard		
Content		
Suggestions		
Creative	Analytical	Practical
• Use the materials to explain . . . • Find an amusing way to show . . . • Create a new way to say . . . • Show how it could be used to . . . • Make connections to other things that show . . .	• Show parts of . . . and how they work. • Make a diagram to show . . . • Explain the key parts of . . . and why they are important. • Write a step-by-step plan to . . . • Describe why . . . works that way.	• Show how you could use this to solve a problem. • Explain why this is important. • Develop a plan to use this information. • Find out how someone uses this information.

task column of the agenda for the class, day, or unit of study. After each task is completed, they detail the progress in the log column and then chronicle their reflections in the next column. Each student and the teacher then conference and sign off in the last column.

Students may also use double-duty log/journals (see Figure 10.8) to monitor steps and record reflections as they work on the assignment. This ongoing assessment helps both teacher and students clearly see the successes, progress, and needs throughout the assignment. It helps the students keep track of their time, reflect on their work, and set goals for the next step.

Adjusting and compacting are two techniques that strategic teachers use to help students feel comfortable and capable in their learning. Most instructional strategies can be used to adjust learning to meet the needs of the differentiated classroom.

Figure 10.7 Personal Agenda to Keep Track of Time and Tasks

Date	Task	Accomplished	Reflections	Next Steps

Figure 10.8 Double-Duty Log/Journal

Date and Task	Completed	Reflections

FLEXIBLE GROUPING

Finding the Right Size

Flexible grouping is often needed to facilitate differentiated instruction. Everyone has strong and weak areas of ability and interest. Students need to be placed in groups that maximize their instructional time based on their performance levels. Grouping flexibility allows students to move according to their demonstrated performance, interests, and knowledge base levels and to meet their instructional, emotional, and personal needs. If a group of students gets along socially, they will usually meet the instructional expectations.

When the teacher uses each component of TAPS (*T*otal, *A*lone, *P*artner, *S*mall group) in planning, students' individual social needs have a greater chance of being met. These grouping methods can be used where they fit best in the classroom. Some students can work well in all of these ways, but every learner has preferences (Goleman, 1995).

A person who is very strong in his or her intrapersonal intelligence processes may prefer to solve problems by working alone. Such a student is able to solve the problem independently and does not see the need to work with a group. Often this student will get really quiet in a group situation and become more metacognitive in order to process the learning.

Other students will be very strong in interpersonal intelligence. Sometimes called "social butterflies," they feel the need to talk about concepts to understand them fully. They prefer to work with others rather than alone. These students bring empathy and harmony to the group.

Groups need the following:

- Ample space to work
- Clear directions and procedures
- Rules and guidelines
- Individual roles assigned for group responsibilities
- A time frame assigned for on-task work
- A structure to tap into all members' strengths

Some students learn best while working alone; some work better when grouped with others. Flexible grouping offers students options designed to tap into different readiness levels, interests, talents, and learning modalities. A high-quality pre-assessment helps decide which type of grouping will be the most effective for that particular part of the learning. Flexible grouping is ever present and continuously changing when planning differentiated instruction.

11 Technology Integration

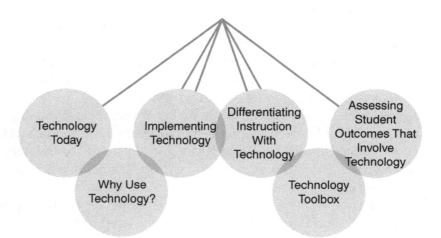

TECHNOLOGY TODAY

The world that today's graduates will enter is very different from the one many teachers grew up in. We are living in a global society that has a whole new set of challenges. Science and technology are changing the world (Stewart, 2007). Thomas Friedman (1997) in *The World Is Flat* described how the "wiring of the world" and the digitization of production since 1998 are making it possible for people to do increasing amounts of work anywhere and anytime. Will Richardson, a guru on the use of web tools in the classroom, has written the extremely useful book *Blogs, Wikis, Podcasts, and Other Powerful Web Tools for Classrooms* (2010). Richardson quoted Marc Prensky, an education theorist, regarding today's students who have been using technology all of their lives: "This online life is a whole lot bigger than just the Internet. This online life has become an entire strategy for how to live, survive and thrive in the twenty-first century where cyberspace is a way of life" (p. 7).

Because of their immersion in technology, many of today's students do not learn the same way that previous generations of students have learned. Educators preparing to use technology in today's classrooms need to be sensitive to how students use technology. Globalization of our communication networks and business marketplace will require graduates to make decisions using a wide knowledge of the world. Graduates will be required to think creatively, work in teams, multitask, and use a variety of technological resources.

Although society is experiencing rapid technological changes, educational institutions are having difficulty keeping up. Despite schools' evident commitment to technology, some research indicates that teachers continue to use computers to maintain their current teaching methods rather than to promote innovative practices (Cuban, 2001). Prensky (2001) uses the term *Digital Immigrants* to describe people who were not born into the digital world but have learned how to use computer technology later in their lives. Most educators today were born before the majority of the technology currently used in the classroom was invented. The World Wide Web is less than 20 years old. Prensky writes that Digital Immigrants have a tendency to use current technology piecemeal, in a disjointed fashion, as compared to most Digital Natives. However, Digital Immigrants, because of their maturity, often use technology more effectively in educational and business settings.

Educators have not yet tapped the potential of technology to enhance learning in many ways. Some schools that use block schedules have found that the extended class periods provide an increased opportunity to integrate technology into the curriculum. Teachers can use the longer preparation time to prepare interactive lecture outlines using presentation software. They can also plan project-based learning and increase their personal use of technology as a management tool. Students benefit by having longer periods to work on individual or group projects.

This chapter addresses the following questions:

- Why use technology in the classroom?
- How can a teacher effectively implement technology in the classroom?
- How can teachers use technology to differentiate instruction?
- What technology tools are available for educators?
- How can we assess student work that uses technology?

WHY USE TECHNOLOGY?

Students today live in a digital world, which means schools must adapt instruction to complement learning in a technological environment. Educators today have the opportunity and the responsibility to utilize research-based, technology-enabled practices to thrill, to inspire, and to capture the imagination of our students. Integrating technology can create environments that foster deeper cognitive development through inquiry, real and relevant project-based learning, and differentiated instruction. The strength of technology is that it provides an excellent platform where students can collect information in multiple formats and then organize, link, and discover relationships among facts and events. An array of tools for acquiring information and for thinking and expression allows more students more ways to enter the learning enterprise successfully and to live productive lives in the global, digital, and information-based future they will face (Statham & Torell, 1996).

As technology advances, the need for teachers to make the best use of these new tools requires a paradigm shift from traditional methods of instruction to student-centered approaches. As schools move from traditional schedules to block schedules, some teachers find that reforming instruction is inevitable. Research shows a relationship between educational reform and using a range of instructional technologies (Means, 1994). The following are examples of educational reform features:

- Heterogeneous grouping
- Interactive modes of instruction
- Student exploration
- Collaborative work
- The teacher's role as a facilitator
- Authentic and multidisciplinary tasks
- Performance-based assessment

Implementing technology can help transform a traditional classroom into one that uses a constructivist model. In this context, students take charge of their own learning and learn to think critically while they work in collaboration. Technology provides many new opportunities for students. Means (1994) stated:

> Reformers argue that all students should have the opportunity to practice *advance skills* within the context of tasks that are personally meaningful and challenging to students. . . . The fact the tasks will be more complex suggests that longer blocks of time will be

required to work on them, again conflicting with the notion of fixed, short periods of time for distinct subject areas. (p. 6)

Block schedules provide longer periods for teachers to collaborate on planning interdisciplinary activities that integrate technology. Students who engage in complex tasks using technology change roles, evolving from passive learners to active learners. Following block schedule implementation, some teachers find that using technology affects students in many ways. Students have been observed spending more time on-task, their motivation toward learning has increased, they have shown more pride in their work, and their computer skills have increased, as has overall student performance. Teachers find that they are no longer the center of attention but adopt a new role as facilitator in which they move from group to group, suggesting ways to facilitate the students' search for knowledge, guiding students to new resources, checking timelines, and monitoring student progress.

Technology can positively affect teachers in many ways as well. Some teachers have increased their use of technology in both classroom instruction and classroom management. In addition, teachers create lessons by using current information, as well as by increasing communication between school and home. Increased teacher collaboration within schools is one of many benefits of technology integration. The following list of reasons to use technology, written with the student's perspective in mind, is drawn from the experiences of teachers who have successfully integrated technology. Technology

- develops higher-level thinking by using software designed to teach problem-solving skills.
- increases student responsibility by requiring them to take charge of their own learning through direct exploration and expression.
- engages students in meaningful, authentic tasks.
- promotes student learning.
- creates more opportunities for students to develop multiple intelligences: bodily/kinesthetic, verbal/linguistic, interpersonal, intrapersonal, musical/rhythmic, visual/spatial, logical/mathematical, and naturalistic.
- increases student motivation: students demonstrate more perseverance in solving problems.
- increases collaboration among students as a consequence of cooperative work and peer tutoring.
- increases student self-esteem fostered by success.
- provides more opportunities to display student work.

- increases students' computer skills, thus preparing students for the world after school.
- increases student use of outside resources.
- provides students with a medium to integrate subject areas.
- exposes students to another learning method when teachers facilitate, rather than direct, instruction.
- increases student achievement when it is implemented appropriately.

IMPLEMENTING TECHNOLOGY

Classroom teachers have much to consider as they plan for technology integration. Like any good tool, its use is only as good as the user. Effective teachers use technology in an organized way and develop quality lesson plans that align with school improvement plans and curriculum content standards. Technology planning also requires the teacher to ask—and answer—the following questions:

- Does the plan take into account any district "acceptable use guidelines"?
- Can I find grants and other funding methods to help pay for classroom technology?
- What equipment at my site is available and how often?
- How proficient am I in using technology?
- To what extent are my students proficient in using technology?
- How much time do students need to complete the activity being planned?
- How do I know that the technology chosen is effective and of good quality?

Answering these types of questions can be overwhelming to teachers who are just beginning to use technology. The vast number of products and information available can be challenging to wade through. Teachers need to be selective in the beginning. They need to work with the technology with which they are comfortable. Listed below are tips from teachers who have integrated technology.

- *Survey students to identify their computer skills.* Students come to the classroom with varying degrees of computer experience. Survey results are helpful in determining the type of activity to assign so that students can apply computer skills in meaningful ways. The survey may include questions like "Do you have access to a computer after school?" "Do you know how to save a document?" or "Have you ever used a web browser?" The questions should be framed around the skills students need to complete the activities planned. Figure 11.1 shows an example of a checklist/survey that can be given to students in order to determine their level of technological expertise.

- *Use survey results to assign project groups.* By building groups with prior knowledge of computer skills, the opportunity for peer tutoring naturally augments the group learning process.

- *Use survey results to assign "tech buddies."* Pairing students who are more technologically advanced with those who are less experienced can be very effective.

- *Start simply.* Use only the technologies with which you are most comfortable. Integrate them into a lesson that has been successful in the past.

- *Identify which technology skill students will need to complete the assignments.* An example is basic word processing and insertion of a graphic or picture.

- *Evaluate carefully each lesson in which technology is used.* Document what worked well and what did not. Think of any revisions that could be made for future use.

- *Draw diagrams showing how to connect equipment correctly.* Laminate them. These can be very useful when equipment has to be moved.

- *Collaborate with other teachers whenever possible.* Block schedules often create common planning times for those teachers who teach the same courses. Teachers can take advantage of this and use the time to plan projects that authentically use technology.

- *Back up all work.* If the computer fails for any reason, stored information may be lost. The rule of thumb is to back up or copy any data or projects you do not want to re-create from scratch. Some school districts let teachers back up their work onto a server. If this is not an option, use an external hard drive.

At times, teachers find it necessary to incorporate teaching computer skills directly into the curriculum. By letting the curriculum drive the technology, some teachers will use content to teach the computer skills they believe are necessary. For example, assigning a single-page individual project related to the current topic of discussion can provide the opportunity for students to demonstrate their current technological skills as well

Figure 11.1 Basic Technology Skills Checklist

Student Name: _____

- ☐ Can identify computer hardware.
- ☐ Can turn on a computer.
- ☐ Can shut down Windows properly.
- ☐ Can move the mouse pointer and make it go where I want it to go.
- ☐ Can click and drag a mouse.
- ☐ Can use the keyboard.
- ☐ Can physically adjust the monitor.
- ☐ Can use an educational software program when given a sequence of steps to follow.
- ☐ Can move and resize windows.
- ☐ Can use menus and toolbars.
- ☐ Can use scroll bars.
- ☐ Can use tutorials and/or educational software with minimal assistance.
- ☐ Can explain the difference between a program and a document.
- ☐ Can start a program by double-clicking an icon.
- ☐ Can start a program from the program manager/start menu.
- ☐ Can open a document using a word processing program.
- ☐ Can save a document using a word processing program.
- ☐ Can close a document using a word processing program.
- ☐ Can create a document using a word processing program.
- ☐ Can format text within a word processing document.
- ☐ Can edit text within a word processing document.
- ☐ Can print a word processing document.
- ☐ Can open a spreadsheet.
- ☐ Can save a spreadsheet to the hard drive or a disk.
- ☐ Can close a spreadsheet.
- ☐ Can create a simple spreadsheet.
- ☐ Can print a spreadsheet.
- ☐ Can enter data into a spreadsheet.
- ☐ Can open the Internet and type a web address in a search engine.
- ☐ Can open a PowerPoint presentation.
- ☐ Can create a PowerPoint presentation.
- ☐ Can insert graphics into documents and PowerPoint presentations.
- ☐ Can use e-mail as a communication tool.
- ☐ Can add an attachment to an e-mail.

as learn new ones. These skills could be inserting a picture, object, or clip art into a page of a word processing document (see Figure 11.2). Peer tutoring can be a useful strategy in which students with good technological skills can help those students who lack those skills. Students can also research their topics using resources on the Internet. Each student may use the computer to write a paragraph discussing his or her assigned topic. The teacher may give specific directions—for example, to use a specific font and size for the paragraphs; to give their work titles, which have to be centered, boldfaced, and in a larger-size font than the main body of text; to insert an object such as a graph, clip art, or picture that relates to the assigned topics. Students could later share their "one pagers." Teachers can model the required skills for students at the beginning of the lesson.

DIFFERENTIATING INSTRUCTION WITH TECHNOLOGY

Differentiating instruction is an approach to teaching and learning that provides multiple options for students to gather information and make sense of ideas and concepts. Instructional approaches should be adapted to accommodate the individual and diverse needs of the students in the classroom. Doing so allows teachers to maximize each student's potential. Technology offers many tools that can assist teachers in varying strategies and outcomes. Pre-assessing students' technological skills will determine at what level of complexity the tasks should be. See Figure 11.3.

Some school districts build competency matrices in their technology plans to assess students' technical skills. These are useful instruments for both students and teachers. Students can use them to track their own progress and incorporate them into their electronic portfolios. Teachers can use them as a guide for planning for differentiating instruction. Teachers can assign activities that will challenge the students to enhance their skills, while at the same time addressing the content that they need to know that aligns with the standards and curriculum. See Figure 11.4.

Assessing students' technology skills allows teachers to choose projects that will both challenge the student and allow the student to learn new skills. Assessing student skills on a regular basis will benefit both the teacher and student. Competency matrixes are one way to accomplish this task, and the teacher and student can complete these together. Allowing students to self-assess their skill set will provide them ownership of the learning process.

When designing differentiated lessons, it will be necessary to vary the learning activities or strategies that provide appropriate methods for the

Figure 11.2 Template E-Sheet

Internet Research E-Sheet

Name:

Date:

Topic:

URL:

[Insert image here.]

Research Question 1

Research Question 2

Research Question 3

[Insert graphic.]

List Three New Things You Learned

1.

2.

3.

Figure 11.3 Differentiating Instruction

Technology	
Content/Topic	**Process/Activities**
Pre-Assessment Surveys	Databases Spreadsheets Word Processing
Computer Skills Survey	Digital Photography PowerPoint Presentations Podcasts
Technology Competency Matrix	
Pre-Designed Templates	Electronic Field Trips Blogs/Wikis
Product	**Environment**
Vary Levels of Complexity Choices	Learning Styles Grouping
Alternative Product Ideas	Compacting Curriculum
Can Be Shared With Small and Large Audiences	Build on Prior Knowledge
Assessment	Equipment Internet Software

Figure 11.4 Competency Skills Matrix

	B	D	A
Keyboarding			
• Practice throughout the curriculum.			
Database and Spreadsheets: Master Microsoft Excel			
• Develop various spreadsheets.			
• Interpret and use data within spreadsheet.			
• Manipulate columns and rows to communicate information effectively in a spreadsheet.			
Presentations: Master Microsoft PowerPoint			
• Develop PowerPoint using various media sources.			
• Use different slide formats and transitions.			
• Use different forms of media effects.			
• PowerPoint slideshow conveys information appropriately to intended audience.			
Research Strategies			
• Use preexisting databases to collect research.			
• Brainstorm possible topics and narrow the focus by asking questions that identify a "driving question."			
• Develop a search strategy using keywords that define the topic.			
• Learn strategies for online searching that aid in the management and movement of data.			

• Explain and use online resources that are appropriate for the learner and the topic.					
• Organize and analyze information in order to draw conclusions and implications based on the online investigation.					
• Utilize other print and nonprint sources as necessary.					
• Produce a product using online sources combined with other resources.					
• Evaluate search results, making a decision about accuracy of the data and reformulating the search if necessary.					
Online Communications					
• Learn to evaluate a website.					
• Become familiar with Internet procedure.					
• Practice e-mail skills to communicate with the online community.					
• Learn and model ethical, legal, and responsible behavior in the online community.					
Skills B = *Beginning*. Student has just begun to learn this skill. D = *Developing*. Student is working toward attaining this skill. A = *Accomplished*. Student shows evidence of skill mastery.					

student to explore the concepts. For example, a student may use a PowerPoint to display his or her comprehension of the concepts covered, and varying the complexity of the PowerPoint slideshow can allow for different levels of student reasoning skills.

Many technology products allow students to create evidence of their learning. One aspect of differentiation is to build in choices for students. Students working above grade level may be asked to produce work that requires higher-level thinking skills, and those working below grade level may have reduced expectations. A tic-tac-toe strategy allows students to select three assignments by choosing one box from each row (see Figure 11.5). All students will use the Internet to gather information, but their end products will vary.

Figure 11.5 Tic-Tac-Toe Strategy

Paper Product	Collaboration	Multimedia
Pamphlet Create a pamphlet that contains information on a genetic disease. Be sure to include the inheritance patterns and the probability factors for three generations.	**Blog** Find a blog that discusses genetics or a genetic disease. Post three questions and record the responses to your questions.	**PowerPoint** Create a PowerPoint presentation showing the structure and function of plant and animal cells.
Poster Design a wanted poster for a specific type of mutation that causes a disease. Include graphics and diagrams and an explanation of how the mutation occurred.	**Project** Create an online project that lets you collect information and statistics on several human traits (minimum 5).	**Digital Slide Show** Create a digital slide showing tools used by genetic counselors. Be sure to include examples of pedigree charts and how they can influence human decisions.
E-Sheet Create an Electronic Sheet, using the template provided, of the work of Gregor Mendel. Be sure to include a picture and graphic and place them in the boxes provided.	**WebQuest** Locate a WebQuest that covers the current class topic. Once approved by the teacher, complete the WebQuest and document any information you learn from this activity.	**Podcast** Create a podcast to show how the work of Gregor Mendel has influenced today's knowledge of genetics. Provide specific examples of new technologies, such as recombinant DNA.

Technology can be an invaluable tool for teachers to use to accommodate students' diverse learning styles when combined with Gardner's (1983) nine multiple intelligences. Each of the multiple intelligences can be integrated with technology in many ways. Examples of these are shown in Figure 11.6.

TECHNOLOGY TOOLBOX

Videos

Videos can easily be integrated into classroom instruction and assist in differentiating instruction. There are many benefits to using videos. Videos can take students on field trips inside the human body or on an exploration of the solar system. Students who may not have the opportunity to travel can visit countries around the world. Videos can also be a means to present complex concepts through animation and three-dimensional images.

Teachers who use videos effectively can reach students with a variety of learning styles, engaging them in the learning process.

Applications

Here are some ways videos can be used:

- Videos can introduce a new topic or be an anticipatory set.
- Video clips can be embedded into PowerPoint presentations, accommodating visual learners.
- Videos can provide a common experience, which can generate classroom discussions.
- Videos can allow students to practice critical viewing skills and evaluating multimedia.
- To check for understanding, the teacher can show a video clip and ask questions.
- Videos can be used for closure at the end of a lesson to summarize what has been taught.

The website www.schoolvideos.com/expert/7_mistakes provides a free video that teachers can download. The video provides instruction on how to use videos effectively and discusses the seven common mistakes teachers make when using videos.

Figure 11.6 Multiple Intelligences Chart

Intelligence	Student	Technology Tools
Verbal/ Linguistic	Learns through the spoken and written word.	Word processing, web development, desktop publishing, chats, audio and video recording, e-mail, reference tools, search engines, interactive books, e-books
Logical/ Mathematical	Learns through reasoning and problem solving.	Database programs such as Access and Excel, graphing calculators, WebQuests, critical-thinking and problem-solving software, online data collection and calculation tools, computer-aided design (CAD)
Visual/ Spatial	Learns visually and organizes ideas spatially.	Computer-aided design (CAD), animation software, web development, mapping tools, visual artwork, digital and video cameras, digital drawing pads, desktop publishing, podcasts, scanners
Musical/ Rhythmic	Learns through patterns, rhythms, and music.	Sound and music files, music clips, DVDs, CDs, video recorders, music presentation software, animation, audio books, synthesizers, electronic keyboards
Bodily/ Kinesthetic	Learns through interaction with the environment.	Keyboarding, scientific probes and microscopes, animation, handheld devices, virtual field trips, Lego/robotic kits, digital and video cameras
Interpersonal	Learns through interactions with others.	Blogs, e-mail projects, chat, video and teleconferencing, forums and discussions, group presentations (PowerPoint)
Intrapersonal	Learns through feelings, values, and attitudes.	Computer-based journaling, problem-solving software, Internet research, blogs, multimedia portfolios
Naturalist	Learns through classification, categories, and hierarchies.	Digital and video cameras, PowerPoint, microscopes and probe ware, geocaching (GPS)

Videos can be expensive and can quickly become out-of-date. Many teachers now use video streaming as a resource, ensuring access to current content. Several websites provide videos for downloading. PBS now has a site, PBS Video (http://video.pbs.org), that hosts its videos in one place. These videos are on-demand and are of excellent quality. Discovery Education (www.discoveryeducation.com/index.cfm) streaming offers 9,000 full-length clips and 71,000 content-specific clips that can be downloaded.

The template in Figure 11.7 can be used for students to record their learning from and evaluation of a video they watch.

WebQuests

WebQuests involve an inquiry-based and constructivist approach to a lesson in which information is obtained from the web. They require students to use higher-level thinking, and students often work in collaborative groups. Students who surf the Internet in a random fashion without a clear task in mind do not necessarily benefit educationally. WebQuests can provide a purpose and a target for learning. How can educators recognize a good WebQuest? According to Bernie Dodge (1997) at San Diego State University, WebQuests should contain the following parts:

- An introduction that sets the stage and provides some background information
- A task that is doable and interesting
- A set of information sources needed to complete the task. Many (though not necessarily all) of the resources are embedded in the WebQuest document itself as anchors pointing to information on the World Wide Web. Information sources might include web documents, experts available via e-mail or real-time conferencing, searchable databases on the Internet, and books and other documents physically available in the learner's setting. Because pointers to resources are included, the learner is not left to wander through cyberspace completely adrift.
- A description of the process the learners should go through to accomplish the task. The process should be broken out into clearly described steps.
- Some guidance on how to organize the information acquired
- A conclusion that brings closure to the WebQuest, reminds the learners about what they have learned, and perhaps encourages them to extend the experience into other domains

Figure 11.7 Video Evaluation Form

Name: _____

Period: _____ Date: _____

Title of Movie: _____

Topic of Movie: _____

1. Discuss *three important points* mentioned in the video.

   a.

   b.

   c.

2. How informative was the film/video?

3. Did it hold your interest?

4. Did the production/graphics/design help you to understand the content?

Rate this film using the following criteria:

   1. Does not meet expectations.

   2. Meets expectations.

   3. Exceeds expectations.

My Rating: _____

Explain your rationale for the rating you gave.

Some other, noncritical attributes of a WebQuest include these:

- WebQuests are most likely to be group activities, although one could imagine solo quests that might be applicable in distance education or library settings.
- WebQuests might be enhanced by wrapping motivational elements around the basic structure by giving the learners a role to play (e.g., scientist, detective, reporter), simulated personae with whom to interact via e-mail, and a scenario to work within (e.g., you've been asked by the Secretary General of the United Nations to brief him on what's happening in sub-Saharan Africa this week.)
- WebQuests can be designed within a single discipline, or they can be interdisciplinary. Given that designing effective interdisciplinary instruction is more of a challenge than designing for a single content area, WebQuest creators should probably start with the latter until they are comfortable with the format.

The best use of the WebQuest format is for topics that are less well defined—tasks that invite creativity and problems with several possible solutions. WebQuests can address open-ended questions like these:

- What should be done to protect America's coral reefs?
- What kinds of people were most likely to survive the sinking of the *Titanic?* Why?
- What was it like to live during the California Gold Rush?
- What would Mark Twain think about the lives that children live today?
- How do other democracies deal with social problems like crime, and what, if anything, can the United States learn from them?

Figure 11.8 lists useful WebQuest sites.

Online Projects

Online projects are a great way to expand the classroom experience, and they encourage collaboration among students and teachers throughout the world. Using the Internet this way can enhance curriculum-based lessons.

Figure 11.8 WebQuest Sites and Tools

WebQuests Sites	
All About WebQuests www.suelebeau.com/ webquests.htm	This site contains general information on WebQuests, sample WebQuests, and literacy, science, math, and social studies WebQuests.
Best WebQuests.com www.bestwebquests.com	This site contains WebQuests on a variety of topics. Tom March, the site developer, team-taught with Bernie Dodge (the inventor of WebQuests).
Zunal.com www.zunal.com	This site allows teachers/students to create WebQuests using free software that does not require writing HTML code. You can save and print your WebQuests and browse through those posted. Step-by-step tutorial available.
Tools	
4Teachers.org www.4teachers.org	This site helps you integrate technology into your classroom by offering free online tools and resources. It helps teachers locate, create, and use web lessons, quizzes, rubrics, and classroom calendars.
TeacherPlanet.com www.rubrics4teachers.com	This site provides a complete guide for teacher rubrics and assessment.
Pics4Learning.com www.pics4learning.com	Pics4Learning is a copyright-friendly image library for teachers and students. The Pics4Learning collection consists of thousands of images that have been donated by students, teachers, and amateur photographers. Unlike many Internet sites, permission has been granted for teachers and students to use all of the images donated to the Pics4Learning collection.
FindSounds www.findsounds.com	At this free site, you can search the web for sound effects and musical instrument samples.
Internet4Classrooms www.internet4class rooms.com	This site contains lesson plans that integrate technology, ideas for using digital cameras in the classroom, and technology self-assessment tools. The site also lists "idea starters" for using technology. Their planning templates are very useful tools.
Education World www.educationworld.com	The "Educator's Best Friend"—make it your home page.

Applications

The following are useful resources for online projects:

- *GlobalSchoolNet (www.globalschoolnet.org)*. This is a clearinghouse for collaborative projects across the globe.
- *Center for Innovation in Engineering and Science Education (CIESE; www.k12science.org/currichome.html)*. CIESE sponsors and designs interdisciplinary projects for students around the world to use. The focus is on projects that use real-time data.
- *Web-Based Inquiry Science Environment (WISE; http://wise.berkeley .edu)*. This is a free online science learning environment that uses a web-based inquiry approach. Students learn about and respond to contemporary scientific controversies through designing, debating, and critiquing solutions, all on the WISE system. The WISE system promotes lifelong learning as well as language and technology literacy (Linn & Slotta, 2000).

Research/Search Engines

Today's students grew up with the Internet, but they need direction on how to use it as a tool for learning. It is essential for students to be able to find websites quickly, conduct sound research, and work independently. Many search engines are available today; Figure 11.9 lists some that are used frequently. Students will need to learn how to construct presentations or other products that demonstrate their understanding of what they have learned. A challenge for teachers whose students use the Internet as a resource is plagiarism. One way to reduce this tendency is to address this in a lesson. Students need to understand what plagiarism is and be shown examples of how to use information without plagiarizing other people's work. Some teachers require students to provide a list of their resources with the work they submit or showcase. Plagiarism contracts are a way to make students accountable for their work. It is essential for students to understand the consequences of plagiarism.

Electronic Field Trips

Electronic field trips expand learning beyond the four walls of the classroom, bridging the gap between the classroom and the world outside. One of the advantages of electronic field trips over real field trips is that they provide the opportunity to experience an event several times. Video

Figure 11.9 Search Engines

Search Engine	Description
www.ask.com	The Ask.com search engine allows users to find online information by asking a question, entering a phrase, or giving a keyword. (Formerly Ask Jeeves.)
www.google.com	Google allows users to search the web for images, news, products, video, and other content.
www.hotbot.com	This search service relies on the databases of other search engines.
www.dogpile.com	Dogpile fetches and ranks results from multiple search engines, letting user search for keywords, pictures, audio, video, news, or phone numbers with one click.
www.webcrawler.com	Produces metasearch results from popular engines and directories.
www.search.com	Finds content on the web by searching with the best engines from one place.

clips can be viewed again if necessary. These trips offer combinations of many features. Following are some examples:

- Website with activities and teachers' guides that include blackline masters
- Live broadcasts
- Online discussions
- Audio and video components
- Access to experts

Applications

One can find many sources for electronic field trips. Here are some examples:

- *NASA (http://quest.arc.nasa.gov/lfs/scott-intro.html)*. Offers free web-based, interactive explorations.
- *eFieldTrips (www.efieldtrips.org)*. These field trips consist of four components, a downloadable copy of a printed trip journal, a virtual visit, "ask an expert," and live chats.
- *Colonial Williamsburg (www.history.org/history/teaching/eft/eft.cfm)*. Teachers can register for the electronic field trips for the current school year.

Blogs/Wikis/Podcasts

Blogs

Blogs (short for "web logs") are websites that make it easy for authors to publish from any Internet connection. These sites are simple to update, and users can track conversations with readers who leave comments on the postings. Many teachers and students are using blogs as class portals where curriculum is incorporated into the blog, as online filing cabinets, and as a staging area for student e-portfolios. A good example of a blog set up by a technology educator is Tim Wilson's "The Savvy Technologist" (http://technosavvy.org). There are many advantages to using blogging. It allows students to share their work and provides an immediate record of their progress. Students can easily incorporate text and pictures into their blogs. Parents also will have access so that they can see the work of their children.

School districts may block blogs for safety and security reasons but still allow access to tools like Google, Bing, Blackboard, and Yahoo! that have blogging features built in. A good site for educators who are interested in blogging is The Edublogger (http://theedublogger.edublogs.org), which offers a series of webinars (web-based seminars) for beginners. An example of an easy-to-use blog site to get started with is Google's Blogger (www.blogger.com).

Wikis

Wikis are online encyclopedias that are easy for anyone to add to or edit. Wikipedia.org is the most famous and often-used wiki on the Internet. In some schools, teachers and students are using private wikis to create their own textbooks and resource sites (Richardson, 2010).

Podcasts

Podcasts are amateur radio-style broadcasts that are easy to create and distribute to a variety of media. With the widespread use of digital voice recorders, including in cell phones, anyone can create an MP3 file and upload it to a blog site. Audio/video files can be uploaded to a blog as well. Teachers can incorporate podcasting as a presentation methodology option for their students. Good examples of how podcasting is being used by educators are available at the Education Podcast Network (http://epnweb.org).

ASSESSING STUDENT OUTCOMES THAT INVOLVE TECHNOLOGY

Chapter 9 focused on assessing student learning in a differentiated block schedule. Many strategies presented in that chapter can be adapted for assessing student products that use technology.

Students often use presentation software to demonstrate their learning, showcase their research, and present group projects. Creating projects using technology motivates students. However, students need to be taught the skills necessary for creating good presentations. Some teachers have found that taking the time to stress the importance of presentation design helps students stay focused on the problems they are trying to solve and not on the "bells and whistles" that may be included in the software.

Students also need to be taught how to plan a project and create action plans and timelines. When using project-based learning and technology, it becomes essential that assessments match the targets that have been set for the students. Teachers can develop rubrics using indicators that are student generated. Students who are shown examples of poor or weak presentations, average presentations, and good presentations will have a better understanding of what is expected from them. The rubric shown in Figure 11.10 can be used in assessing student oral presentations.

Students today have been born into a world that embraces technology. These Digital Natives easily immerse themselves in a technological learning environment. Teachers often find themselves lagging behind their students in technology and become frustrated due to their own lack of skills in this arena. Those teachers who embrace technology, learn new skills, and are willing to take risks will discover how valuable technology can be as learning tool.

Technology is here to stay and will continue to evolve. Dr. Douglas Brooks, a professor at Miami University in Oxford , Ohio, is a writer for the website HotChalk (www.hotchalk.com). In one posting, he lists skills that teachers should be trained to do when planning curriculum, when delivering instruction, and when working with students and parents. This list was derived from what vendors at a National Educational Technology Conference believed. Some of these skills are the following:

- Create a classroom website.
- Have and be able to use an interactive whiteboard.
- Use wireless tablets that enable the teacher to face students when using a whiteboard.
- Create instructional lessons in a web-based environment.
- Stream videos from current sources.
- Be able to use student response systems.
- Differentiate instruction using technology.
- Have students work collaboratively on wiki sites.
- Network with colleagues in a collaborative learning environment and use web-based professional portals.

Figure 11.10 Rubric for Student Presentations

Criteria	1	2	3	4
Content *Facts*	• Content not addressed. • Content irrelevant. • Information presented was opinion, not fact.	• Content addressed adequately. • Some irrelevant content included. • Difficult to distinguish fact from opinion.	• Content is addressed. • Most facts presented are relevant. • Some mixing of fact and opinion.	• Content clearly addressed. • Facts reported are relevant. • Clearly distinguished fact from opinion.
Volume *Eye Contact* *Participation*	• Presentation cannot be heard. • No eye contact. • More than two group members do not speak.	• Volume varies and voice is difficult to understand. • Some eye contact. • One group member does not speak.	• Volume is appropriate for part of presentation. • Eye contact is intermittent. • All group members speak but not equally.	• Volume is appropriate throughout presentation. • Good eye contact. • All group members speak equally.
Media Aid	• No media aid used.	• Media aid used distracts from content. • Media aid is illegible.	• Media aid helps presentation but contains one distracting element. • Media aid difficult to read in some places.	• Media aid used enhances presentation and keeps one's attention. • Media aid is legible.
Organization	• No organization. • No logical flow. • Confusing.	• Presentation off track in places. • Gaps may exist. • Some of presentation is logical and organized.	• Good organization. • Demonstrates a clear plan. • Most of presentation logical and organized.	• Well organized. • Demonstrates a clear and complete plan. • All of presentation logical and organized.
Conclusions	• No conclusions reported. • Presenter/group cannot answer questions.	• Some conclusions reported and supported by data. • Presenter/group able to answer some questions.	• Most conclusions reported are supported by data. • Presenter/group able to answer most questions.	• All conclusions reported are supported by data. • Presenter/group able to answer all relevant questions.

The challenges facing most educators who wish to integrate technology into their teaching are the time needed for training and budgetary constraints for purchasing equipment and software. However, many schools are using the technology highlighted in this chapter, and students continue to amaze teachers with their expertise and accomplishments.

12 Final Thoughts

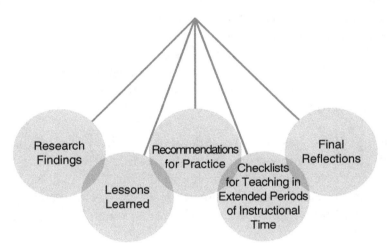

Research Findings

Lessons Learned

Recommendations for Practice

Checklists for Teaching in Extended Periods of Instructional Time

Final Reflections

Individual differences in students, parents, teachers, school leadership, budget, resources, belief systems, and the school culture of each site play a profound role in the success of implementation of the block schedule. Research and practice suggest that one major way to influence the prospects for and probability of success is careful planning, preparation, monitoring of implementation efforts, and incorporation of feedback.

One crucial component of this process is the preparation of staff to teach in extended periods of instructional time. When lessons are engaging, meaningful, and relevant, students and parents are pleased. Teachers feel good about students' responses, attention, and learning. Time flies! In contrast, when teachers simply take lessons from two traditional 45-minute periods and "stick them together" in a 90-minute block, the results can be horrendous and frustrating for all.

RESEARCH FINDINGS

Although few large-scale studies have been undertaken, individual school evaluation reports and dissertations have examined grade point average, honor roll achievement, numbers of failures and dropout rates, discipline referrals, and students' performance on standardized tests.

> Consistent evidence shows that students' grades improve and the number of students on the honor roll increases. . . . Studies show declining failure rates in 4/4 schools and a greater likelihood that students labeled "at risk" will remain in school, especially in the 4/4 schedule, probably because students may repeat several classes but still graduate with their class. . . . The number of discipline referrals to the office is reduced, typically between 25 and 50 percent. . . . In-school suspensions decline, teacher and student attendance improves slightly and . . . the number of class tardies is reduced. (Rettig & Canady, 1999, p. 15)

Although there has been considerable controversy regarding "hard data" on student achievement, many individual schools have reported improved test scores on state exams and on the SAT and ACT. Student achievement on Advanced Placement tests has also increased. Many schools report that students earn more credits when block scheduling is implemented.

LESSONS LEARNED

When a school is making the decision to go to a block schedule, it is essential that

- all stakeholders be involved.
- the schedule that is selected or designed is one that meets the needs of staff and students.
- careful study takes place that involves readings, visitations, research analysis, and interviews.
- planning engages all stakeholders after a schedule is selected.
- implementation efforts be carefully monitored and adjustments made based on feedback.
- celebrations of even small accomplishments be organized to increase momentum.

- all stakeholders realize that change is difficult and involves loss of "the familiar."
- support be provided to enable those serving students to learn new behaviors to enhance classroom success.

To enhance the process of transitioning to the block, the following actions are essential for those involved in the planning efforts:

- Continue to *build trust* between and among everyone engaged in transition planning efforts and the faculty.
- Provide training to enable teachers and other staff to *increase their repertoire of strategies* for serving students; this helps staff feel less vulnerable and more in control.
- Recognize that some faculty members may be fearful about being "out of control" in an extended period of instructional time. Provide opportunities to *problem-solve and discuss concerns* in a supportive environment.
- Realize that some faculty members may feel reticent. Seek ways to *lessen their perception of vulnerability.*
- Help staff see the *relevance* of the block to their discipline area, especially with recognition of thinking skills.
- Invite staff to see how it might be *feasible* to teach lessons in their subject areas within an extended period of instructional time. For example, they might visit other schools where teachers are using the longer schedule.

RECOMMENDATIONS FOR PRACTICE

The National Council of Teachers of Mathematics, National Science Teachers Association, American Association for the Advancement of Science, and National Commission on Social Studies offer several recommendations that can be accommodated within extended periods of instructional time:

- *More* active learning in the classroom, with all the attendant noise and movement of students doing, talking, and collaborating
- *More* deep study of a small number of topics so that students internalize the field's method of inquiry
- *More* cooperative, collaborative activity, developing the classroom as an interdependent community

- *More* experiential, inductive, hands-on learning
- *More* responsibility transferred to students for their work: goal setting, record keeping, monitoring, evaluation
- *More* choice for students; for example, picking their own books, writing topics, team partners, and research partners
- *More* attention to affective needs and the varying cognitive styles of individual students
- *More* reliance on teachers' descriptive evolution of student growth, including qualitative/anecdotal observations

What Practitioners Tell Us

When asked, "What skills do students need in 80- to 100-minute classes?" teachers reported the following:

- Organizing time, materials, information
- Taking responsibility for their own learning
- Self-direction
- Using notes
- Achieving goals
- Understanding directions
- Skillful listening
- Cooperative learning
- Using resources to find information or to problem-solve
- Problem solving
- Finding main ideas
- Memory strategies
- Reading for meaning
- Observing
- Reading textbooks
- Asking questions
- Taking notes
- Setting goals
- Studying and test taking
- Interpreting and creating tables (Davenport & Tobin, 1997)

These skill areas served as a basis for the thinking behind chapters in this book.

Teachers have also commented about the advice they would give to those teaching in the block:

- Don't lecture for more than 12 minutes without processing time. Students won't remember.

- Chunk activities within the 80- to 100-minute period at least four times. Relate one activity to the next with thoughtful transitions so that students don't lose a sense of continuity.
- Provide frequent opportunities for movement built into academic activities; for example, use gallery walks, stand-pair-share, or round-the-room brainstorming.
- Increase student responsibility and accountability. Foster reflection and metacognition.
- Make homework meaningful and relevant.
- Use journals to promote long-term memory of content.
- Design extension projects to provide enrichment for students who finish early.
- Seize opportunities to integrate the curriculum; doing so reinforces content and skills.
- Teach for depth, not coverage.
- Be clear about the KUDOs (*k*now, *u*nderstand, be able to *do*). When planning for instruction, first identify standards, benchmarks, and essential concepts and then work backward. Decide what is most important for students to know and be able to do. Exercise selective abandonment based on pre-assessment.
- Plan transitional activities (2–5 minutes), such as brain breaks, to energize students.
- Use cooperative learning for flexible grouping situations.
- Foster feedback, not grading, to increase growth.
- Use daily agendas and outcomes with time chunks if possible.
- Collaborate and share with other teachers; it's a great way to maximize your strategies and your attitude.
- Use simulations, case studies, problem-based learning, role-playing, community service learning, inquiry, and research to make standards and benchmarks relevant to students' lives.
- Recognize that meaningful assignments will keep students on-task for longer periods of time.
- Overplan.
- Use authentic assessment.
- Be creative: there is not just one way.
- Remember that you have spent many years perfecting the old system. It will take just as long to master the new system.

Many teachers have admitted to worrying about student absences. Strategies they have recommended for working with student absences follow:

- Keep a daily file folder of assignments so that students have a central location in which to retrieve missed work.

- Set aside a separate corner in the room where assignments are posted and copies of handouts can be found.
- Link students with study buddies. If one is absent, another can fill the other in.
- Identify a student on a rotating basis to take notes on a laptop computer. Print out these notes and make them available to the class. If a laptop is not available, have students take turns taking notes and photocopy them.
- Audiotape discussions or instruction. Ask specific students to share class notes.
- Identify a student assistant "to fill students in" when they return from an absence.
- Develop a homework hotline.
- Create a "help wanted" form. Students can fill this in and make an appointment to meet with the teacher about missed instructional time.

CHECKLISTS FOR TEACHING IN EXTENDED PERIODS OF INSTRUCTIONAL TIME

The following checklists have been developed as "ticklers" for planning assessment, instruction, curriculum, and classroom environment. These questions represent aspects of planning linked to block schedule implementation success.

Assessment

- ❑ Are the standards I am assessing and the criteria clear?
- ❑ How will I assess?
- ❑ How will I use assessment results for planning?
- ❑ Will the feedback to students be substantive, specific, constructive, and timely?

Curriculum

- ❑ To what standards does this relate?
- ❑ What do they already know?
- ❑ What content will I teach?
- ❑ In what order?
- ❑ In what "chunks"?
- ❑ What resources can be used (e.g., texts, CD-ROMs, Internet, videos)?

Instruction

- ❐ How will I hook students' attention?
- ❐ How will I relate today's topics to students' real world?
- ❐ In what way will I share the lesson outcomes?
- ❐ How will I get students to recall previous knowledge that relates to this topic (opening mental files)?
- ❐ How will I present the content of the lesson: lecturette, video, text, jigsaw?
- ❐ What questioning strategies will I use?
- ❐ How will I keep things moving?
- ❐ Have I considered multiple intelligences and visual, auditory, and kinesthetic learners? Receptive/expressive language?
- ❐ How will I actively involve students?
- ❐ How will I incorporate TAPS for flexible groups of students?
- ❐ How will I check for understanding (use formative assessment)?
- ❐ How will I monitor and adjust instruction?
- ❐ How will I provide for perfect practice?
- ❐ How will I ask students to summarize their learnings?
- ❐ How will I ask students to demonstrate authentically what they know and can do?
- ❐ How might homework reinforce learnings?
- ❐ How will I revisit this lesson's key points/skills to promote long-term retention?

Classroom Environment

- ❐ How can I create an environment characterized by high challenge and low threat to create relaxed alertness (flow)?
- ❐ How can I create a climate of high expectations?
- ❐ How can I promote positive relationships in the classroom?
- ❐ How can I help students develop social and emotional skills, including the following?
  - o Self-awareness
  - o Managing emotions
  - o Motivating oneself/delaying gratification
  - o Empathy
  - o Handling relationships (Goleman, 1995)
- ❐ How can I support students in developing responsibility for the following:
  - o Attendance
  - o Coming to class with necessary materials

- o Class participation
- o Completing assignments
- o Monitoring their progress
- ❏ How can I manage time well with respect to the following?
  - o Pacing
  - o Transitions
  - o Beginning and ending class
  - o Handling distribution/collection of materials/supplies
- ❏ How can I create and maintain a sense of learning community and pride among students?

FINAL REFLECTIONS

No doubt about it: change is difficult, even if it is desirable. As educators strive to create meaningful learning environments within a block schedule for both adults and students in the school, there will be times of feeling overwhelmed, wanting to go back to more familiar ways, and perhaps even frustration. It is crucial to remember that collaboration, careful planning, problem solving, resource seeking, sharing, and a spirit of hope and optimism are powerful ingredients for facilitating this change process.

Adult learners (Brookfield, 1983; Knowles, 1980) value opportunities with the following characteristics:

- *Experiential.* Adults need to connect new ideas or actions to what we know and do well.
- *Self-Directed.* Adults need choice and opportunities to prioritize the work.
- *Life Applicable.* Adults need learning that has real-life uses and is transferable to their unique circumstances.
- *Performance Centered.* Adults like learning that is hands-on, engaging, or gives them an opportunity for reflection.
- *Impact of Professional Learning Communities.* Benefits for teachers who participate in high-quality professional learning teams include the following (Hord, 1997):
  - o Reduction of isolation
  - o Increased commitment to the school's mission/vision
  - o Shared responsibility for the total development of students
  - o Collective responsibility for student success
  - o Increased meaning and understanding of content
  - o Higher likelihood that teachers will be well informed, professionally renewed, and inspired
  - o More satisfaction, higher morale, and lower absenteeism
  - o Significant advances in modifying teaching strategies
  - o Commitment to making significant and lasting changes

The same research indicates results in terms of specific benefits for students, if their teachers dialogue and interact with peers:

- Decreased dropout rates and fewer missed classes
- Lower rates of absenteeism
- Increased learning
- Greater gains in math, science, history, and reading
- Smaller achievement gaps between students from different backgrounds

> Getting the maximum benefits from commitment, involvement, strong initiative, good inquiry, open advocacy, effective conflict resolution, solid decision making and extensive use of critique is what spectacular teamwork is all about. (Blake, Mouton, & Allen, 1987, p. 9)

Professional learning communities (PLCs) are a strong support system for teachers who are transitioning to a differentiated block schedule. As grade-group teams of teachers or subject-alike PLCs meet, they have the opportunity to share successes, ideas, and strategies that worked in their classroom and to problem-solve issues that are causing concern or management situations that need to be dealt with.

Administrators need to be an integral part of staff development with teachers and foster collaboration and provide time for teams to meet and dialogue. The role of encourager, cheerleader, and resource provider is essential for the school leaders. Listening to teacher issues and concerns, providing resources, and meeting "just in time" needs are crucial to success of the implementation and fostering an overall positive attitude among faculty.

As a final thought, let's reflect on why we all entered the teaching profession . . . because we wanted to make a difference for students. Imagine the power of influence that could be generated within a school when all the stakeholders, committed to making a difference, work together to provide meaningful learning experiences within extended periods of instructional time. A vision of this reality can help those within the schoolhouse and the surrounding community hold on to their convictions about what working within the block should be like. This vision and those convictions can steer the school through rough seas and keep it on course—a course guided by the needs of students, needs that can be satisfied when exposed to a challenging educational experience in a climate nurtured by caring adults.

References

Anderson, T. H., & Armbruster, B. B. (1984a). Content area textbooks. In R. C. Anderson, J. Osborn, & R. J. Tierney (Eds.), *Learning to read in American schools* (pp. 193–224). Hillsdale, NJ: Lawrence Erlbaum.

Anderson, T. H., & Armbruster, B. B. (1984b). Studying. In P. D. Pearson, R. Barr, M. L. Kamii, & P. Mosenthal (Eds.), *Handbook of reading research* (pp. 657–679). New York: Longman.

Aronson, E. (1978). *The jigsaw classroom.* Beverly Hills, CA: Sage.

Baron-Cohen, S. (2003). *The essential difference: The truth about the male and female brain.* New York: Basic Books.

Bellanca, J., & Fogarty, R. (1991). *Blueprint for thinking in the cooperative classroom.* Arlington Heights, IL: IRI/Skylight.

Bennett, B., Bennett-Rolheiser, C., & Stevahn, L. (1991). *Cooperative learning: Where heart meets mind; An interactive resource book.* Toronto, Canada: Education Connections.

Berte, N. R. (1975). *Individualizing education through contract learning.* Tuscaloosa: University of Alabama Press.

Blake, R. R., Mouton, J. S., & Allen, R. L. (1987). *Spectacular teamwork: How to develop leadership skills for team success.* New York: Wiley.

Bloom, B. S. (Ed.). (1956). *Taxonomy of educational objectives: Book 1. Cognitive domain.* New York: David McKay.

Blum, D. (1997). *Sex on the brain: The biological differences between men and women.* New York: Viking.

Burns, E. T. (1992). *Our children, our future: Defining the stakes in a battle we must not lose* (2nd ed.). Dallas, TX: Marco Polo.

Burz, H. L., & Marshall, K. (1998). *Performance-based curriculum for social studies: From knowing to showing.* Thousand Oaks, CA: Corwin.

Bybee, R. W., Taylor, J. A., Gardner, A., Van Scotter, P., Carlson Powell, J., Westbrook, A., & Landes, N. (2006). *The BSCS 5E instructional model: Origins, effectiveness and applications.* Retrieved from http://www.bscs.org/pdf/bscs5eexecsummary.pdf

California Polytechnic State University Student Academic Services. (2010). *Notetaking systems.* Retrieved April 2, 2010, from http://sas.calpoly.edu/asc/ssl/notetaking.systems.html

Canady, R. L., & Rettig, M. D. (1995). *Block scheduling: A catalyst for change in high schools.* Princeton, NJ: Eye on Education.

Cantelon, T. (1991a). *The first four weeks of cooperative learning, activities and materials.* Portland, OR: Prestige.

Cantelon, T. (1991b). *Structuring the classroom successfully for cooperative team learning.* Portland, OR: Prestige.

Carskadon, M. A. (Ed.). (2002). *Adolescent sleep patterns: Biological, social, and psychological influences.* Cambridge, UK: Cambridge University Press.

Carter, R. (1998). *Mapping the mind.* Los Angeles: University of California Press.

Charles, C. M. (1996). *Building classroom discipline.* White Plains, NY: Longman.

Clarke, J., Wideman, R., & Eadie, S. (1990). *Together we learn.* Scarborough, Canada: Prentice-Hall.

Conference Board of Canada. (2000). *Employability Skills 2000+.* Retrieved April 2, 2010, from http://calsca.com/conference_board.htm

Cowan, G., & Cowan, E. (1980). *Writing.* New York: John Wiley.

Csikszentmihalyi, M. (1990). *Flow: The psychology of optimal experience.* New York: HarperCollins.

Cuban, L. (2001). *Oversold and underused: Computers in the classroom.* Cambridge, MA: Harvard University Press.

Davenport, E., & Tobin, K. (1997). *HM network, HM learning and study skills group.* Newton, MA: NASSP.

Davey, B. (1983). Think aloud: Modeling the cognitive processes of reading comprehension. *Journal of Reading, 27*(1), 44–47.

De Bono, E. (1976). *Teaching thinking.* London: Temple Smith.

De Bono, E. (1985). *Masterthinker's handbook.* New York: International Center for Creative Thinking.

Dodge, B. (1997). *Some thoughts about WebQuests.* Retrieved April 2, 2010, from San Diego State University website: http://webquest.sdsu.edu/about_webquests.html

Doyle, M., & Strauss, D. (1976). *How to make meetings work.* New York: Playboy Press.

Dunn, R., & Dunn, K. (1987). *Understanding learning styles and the need for individual diagnosis and prescription.* Columbia, CT: The Learner's Dimension.

Ekwall, E. E., & Shanker, J. L. (1988). *Diagnosis and remediation of the disabled reader* (3rd ed.). Boston: Allyn & Bacon.

Evertson, C. M., & Harris, A. H. (1992). What we know about managing classrooms. *Educational Leadership, 49*(7), 74.

Fitzgerald, R. (1996). Brain-compatible teaching in a block schedule. *School Administrator, 53*(8), 20–21, 24.

Fogarty, R., & Stoehr, J. (2008). *Integrating curricula with multiple intelligences: Teams, themes, and threads* (2nd ed.). Thousand Oaks, CA: Corwin.

Friedman, T. L. (2007). *The world is flat: A brief history of the twenty-first century* (Updated & exp. ed.). New York: Farrar, Straus & Giroux.

Gardner, H. E. (1983). *Frames of mind: The theory of multiple intelligences.* New York: Basic Books.

Garmston, R., & Wellman, B. (1995). Adaptive schools in a quantum universe. *Educational Leadership, 52*(7), 6–12.

Gazzaniga, M. L. (1998a). *The mind's past.* Berkeley: University of California Press.

Gazzaniga, M. L. (1998b). The split-brain revisited. *Scientific American, 279,* 50–55.

Gibbs, J. (2001). *Tribes: A new way of learning and being together.* Windsor, CA: Center Source Systems.

Goleman, D. (1995). *Emotional intelligence.* New York: Bantam.

Goleman, D. (1998). *Working with emotional intelligence.* New York: Bantam.

Goodlad, J. I. (2004). *A place called school* (20th anniv. ed.). New York: McGraw-Hill. (Originally published 1984)

Gordon, W. (1961). *Synectics.* New York: Harper & Row.

Gregorc, A. (1985). *Inside styles: Beyond the basics; Questions and answers on style.* Maynard, MA: Gabriel Systems.

Gregory, G. H. (2008). *Differentiated instructional strategies in practice: Training, implementation, and supervision* (2nd ed.). Thousand Oaks, CA: Corwin.

Gregory, G. H., & Chapman, C. (2007). *Differentiated instructional strategies: One size doesn't fit all* (2nd ed.). Thousand Oaks, CA: Corwin.

Gregory G. H., & Parry, T. (2006). *Designing brain-compatible learning* (3rd ed.). Thousand Oaks, CA: Corwin.

Gurian, M., Henley, P., & Trueman, T. (2001). *Boys and girls learn differently! A guide for teachers and parents.* San Francisco: Jossey-Bass.

Gurian, M., & Stevens, K. (2004). With boys and girls in mind. *Educational Leadership, 62*(3), 21–26.

Harste, J. C., Woodward, V. A., & Burke, C. L.. (1984). *Language stories and literacy lessons.* Portsmouth, NH: Heinemann.

Havers, F. (1995, March 2). Rhyming tasks male and female brains differently. *The Yale Herald.*

Head, M. H., & Readence, J. E. (1992). Anticipation guides: Using prediction to promote learning from text. In E. K. Dishner, T. W. Bean, J. E. Readence, & D. W. Moore (Eds.), *Reading in the content areas: Improving classroom instruction* (3rd ed., pp. 227–233). Dubuque, IA: Kendall/Hunt.

Hill, S., & Hancock, J. (1993). *Reading and writing communities.* Armadal, Australia: Eleanor Curtain.

Hord, S. M. (1997). *Professional learning communities: Communities of continuous inquiry and improvement.* Austin, TX: Southwest Educational Development Laboratory.

Jensen, E. (with Dabney, M., Markowitz, K., & Selsor, K.). (2003). *Environments for learning.* San Diego, CA: The Brain Store.

Johnson, D., & Johnson, R. (1991). *Cooperative learning.* Edina, MN: Interaction Book.

Johnson, D., & Johnson, R. (1994). *Leading the cooperative school.* Edina, MN: Interaction Book.

Johnson, D. W., Johnson, R. T., & Holubec, E. J. (1988). *Cooperation in the classroom* (Rev. ed.). Edina, MN: Interaction Book.

Johnson, D. W., Johnson, R. T., Holubec, E. J., & Roy, P. (1984). *Circles of learning: Cooperation in the classroom.* Alexandria, VA: Association for Supervision and Curriculum Development.

Kagan, S. (1992). *Cooperative learning.* San Clemente, CA: Kagan Cooperative.

Kain, D. L. (1993). Cabbages-and-kings: Research direction in integrated/intradisciplinary curriculum. *Journal of Educational Thought, 27*(3), 312–331.

Key, N. (1991). *Research and methodologies for whole-brained integration at the secondary level.* (ERIC Document Reproduction Service No. ED347141)

Knowles, M. (1980). Life long learning. *Training and Development Journal, 34*(7), 40.

Knowles, M. S. (1986). *Using learning contracts.* San Francisco: Jossey-Bass.

Levine, M. D. (1990). *Keeping a head in school: A student's book about learning abilities and learning disorders.* Cambridge, MA: Educators.

Linn, M. C., & Slotta, J. D. (2000). WISE science. *Educational Leadership, 58*(2), 29–32.

Marzano, R. J. (2007). *The art and science of teaching: A comprehensive framework for effective instruction.* Alexandria, VA: Association for Supervision and Curriculum Development.

Marzano, R. J., Norford, J. S., Paynter, D. E., Pickering, D. J., & Gaddy, B. B. (2001). *A handbook for classroom instruction that works.* Alexandria, VA: Association for Supervision and Curriculum Development.

Marzano, R. J., Pickering, D. J., & Pollock, J. E. (2001). *Classroom instruction that works: Research-based strategies for increasing student achievement.* Alexandria, VA: Association for Supervision and Curriculum Development.

McTighe, J., & Lyman, F. (1988, April). Cueing thinking in the classroom: The promise of theory-embedded tools. *Educational Leadership, 45*(7), 7.

McTighe, J., & Lyman, F. T., Jr. (2001). Cueing thinking in the classroom: The promise of theory-embedded tools. In A. L. Costa (Ed.), *Developing minds: A resource book for teaching thinking* (3rd ed., pp. 384–392). Alexandria, VA: Association for Supervision and Curriculum Development.

Means, B. (Ed.). (1994). *Technology and education reform: The reality behind the promise.* San Francisco: Jossey-Bass.

Merriam-Webster's Collegiate Dictionary (11th ed.). (2003). Springfield, MA: Merriam-Webster.

Moir, A., & Jessel, D. (1989). *Brain sex: The real difference between men and women.* New York: Dell.

National Center for Education Statistics (NCES). (1996). *Pursuing excellence: A study of U.S. eighth-grade mathematics and science teaching, learning, curriculum, and achievement in international context; Initial findings from the Third International Mathematics and Science Study* (NCES report 97-198). Retrieved April 2, 2010, from http://nces.ed.gov/pubsearch/pubsinfo.asp?pubid=97198

National Sleep Foundation. (n.d.). *Teens and sleep.* Retrieved April 2, 2010, from http://www.sleepfoundation.org/article/sleep-topics/teens-and-sleep

Ogle, D. (1986). K-W-L: A teaching model that develops active reading of expository text. *Reading Teacher, 39*(6), 564–574.

Oliva, P. F. (2001). *Developing the curriculum* (5th ed.). New York: Longman.

Ornstein, R., & Sobel, D. (1988). *The healing brain: Breakthrough discoveries of how the brain keeps us healthy.* Cambridge, MA: Malor Books.

Panksepp, J. (1998). *Affective neuroscience: The foundations of human and animal emotions.* New York: Oxford University Press.

Popham, W. J. (2008). *Transformative assessment.* Alexandria, VA: Association for Supervision and Curriculum Development.

Prensky, M. (2001). *Digital natives, digital immigrants.* Originally published in *On the Horizon, 9*(5). Retrieved April 2, 2010, from http://www.marcprensky .com/writing/Prensky%20-%20Digital%20Natives,%20Digital%20 Immigrants%20-%20Part1.pdf

Queen, J. A. (2000). Block scheduling revisited. *Phi Delta Kappan, 82*(3), 214–222.

Renzulli, J. S. (1992). Using curriculum compacting to challenge the above average. *Educational Leadership, 50*(2), 51–57.

Rettig, M. D., & Canady, R. L. (1999, March). The effects of block scheduling. *School Administrator.*

Rich, B. (Ed.). (2000). *The Dana brain daybook.* New York: Charles A. Dana Foundation.

Richardson, R. (2010). *Blogs, wikis, podcasts, and other powerful web tools for classrooms* (3rd ed.). Thousand Oaks, CA: Corwin.

Robbins, P., Gregory, G., & Herndon, L. (2000). *Thinking inside the block schedule.* Thousand Oaks, CA: Corwin.

Rowe, M. B. (1987). Wait time: Slowing down may be a way of speeding up. *American Educator, 11*(1), 38–43, 47.

Russell, D., & Hunter, M. (1976). *Planning for effective instruction: Lesson design.* Los Angeles: Seeds Elementary School.

Santa, C. (1988). *Content reading including study systems.* Dubuque, IA: Kendall/ Hunt Publishing.

Schmoker, M. J. (2006). *Results now: How we can achieve unprecedented improvements in teaching and learning.* Alexandria, VA: Association for Supervision and Curriculum Development.

Secretary's Commission on Achieving Necessary Skills. (1991). *What work requires of schools: A SCANS report for America 2000.* Washington, DC: U.S. Department of Labor.

Slavin, R. E. (1994). *Cooperative learning: Theory, research, and practice.* Boston: Allyn & Bacon.

Smilkstein, R. (2003). *We're born to learn: Using the brain's natural learning process to create today's curriculum.* Thousand Oaks, CA: Corwin.

Sousa, D. (2006). *How the brain learns* (3rd ed.). Thousand Oaks, CA: Corwin.

Sperry, R. (1968). Hemisphere disconnection and unity consciousness awareness. *American Psychologist, 23,* 723–733.

Spinks, S. (Writer, Director, Producer). (2002). *FRONTLINE: Inside the teenage brain* [Transcript]. Boston: WBGH. Retrieved April 2, 2010, from http://www.pbs .org/wgbh/pages/frontline/shows/teenbrain/etc/script.html

Statham, D. S., & Torell, C. R. (1996). *Computers in the classroom: The impact of technology on student learning.* Boise, ID: U.S. Army Research Institute and Boise State University.

Stepien, W., Gallagher, S., & Workman, D. (1993). Problem-based learning for traditional and interdisciplinary classrooms. *Journal for Gifted Education, 16,* 338–357.

Sternberg, R. J. (1996). *Successful intelligence: How practical and creative intelligence determine success in life.* New York: Simon & Schuster.

Stewart, V. (2007). Becoming citizens of the world. *Educational Leadership 64*(7), 9–14.

Stiggins, R. J. (1997). *Student-centered classroom assessment* (2nd ed.). Upper Saddle River, NJ: Prentice-Hall.

Tapscott, D. (2009). *Grown up digital: How the Net Generation is changing your world.* New York: McGraw-Hill.

Taylor, S. (2002). *The tending instinct.* New York: Times Books.

Tomlinson, C. A. (1999). *The differentiated classroom: Responding to the needs of all learners.* Alexandria, VA: Association for Supervision and Curriculum Development.

Tomlinson, C. A. (2001). *How to differentiate in mixed ability classrooms* (2nd ed.). Alexandria, VA: Association for Supervision and Curriculum Development.

Tomlinson, C. A., & McTighe, J. (2006). *Integrating differentiated instruction and understanding by design: Connecting content and kids.* Alexandria, VA: Association for Supervision and Curriculum Development.

Walberg, H. J., & Paik, S. J. (2000). *Effective educational practices.* (ERIC Document Reproduction Service No. ED443788)

Whetzel, D. (1992). *The Secretary of Labor's Commission on Achieving Necessary Skills* (ERIC Digest). (ERIC Document Reproduction Service No. ED339749) Retrieved April 2, 2010, from http://www.ericdigests.org/1992-5/skills.htm

Wiggins, G. (1992). Creating tests worth taking. *Educational Leadership, 49*(8), 26–33.

Wiggins, G., & McTighe, J. (1998). *Understanding by design.* Alexandria, VA: Association for Supervision and Curriculum Development.

Winebrenner, S. (1992). *Teaching gifted kids in the regular classroom.* Minneapolis, MN: Free Spirit.

Witelson, S. (2004, May). *The male and female brain: The same but different* [Speech]. Hamilton, Ontario, Canada.

Wolfe, P., & Nevills, P. (2004). *Building the reading brain, preK–3.* Thousand Oaks, CA: Corwin.

Wolfe, P., & Sorgen, M. (1990). *Mind, memory and learning: Implications for the classroom.* Napa, CA: Author.

Wong, H. K., & Wong, R. T. (1991). *The first days of school: How to be an effective teacher.* Sunnyvale, CA: Harry K. Wong.

Index

CORWIN
A SAGE Company

The Corwin logo—a raven striding across an open book—represents the union of courage and learning. Corwin is committed to improving education for all learners by publishing books and other professional develop ment resources for those serving the field of PreK–12 education. By providing practical, hands-on materials, Corwin continues to carry out the promise of its motto: **"Helping Educators Do Their Work Better."**

CPSIA information can be obtained
at www.ICGtesting.com
Printed in the USA
LVHW052105040821
694541LV00005B/191